When
Workers
Organize

When Workers Organize

New York City in the Progressive Era

Melvyn Dubofsky

The University of Massachusetts Press   Amherst 1968

Copyright © 1968 by the
University of Massachusetts Press
Library of Congress Catalog Card
Number 68–19669
Set in Linotype Garamond No. 3 &
Goudy Heavyface & printed in
the United States of America by
The Book Press
Designed by Richard Hendel

To my parents

Preface

HISTORIANS HAVE TRADITIONALLY charac-
terized the first two decades of the twentieth century as the Progressive
era, a period during which crusading reformers sought to improve all
aspects of American society. The reformers historians have generally
written about were from the middle and even upper classes, men and
women of education, culture, and sometimes considerable wealth.
Middle- and upper-class Progressivism reflected both American fears
and hopes: fear of revolution or violence by the masses who were not
sharing fully in the rewards of industrialism, and a more generous hope
for a better America, in which the fruits of capitalism would be more
widely distributed.

The reform impulse quite naturally benefited the American working
class. Under increasing pressure from reform societies, labor lobbyists,
and lower-class voters, state legislatures enacted social welfare legislation. Restrictions against child labor were strengthened; the hours
of labor for women were restricted by statute; laborers gained employers' liability or workmen's compensation laws; factory safety and
sanitary codes were expanded and tightened; and some states made
gestures in the direction of minimum wage legislation. Historians
have also to some extent explored and written about this aspect of the
Progressive era.

But welfare and factory legislation did not satisfy many militant workingmen. Such workers did not refuse legislative gifts; on the contrary, they usually demanded reforms. But what legislatures could give, they could also take away. Moreover, since there was no assurance that state agencies would enforce new laws effectively, labor determined to use its own collective power to achieve social and economic betterment, and, perhaps, to reshape the future of American society. Workers turned to the trade-union as the most effective means to obtain power and security. Many workers devoted their time, their meager funds, and sometimes their very lives to building trade-unions.

The impulse to organize the working class dominated the thoughts and actions of those who created the Progressive era's unions. However, organizers usually failed to establish stable unions when they adopted the method of slow and tedious recruiting among the workers. Frequently, it was the dramatic, sometimes spontaneous, mass strike that galvanized the working people and produced a massive influx into the unions. Thousands of previously uninterested workers rushed to enroll in trade-unions when they struck and clearly demonstrated the possibilities of collective action.

A history of labor during the Progressive years must give special emphasis to the organizational strike as a factor in union growth. I have written this account of industrial conflict within a single urban community—New York City—in an effort to explore the extent to which an environment conducive to reform affected labor's attempts to organize. By focusing upon an important and controversial period in American history—the Progressive era—and limiting the study to a single city, I have hoped to probe fully the relationship between the labor movement and the nonworking-class sectors of the urban community.

I chose New York City because its heterogeneous population, its machine politicians, its legion of social workers and reformers, and its active, often militant, labor movement made it a microcosm of the American nation during the Progressive era. In that singular metropolis teeming masses dwelled in wretched tenement districts where squalor, poverty, and powerlessness brought to the surface the economic, social, and ethnic tensions common to urban America. New York's workers, American-born and immigrant, struggled as did individuals everywhere in the country to come to terms with the new industrialism in a painful, sometimes violent, adjustment.

Working-class history, however, is difficult to reconstruct. Personal papers and records are scarce; those which survive bear on the few unions which did not go under in the successive crises of the period under consideration. For the unorganized worker and the rank-and-file union member sources are rarer still. The inarticulate and often uneducated laborer had little sense of history and less compulsion to record his emotions or thoughts for the benefit of posterity and scholars. Reports of the Federal Bureau of Labor Statistics, various state bureaus, and private charitable organizations comprise the bulk of the materials concerning working-class life. Although these reports offer great masses of statistical evidence regarding wage scales, living standards, and housing conditions, they seldom explore the innermost thoughts and aspirations of the working man or woman.

Fortunately, the student of New York City labor has a firm scholarly foundation upon which to build. The Jewish-American labor movement which emerged directly from New York's needle trades is the subject of a vast literature. Moreover, three recent studies have illuminated vital aspects of the city's working-class history: Moses Rischin, *The Promised City: New York's Jews, 1870–1914* (Cambridge, Massachusetts: Harvard University Press, 1962); Hyman Berman, "The Era of the Protocol: A Chapter in the History of the International Ladies' Garment Workers' Union, 1910–1916" (Unpublished Doctoral Dissertation, Columbia University, 1955); and Irwin Yellowitz, *Labor and the Progressive Movement in New York State, 1897–1916,* (Ithaca, New York: Cornell University Press, 1965). Each of these works contains valuable insights and information about New York City labor during the Progressive era.

Rischin provides an invaluable account of the rise and growth of the Jewish immigrant community in New York City. I have drawn amply on his book for discussion of the Jewish working people, their lives, attitudes, and responses to trade-unionism. Berman's "Era of the Protocol . . ." is an excellent analysis of internal institutional union development, also largely among Jewish workers, in this case members of the International Ladies' Garment Workers' Union. And Yellowitz delineates clearly the factors that drew labor leaders and middle- and upper-class social reformers into a marriage of convenience and the forces that made for their mutual distrust, while both groups lobbied at the State Capitol for reform legislation.

My reading of the sources, and particularly the labor press, has convinced me that organization and union recognition were always more important to the worker than reform legislation, that labor leaders and rank-and-file members devoted their primary energies to the establishment of trade-unions. Consequently, this book focuses upon the attempts of New York City's unorganized workers to achieve organization and seeks to explain why some groups of workers succeeded while others failed.

Although this book emphasizes the attitudes and activities of organized labor, it is neither a narrative of individual trade-union development nor of the day-to-day processes of industrial relations and collective bargaining. Instead it explores the relationship between the labor movement and the urban community during serious and prolonged industrial conflicts. It seeks to demonstrate that the relationship between organized labor and municipal reformers was more complex than is usually thought to be the case, and it analyzes the strengths and weaknesses of the Progressive attitude toward organized labor and industrial conflict as well as the aspirations and struggles of New York's workers. Finally, my findings suggest that historians should devote less effort to discovering the social origins and status of Progressives and more to analyzing the differing fashions by which Americans from all classes of society responded to the challenge of industrialism.

The book could not have been completed without the assistance of numerous institutions and individuals. A fellowship from the University of Rochester gave me the opportunity to begin the study, and subsequent grants from the American Association for State and Local History and the Dean's Fund of Northern Illinois University allowed me to complete the research and writing.

From the very beginning my research efforts benefited from the kind attention and patience of numerous librarians and archivists. Untold hours were spent utilizing the resources of the New York Public Library, especially in the Divisions of Economics and Jewish Studies. The directors of special collections and of the oral history project at Columbia University's Low Library allowed me to review the relevant materials there. The State Historical Society of Wisconsin opened its collection of American Federation of Labor papers as well as the Morris Hillquit papers. At the New York State School of Industrial and Labor Relations, Miss Leone Eckhart, Director of the Library, guided me through the sources there, and Professor Jesse T.

Carpenter most generously allowed me to roam at will through the Paul Abelson papers, which are in his personal possession. Mr. Louis Falco of the New York City Municipal Archives introduced me to the little used but particularly important collections of New York's municipal administrations. My greatest debt, however, is owed to Mrs. Louise Heinze and her staff at the Tamiment Institute Library where I spent many a treasured and delightful hour reading trade-union publications and Socialist Party minute books and correspond-ence, while old radicals drifted in and out of the library for a few minutes conversation; Mrs. Heinze offered me what amounted to my own personal library in labor and radical history. I cannot offer thanks enough to Messrs. Joseph Schlossberg, Louis Waldman, and J. B. S. Hardman and Misses Rose Schneiderman and Pauline Newman for sharing with me their experiences and memories of working-class life in early twentieth-century New York.

Numerous friends read the manuscript at various stages, and their criticisms proved of immense value. Of particular assistance were the critiques offered by Professor Glyndon G. Van Deusen, under whom this study originated as a doctoral dissertation at the University of Rochester, Professor Moses Rischin, Professor Sidney Fine, and my colleagues at Northern Illinois University, Professors Charles Freede-man, Alfred Young, and Benjamin Keen, all of whom read the manu-script in its entirety. Their kind and learned advice saved me from innumerable blunders and improved the book's quality. Last but not least I must thank my untiring wife, Joan, for taking precious time away from home and children in order to edit and type the manuscript.

Amherst, Massachusetts   MELVYN DUBOFSKY
April 1968

Contents

1.
Working-class Life &
Labor in New York City

NEW YORK CITY WAS, in Samuel Gompers' words, "the cradle of the American labor movement."[1] From the Locofocos and Workies of Jacksonian America, to the Henry George Mayoralty campaign of 1886, to the labor upheaval of 1909–1916, the city occupied a significant place in American labor history.

The metropolis had a well-developed tradition of working-class organization long before the advent of the Progressive era. In the days of Jefferson and Jackson New York's artisans founded craft unions, struck, bargained collectively, organized politically, and elected a spokesman of their own, Ely Moore, to Congress. In the 1850's, local printers and cigar makers constructed stable craft unions and resumed the collective bargaining patterns established during the Jacksonian era. Later in the century local labor leaders organized political protest movements which included the Tompkins Square "Riot and Massacre" of 1874 and the Labor Party, which in 1886 ran Henry George for Mayor.

Immigrants too had a long history of labor organization. Just before and after the Civil War the German-American labor movement grew in a city where European methods and ideas met a receptive audience. Subsequently, the Jewish-American trade-unions established their roots in New York. And, of course, Samuel Gompers, for 50 years the symbol of the American labor movement, received his education in trade-unionism as a New York cigar maker.[2]

In 1900, however, the strength of organized labor in New York City was concentrated in several industries whose employees possessed, thanks to the nature of their crafts, an unusual degree of bargaining power. These employees were largely American-born or of Irish and German origins. Craft unions flourished in those industries where labor possessed irreplaceable skills and the industry faced little external competition. The building trades, the printing trades, the brewery trades, and parts of the machine trades represented the core of organized labor's strength. New York's brewing and building trades included large numbers of Americanized Irish and German laborers, and the printing trades possessed a labor force "remarkable for its high degree of ethnic and cultural homogeneity."[3]

During the Progressive period these older, better established craft unions cemented their past gains. Organized and skilled workers sought and eventually achieved further improvements in working conditions and, particularly in the printing trades, union control of job rights. They employed strikes occasionally—usually with gratifying results—to attain limited objectives: wage increases, reduced hours, the protection of established labor agreements. In these trades mass organizational strikes had outlived their utility. By the turn of the century many of the craft unions had reached equality of bargaining power with the small employers who hired their members; on occasion unions became more powerful than employers. And by 1910 most of the craft unions were tightly knit organizations of skilled workers wielding effective economic power through closed shop contracts.

Labor contracts achieved through collective bargaining became the primary means of improving conditions. Craft unionists were therefore unwilling to break hard-won contracts by engaging either in sympathetic walkouts or a general strike in order to defend fellow laborers' theoretical right to organize.[4] In New York, as elsewhere in the nation, the security of separate craft unions and the philosophy of *sauve qui peut* prevailed over the concept of labor solidarity and the ideal that "an injury to one is an injury to all."[5]

In the building, printing, brewing, and machine trades a union card became the passport to employment. Where the closed shop existed, unions had little reason to conduct fresh organizing campaigns.

Here it was unnecessary for the union organizer to reach indifferent laborers; instead, workers approached the union. These fortunate craft unionists dispassionately observed the bitter conflicts in progress on other labor fronts; they offered sympathy, guidance, and sometimes funds to embattled workers still struggling to organize, but themselves remained aloof from the struggle. Craft unionists, however, had special problems of their own.

Craft unions and their officials frequently practiced union corruption and machine politics. The best known New York labor leader at the start of the new century, Sam Parks, business agent for the Structural Iron Workers' Union local, transformed the strike from a means of improving labor's condition into an instrument for enriching the unscrupulous business agent. Parks and other building trades' union business agents all too commonly used the threat of a work stoppage to extort cash payments from contractors. However, even as they enriched themselves, they protected their followers' high wages and relative job security. Corruption and crime hardly diminished such business agents' popularity with the union rank and file. Even after Parks was convicted of extorting money from intimidated contractors and sentenced to a term in the state penitentiary, his own union re-elected him as business agent.[6] Other labor leaders in the building and printing trades, instead of devoting their time to exacting favors from employers, bargained with Tammany Hall for personal and union favors. These leaders, in return for promising the political support of their organizations, demanded patronage plums for themselves, generous treatment for their unions on municipal projects, and city contracts for family, friends, and pro-union contractors.[7]

A fortunate minority of the city's working class, then, belonged to powerful craft unions, received adequate wages, and tolerated corrupt leaders. But the majority of New York's laborers remained unorganized in 1900. The mass of Jewish and Italian immigrants, laboring in the needle trades, and other unskilled and semiskilled laborers in large municipal and private service occupations, had no unions to protect them. Labor's 1909–1916 organization upheaval struck the unorganized sectors of the metropolitan economy, the workers of which recaptured the *élan* and heroism long since lost by the skilled craft unionists.

New York's unorganized workers turned to the strike as their major organizational weapon. From 1910 to 1913 strikes in New York

State involved at least 95,000 workers annually. In 1913 alone, over 300,000 employees left their jobs to walk picket lines. Frequent and sometimes violent labor disputes were part of New York life until America's entry into the First World War.[8]

The organizational strike expanded the number of trade-unionists in New York almost four times as rapidly as the growth of the city's total population.[9] Unskilled and semiskilled workers in the needle trades were the special beneficiaries of union expansion. In 1909, fewer than 30,000 garment workers belonged to trade-unions; at the end of 1910, however, the membership of the needle trades unions numbered more than 100,000 men and women; and by 1913 total membership had passed the quarter million mark. By 1912 the garment workers had assumed first place in state-wide union membership and they represented almost one third of the state's total union membership.[10]

Women benefited equally. After 1909, owing largely to the success of labor organization in the needle trades, New York City's women workers for the first time entered trade-unions in significant numbers. Even in some nongarment trades, such as bookbinding, women began to move into positions of union leadership. This rapid increase in the number of organized female workers delighted the Women's Trade Union League.[11]

Men and women struck and risked physical danger and economic privation to secure employer recognition of their unions. In every major conflict strikers sought explicit union recognition. Whenever employers refused to concede to recognition, bitterness and violence ensued. Concessions on wages and hours appeared worthless to the strikers without formal recognition of their organizations by employers. As Morris Hillquit, Socialist party leader and labor lawyer, warned union members: "If the employers were today to concede all the demands of the strikers, but be allowed to destroy or even weaken the union, they could and would restore the old conditions of servitude."[12]

However, before the efforts of New York's unorganized workers to build trade-unions of their own choosing are considered, the economic and social environment out of which working-class discontent arose should be described. With that in mind, the remainder of this chapter analyzes briefly the city's economic structure and considers in more detail the working and living conditions endured by the unorganized masses.

I

The men's and women's clothing industries reflected New York's economic growth and structure. Between 1900 and 1910 both industries more than doubled their capitalization and labor force. New York became the nation's garment-making capitol, with 69.3 per cent of all women's clothing made in the United States and 38.4 percent of men's wear produced there. By 1919 the annual product of the women's garment industry nearly doubled that of its nearest competitor—men's clothing—and even bettered the combined efforts of printing and publishing, the metal trades, the food industries, and textiles. Over 160,000 workers, almost one of every six New York laborers, earned their livelihoods in the clothing trades.[13]

Although the clothing trades' economic growth was remarkable, most manufacturers shared in the material advance. The value of manufactured goods produced in New York City exceeded that of any *state* in the Union except New York and Pennsylvania. And New York City possessed (in round numbers) 26,000 of the State's 31,000 manufacturing concerns and 1.37 billion of the State's total capitalization of 1.91 billion dollars.[14]

Although aggregate statistics project an image of the city as an industrial giant, diversity of manufacture and small firms predominated. Other great American manufacturing cities developed and expanded around heavy industrial complexes. New York City deviated from this national pattern. Nationally, manufacturing firms combined and concentrated their productive facilities and management structures with an accompanying growth in the scale and size of their operations. In New York, the reverse occurred: the number of businesses increased and their size dwindled. In the age of Standard Oil, American Tobacco, and United States Steel, small firms with minimal capital investments, carrying on limited production, characterized New York's industrial structure.[15]

Businesses like those in the garment and printing trades face frequent fluctuations in market and product. They cannot invest large sums of capital in production or carry large inventories; they must rely upon subcontractors and other external sources for goods and services that large firms provide for themselves. New York provided an ideal location for such small businesses. There they found specialized subcontractors serving many different firms efficiently and effectively and a diversity of services and markets which meliorated the uncertainties of demand and style shifts, and they were able to meet increased demands without maintaining a great inventory. Thus nearly two dozen manufacturing industries dominated by comparatively small plants concentrated in the city's core.[16]

Statistics reveal the limited size of most New York manufacturing firms and the continuing trend toward smallness. Federal census data show a reduction in the size of women's garment plants in New York between 1879 and 1921, with only one pause. By 1921 the typical shop had only 18 employees. Shops in the men's clothing industry averaged fewer than 50 employees in 1917, and 43.4 percent of all factories had only one to four workers. Printing and publishing establishments as well as the metal trades also showed more rapid growth in the number of business units than in the size of the labor force and a constant trend toward smaller units of production. The textile, bakery, and woodworking industries illustrated similar structures and trends.[17]

The city's industrial structure based on modestly capitalized and widely diversified businesses determined, to some extent, the history, development, and structure of the city's labor movement. Small-scale operations undertaken by countless companies led to intense competition, employer instability, and economic weakness. Business survival required cutting variable costs to the bone. Since the wage bill was the most elastic of variable costs, small employers struggled to maintain low wage rates and bitterly fought trade-unions, making initial organization difficult. On the other hand, workers, once organized, often enjoyed considerable bargaining power in dealing with small employers lacking the capital reserves required to engage in long industrial conflicts. In fact, in New York City during the Progressive era smaller businesses, particularly in the garment trades, proved easier to organize and to bargain with.

II

New York City's labor market was as large and as diversified as its industrial structure. In 1910 it had approximately 70 percent of the combined working force of all first- and second-class cities in the state. More than one quarter of these workers labored in the needle trades, which also employed forty percent of the city's working women.[18]

From its beginnings the city benefited from the economic skills and ambitions of migrants and immigrants. Throughout the nineteenth century ambitious New England Yankees, dispossessed Irish peasants, and German immigrants had provided the city with much needed skills as well as with hordes of unskilled laborers. By 1900, however, Germans and Irish were becoming a minority in a labor force soon to be dominated by east European Jews and southern Italians. In the cigar trade Bohemians had succeeded Germans, only to be displaced in turn by Russian Jews and Italians. On the docks and on public works Irish longshoremen and day laborers ascended the economic ladder, making room for Italian immigrants on the bottom rungs.[19]

The immigrants from Italy's south, like the Irish before them, brought to the new world a heritage of dire poverty and social immobility. They brought few industrial skills and were poorly trained for the demands of an urban-industrial society. Italian immigrants included the greatest proportion of unskilled laborers among all nationalities. According to one estimate, throughout the period of mass immigration, 1881–1914, the percentage of general laborers among Italian immigrants fluctuated between 45 and 60 percent. Italian immigrants' lack of economic skills, and their Old-World traditions, which transcended all other social obligations and institutions, limited their effective participation in New York's labor movement.[20]

The east European Jews were also emigrants from an economically backward region of Europe. Many, however, had been petty merchants or skilled handicraft workers. As a result the proportion of skilled workers, excluding farmers, among Jews immigrating to America surpassed that of all other immigrant groups. Though Jewish immigrant workers found employment in more than 50 important New York trades, they concentrated in the clothing industry which came to be known as the Jewish trades. A sample of New York's Jewish workers indicated that before coming to the United States 64.4 percent of them had engaged in the manufacture of clothes. Their skills, their old-world heritage, and their relatively rapid adjustment to a new environment made Jewish immigrants the cutting edge of New York City's 1909–1916 working-class movement.[21]

III

While working conditions and living standards improved during the Progressive era, the hours of labor remained long and wages low.

Moreover, improvements in wages and conditions were uneven; the highly skilled and the better organized received a disproportionate share; frequently the unskilled and unorganized were barely able to maintain existing standards. Some labor economists have estimated that during the Progressive period three fourths of the adult male wage earners did not earn incomes sufficient to provide standard families (four members) with a minimum level of health and decency.[22] New York City proved no exception to their findings, as the following evidence drawn mostly from investigations of the city's less skilled and unorganized workers reveals.

In the needle trades prior to the emergence of strong, stable trade-unions long working hours prevailed. A usual working week consisted of from 56 to 59 hours exclusive of overtime. The clothing industry's seasonal nature aggravated conditions; during the busy season a 70-hour week was not uncommon, while in slack periods many workers went entirely without employment. Laborers in other occupations fared no better. Carmen on the city's extensive transit system labored seven days a week without provision for a day of rest. The transit worker's basic day required 10 hour's time actually spent on a car run; often, however, to earn 10 hours pay took 14 or 15 hours. The unionized bakers toiled 10 hours daily, six days a week; their nonunion brethren, owing to the Supreme Court's famous *Lochner* decision of 1905, worked a minimum 12-hour day. Only the men belonging to the older, established building trades' craft unions and, after the 1907 strike, to the typographical unions enjoyed the eight hour day and the six day week.[23]

Until the state passed remedial factory legislation in 1912 limiting women's working hours to 54 weekly, women toiled as long as, if not longer than, men. A social worker investigating working conditions among women employed at a twine factory observed:

> The women come out. Pale, narrow-chested, from hand to foot they were covered with fibrous dust. . . . They were types of factory workers—pale, haggard feeders of machines—like those described in the days of a century past in England. The fibre must rest heavily in the lungs of women who bend over rushing, whirring machines ten hours a day without fresh air and exercise.[24]

As late as 1914 the State Factory Investigating Commission reported repeated violations of the 54-hour law affecting women workers in the paper box and confectionery trades. Further surveys taken by the Commission from 1915 to 1918 revealed grosser violations of the hours law. The Commission discovered in a small sample of female laborers, 115 toiling over 60 hours weekly, and 11 working 70 hours or more. Violations were found in most industries employing women, and respect for the law seemingly depended entirely on the employers' preferences. Lax enforcement of factory laws exposed women to excessive and debilitating hours of labor.[25] It also demonstrated why workers turned to collective action through the trade-union.

Working women actually faced a cruel dilemma. Had the state law been enforced without exception many would have had earnings reduced below the necessary minimum. While maximum hours were set by law, no enforced minimum wage protected the total earnings of women. Most females toiled in industries or trades where employers operated on the smallest of margins and survived only by cutting corners and expenses. For both worker and boss, given prevailing attitudes and economic conditions, violation of state legislation was necessary for survival. Certainly complete abolition of illegal overtime without accompanying legislation protecting total earnings and stabilizing highly competitive trades would have brought grief to many women workers. Women, under the pressure of material necessity, chose protracted hours to deprivation.

Factory working conditions intensified the ill effects of extended hours. The State Factory Investigating Commission noted that in a selected manufacturing area on Manhattan's middle west side "manufacturers provided most inadequately for the daily comfort of their employees. . . . There can be no doubt that the health of the workers suffers from the hardships and discomforts which they encounter in their daily work. . . . It adds naturally to the strain and fatigue caused by the long hours of work."[26]

Henry Morgenthau, directing a citizens' committee to survey safety conditions in places of employment, discovered one or more fire hazards in most of the buildings. And the City's Fire Commissioner added: "I think that a great many of the fire escapes on buildings today are only put up to be called a fire escape. They are absolutely inadequate and absolutely useless." The ramifications of improper and insufficient safety precautions had already been indelibly etched in the public mind; on March 25, 1911, during the infamous Triangle Fire, 146 garment workers, predominantly young immigrant girls, lost their lives owing to a combination of fire and negligence in a supposedly fireproof, modern brick and concrete loft building. Morgenthau's Committee uncovered safety violations and inadequacies many months after the Triangle Fire. Again, legislation had proved either ineffective or unenforceable. Such working conditions and dangers recall the apocryphal tale of the Jewish garment worker who came home to celebrate one evening because "at the end of ten years in the garment-making industry, he [remained] alive."[27]

If factory workers endured disheartening conditions, homeworkers toiled in more noisome surroundings. The hoary institution of homework, rather than vanishing from twentieth-century New York, increased markedly. In November 1911, the city contained 13,268 tenements licensed for homework compared to 2,604 in 1904. Each of the licensed tenements included three to 50 apartments in which manufacturing might be established. And these houses represented only those in which state law permitted the manufacture of 41 specified items. At least 60 other items were produced without license and under only cursory state supervision. Unlicensed houses engaged in significant amounts of homework in direct violation of prevailing law. The homework system, for example, dominated the artificial flower industry. Homeworkers, usually representing the poorest strata of urban society, could afford only the cheapest tenements concentrated in notorious slum districts.[28]

Labor in the home, away from the watchful eye of the public and the factory inspector, brought child labor and unregulated hours of work. Wherever the staff employed by the State Factory Commission explored, they discovered children of tender age toiling alongside their mothers. Women with families to tend comprised the great majority of homeworkers; mothers stole the time devoted to manufacturing from the ordinary demands of family existence.

Although the typical day of homework took five hours, many women labored from nine to 11 hours, and some toiled 13 to 18 hours daily. The Factory Commission summarized the homeworker's existence:

> Homework means unregulated manufacturing carried on beyond the possibility of control as to hours of women's work, child labor, night work of minors or cleanliness and sanitation of work places. From the point of view of the community, the greatest objection to homework is its essential lawlessness.[29]

The ordinary homeworker received a pittance. Working with the aid of children, the entire family, if productive, might earn five dollars a week. Some women received as little as one and one-half cents an hour, although five to six cents hourly proved a more common wage. According to published statistics, most homeworkers earned less than four dollars weekly, and many failed to net two dollars.[30]

The Factory Commission wrote what should have been the epitaph for an obnoxious, antiquated system of manufacture: "Far from being socially economic or useful, each industry carried on in the workers' miserable homes was really dragging back that industry as a whole. It was competing unfairly with those carrying on business under the factory laws."[31] But homework persisted.

The homeworkers, of course, labored neither for pin money nor to pass the time of day; necessity was the taskmaster. Homework occupied a paradoxical place in working-class existence. In a community without public, free day nurseries, aid to dependent children, and a broad public relief program, the woman with young children or the woman restricted to the home by social or physical pressures could supplement meager family income only through homework. Many male and female factory workers also brought work home from the shop to escape trade-union or legislative restrictions and supplement regular income. In the case of homework, the means to a higher standard of living or simple sustenance debased and devalued the end, and homework deserved the verdict pronounced by the State Commission.

Factory workers and homeworkers received skimpy rewards for the long hours they labored in unsanitary and dangerous surroundings. During the latter part of the nineteenth century real wages rose and the general economic conditions of the American working class, though not unusually comfortable, improved markedly. The trend of real wages in the Progressive era remains less clear. Two leading authorities on wage rates, Paul H. Douglas and Albert Rees, disagree sharply. Douglas perceives in the early twentieth century a steep rise in the cost of living with a concomitant reduction in real purchasing power; Rees admits that mass immigration and the closing of the agricultural frontier retarded wage rates but insists, upon the basis of a revised cost-of-living index, that from 1899 to 1914 real wages rose slowly but steadily.[32]

Although aggregate statistical analysis and the available evidence indicate from 1890 to 1914 a steady *long run* rise in the real wage level and a commensurate improvement in living standards, individual case and community studies present a less positive account. Moreover, the worker existed in the here and now, not the future; he could not pay rent, purchase clothes, or enjoy a needed and deserved vacation with wages he and his heirs might receive over the *long run;* he would certainly have agreed with John Maynard Keynes's remark that the future promised only one absolute certainty: death.

During the Progressive era individual investigators and welfare organizations made various estimates of the annual or weekly income necessary to sustain a working-class family in New York. The estimates ranged from a necessary yearly income of 800 to 876 dollars for a family of three to four, to 505 dollars for a single man and 466 dollars for a working woman. All estimates supposed the most minimal budgets.[33]

But wages in New York City for the mass of workers fell beneath suggested minima. The United States Immigration Commission reported in 1911 that out of a sample of 10,000 male wage earners, the average yearly income approximated 413 dollars, and nearly half the group earned less than 400 dollars. Women workers investigated earned roughly half as much as the men, two thirds receiving less than 300 dollars annually. For immigrant workers the figures proved even lower. Immigrant families' combined earnings averaged less than the suggested annual sustenance budget of 800 dollars; the more recent arrivals, particularly Italians and Jews, earned considerably less than the better adjusted Irish and Germans.[34]

The State Factory Commission's investigators and other observers found equally dismaying evidence. Of 109,481 workers surveyed, the Commission discovered half received less than 8 dollars weekly, two thirds less than 10 dollars, and only one sixth earned 15 dollars or more. In the garment trades, while more than half the employees earned 10 to 12 dollars weekly, 15 to 30 percent of the work force, classified as learners, received only from 3 to 6 dollars. The Factory Commission observed that in a group of industries—paper box, confectionary, shirt, and millinery—average wages tended to remain beneath the proposed living wage.[35]

Female workers, an increasing proportion of the labor force, fared particularly poorly. Mary Van Kleeck and Louise Odencrantz, investigating the artificial flower trade and the conditions of Italian working women, respectively for the Russell Sage Foundation, found that four out of every five women they questioned required outside financial aid to remain above the minimum standard for health and decency established by the State Commission. One female laborer expressed simply but strongly the circumstances of the poorly paid woman worker:

> I didn't live, I simply existed. I couldn't live that you could call living. I certainly had to deprive myself of lots of things I should have had. It took me months and months to save up money to buy a dress or a pair of shoes. . . . I had the hardest struggle I ever had in my life.[36]

Job insecurity added to the worries of working men and women already frustrated by low wages and poor working conditions. Depressions aggravated anxiety. Twice, in 1908 and again in 1913, economic recessions intensified unemployment. In good times unemployment ordinarily averaged, during June and December when surveys were made, over 10 percent of the unionized work force; during bad times it approached 25 to 45 percent. In 1913, unemployment averaged 40 percent of the clothing industry's work force and 25 percent of that of the building trades. Seasonal changes in the employment level also upset the labor market. In short, few, if any laborers, had secure, year-round employment.[37]

Despite the apparently uninviting economic conditions, workers, native-born and immigrant, continued to enter New York City's labor market. Why? First, workers possessing needed skills and organized in stable craft unions worked and lived amid more pleasant surroundings. Typographical workers, laboring in one of the better organized and more skilled trades, earned average annual wages approximating 2000 dollars; skilled building tradesmen received comparable wages. Unorganized but equally skilled laborers probably earned substantial incomes; prior to the era of effective labor organization in the clothing trades, highly skilled cutters and tailors, despite seasonal employment, maintained above average annual earnings.

The metropolitan economy, however, attracted a large proportion of less skilled immigrant workers who satisfied the needs of small trades with minutely subdivided operations. Lacking both scarce skills and trade-unions, the great majority of the city's workers suffered the anxieties wrought by low wages and economic insecurity. Realizing that conditions were far from ideal, that they were in fact often intolerable, the unorganized refused to accept poor working conditions and unsatisfactory remuneration as either inevitable or permanent.

American-born workers, recalling a harsher past, could cherish the hope of further improvements. Though the economic reality of the new world could not equal the immigrant's expectations, material conditions in America proved remarkably attractive compared to the reality of old-world existence. One Jewish immigrant later recalled:

> Even the slums of the day were beautiful to me compared to the living quarters of Lithuania. For example, even though the toilet was in the hall, and the whole floor used it, yet it was a toilet. There was no such thing in Lithuania. . . . Here there was running water. I saw horse cars and trolley cars, and when I saw a cable car on Broadway, I thought America was truly the land of opportunity.[38]

Moreover, many immigrants as well as native Americans accepted the myth of the self-made man and saw evidence of its truth all around them.

New York's workers sought in different ways to achieve the promise of a brighter future. Some dreamed of rising within the prevailing structure of society by individual effort or by membership in a trade-union which had already made its peace with capitalism and the American system. Still others sought to construct a new and better social order.

But during the Progressive era, whatever the ultimate objective, hundreds of thousands of previously unorganized New York working-men and women turned to the trade-union in an effort to make American society more equitable and to exert positive human control over impersonal economic forces. By militant action and frequent strikes they attempted to build labor organizations, which would reform society to the advantage of the working class. The magnitude of the Progressive reform movement in New York City, the influence of local reformers, and the city's social structure resulted in a community environment more hospitable than ever before to the establishment of independent trade unions.

IV

Just as the city's economic structure and its working conditions helped shape the labor movement, metropolitan patterns of life established the community environment in which the working class forged its own instruments of organization and economic power.

From its seventeenth-century Dutch origins, New York's population had been remarkable for its heterogeneity; with each succeeding generation its religious and ethnic groups multiplied. Of the more than 18 million immigrants entering the United States from 1890 to 1919, over 13 million debarked at the Port of New York, lending substance to the oft repeated anecdote: "An Irishman landing there cries, 'Be dad! it's for the wurrld loike Corrk!'; a German exclaims, 'Ganzwie Berlin!'; the Chicagoan bluntly asks, 'What's the next train for the United States.' "[39]

By 1910 the city's foreign-born population numbered 1,927,203, with most having emigrated from Germany, Ireland, Italy, and Russia. Almost two million New York residents were also the children of parents born in the above four countries.[40] The city's population mixture reflected faithfully the shifting tides of European emigration. From 1880 to 1890, Germans and Irish dominated New York's ethnic mix, followed closely by natives of England, Scotland, and Wales. But as European emigration shifted to the south and east of the Continent, Russian and Italian immigrants began to arrive in large numbers. By 1910 Russian Jews and Italian Catholics had become the city's two largest ethno-religious groups.[41]

Each new wave of immigrants experienced the cycle of acculturation described so well in Oscar Handlin's *The Uprooted*. The newcomers at first found themselves isolated from the mainstream of American life—in the country but not of it. Hampered, except for the Irish, by their inability to speak English or to grasp the social and cultural mores of their adopted land, immigrants sought refuge among their own kind. They congregated in self-circumscribed areas, forming their own distinctive communities within the larger city. These ghettos became the newcomers' private world within the often inhospitable New World. "I did not know that the part of the city where I was living was called the East Side, or the Slums, or the Ghetto," remembered one immigrant Jewish girl.[42]

Jewtowns, Little Italys, Bohemias, and Hungarys, as well as a Chinatown, developed and thrived. These immigrant communities established their own religious institutions, coffee shops, newspapers, entertainment forms, and social institutions. Often subcommunities based upon the extended family or the village of origin developed within the broader immigrant community. And sometimes the narrower ties and loyalties constructed upon family relations and village associations vitiated the more catholic influences of immigrant welfare societies and trade-unions.[43]

Ethnic traditions and institutions assumed a dominant role in the acculturation of displaced and perplexed newcomers who sought security within their own ethnic community and leadership from their more successful compatriots. In the nineteenth century the Irish had turned for leadership to the new breed of Tammany politician and wardheeler, and the Germans to their successful businessmen, newspaper publishers, and Socialists. Later immigrants continued to seek counsel from men of wealth and status—attorneys, politicians, clergymen—and in the twentieth century more and more often from trade-union leaders.[44]

East European Jews and southern Italians, the largest and newest immigrant groups and those affected by the 1909–1916 labor upheaval, brought to America different traditions which governed their respective adjustments. Of course, like all newcomers, they began life in America at the bottom of the economic ladder, engaging in the more laborious, less skilled, less remunerative, and less secure jobs.[45]

Jewish immigrants concentrated in New York City. Almost two thirds of all the Jews entering the United States between 1899 and 1914 settled there; by 1914 about 1,300,000 Jews resided in New York. Furthermore, Jewish immigrants, unlike other nationalities, harbored little desire to re-emigrate; their total net immigration exceeded that of all other ethnic groups.[46]

The Jews, like other immigrants who had come from socially and economically backward regions of Europe, found metropolitan existence unfamiliar and frequently unrewarding. Transported from the handicraft and village system of Tsarist Russia to a bewildering new-world industrial metropolis, the Jews floundered economically. Many followed the path of earlier Russian immigrants to the door of the sweatshop where they would labor with compatriots; there, they found employers who, in return for low wages, understood the immigrants' religious and cultural peculiarities and needs. Although the Jews brought varied trades and skills to America and readily found employment in the needle trades, they met economic hardship before outgrowing the sweatshop stage. Thus, many first generation immigrants unable to rise rapidly on the economic ladder in the land of freedom and prosperity discovered a congenial home and a pertinent philosophy in militant trade-unionism and the Socialist Party.[47]

Many of the Jews arriving in America in the late nineteenth and early twentieth centuries had already participated in and created a tradition of working-class, political-economic action. The Russian-Jewish labor movement or *Bund* emerged amidst the general revolutionary ferment sweeping Tsarist Russia. It grew rapidly and in 1905 exerted significant influence in the labor uprisings of that year, which helped precipitate the abortive revolution. Unlike the AFL affiliated trade-unions predominant in the United States, the *Bund* emphasized the unity of political and economic efforts, operating simultaneously for material betterment and political reform. After the failure of the 1905 Russian Revolution, numerous Russian-Jewish radicals fled to the New World for sanctuary.[48]

Trade-unions and labor leaders, however, occupied an ambivalent place in the Jewish community. For many Jews hoping to go into business for themselves, or linked closely to their families or *lansmannschaften,* unions became a hindrance and a nuisance; for other Jews demanding improved conditions of life and labor or enhanced prestige and status, unions offered hope. Just as politics became the *metier* of the Irish (and Al Smith's career epitomized its reward), trade-unionism attracted the immigrant Jews excluded from the overwhelmingly Irish world of urban politics. Jews interested in bettering society and winning the respect of their peers and superiors could look to the careers of Samuel Gompers and other immigrant labor leaders. In brief, what politics accomplished for the Irish, trade-unionism promised New York's Jews.[49]

While rapid industrialization in Tsarist Russia undermined the economic security of Jewish merchants and artisans causing them to leave Russia, industrial progress in northern Italy weakened further the backward economy of Italy's south, resulting in increased emigration by an already poverty wracked people. The southern Italian immigrants arriving in New York had fled one of the most depressed regions in Europe, an area combining a basically agrarian economy with a pseudourban existence lacking the amenities of city life. Italian newcomers, educationally deprived in the Old World and bound by a superstitious, almost pagan, village and family code, became acclimated to American society even more slowly and with greater difficulty than other immigrants. Thus bad times stimulated considerable re-emigration among Italians, and in some depression years departing Italians actually exceeded new arrivals.[50] Although Italians, like other newcomers, found sanctuary within their own ghettos, their basic ties were to the family, not to the church, or trade-union, or workmen's circle, or political organization. Relative impermanency in America and primitive, almost antisocial, old-world traditions weakened Italian immigrants' ability to establish stable community organizations and to rise socially and economically.[51]

Immigrant leaders perceived the inability of the Italian community to create effective social organizations. Father Bassi of St. Lucy's Church commented sadly:

> The Italian institutions are very few and very poor, and most of the big organizations do nothing to help them. . . . I should like to see the eyes of the public open to the fact that very little is done here for Italians by Italian organizations. . . . We should all unite as the Jewish people do.[52]

Only intense family ties and village loyalties gave Italians a sense of security.

Economic conditions further undermined the Italian male's position in the New World. Most male Italian immigrants left their families in the old country, and once in America they accepted poorly paid work, long hours, backbreaking effort, cheap accommodations, and minimal expenditures for food, clothing, and recreation so as to save enough to bring their families to America or to sustain them in the Old World. In his intense desire to save, the Italian worker sometimes proved hostile to unions, strikes, and radicalism, particularly when they threatened employment and wages. However, where unions were strong, promised substantial improvements in wages and working conditions, and welcomed Italian members, they flocked to the union; higher wages increased savings. But Italian immigrants' social traditions, educational deficiencies, lack of community organizations, and economic needs rendered them less significant than Jews in the creation of immigrant-led labor unions.[53]

The diverse nationalities struggling to adapt to metropolitan life exhibited marked animosity among themselves. The most discernible split arose between older and newer immigrants, Irish and Germans against Jews and Italians. Older immigrants, those who already had achieved some status in their adopted land, tended to patronize and even, on occasion, to antagonize the newcomers. For example, the riot of July 30, 1902, at the funeral of Rabbi Jacob Joseph resulted from the resentment of lower east side Irish forced out of their original areas of settlement by newly arrived Jews. To make matters worse the Jewish community itself was split. German Jews, living uptown and representing both an older wave of immigration and relative affluence and prestige, often disdained their less advanced and less wealthy coreligionists from eastern Europe. And the two largest recent immigrant groups—Italians and Jews—showed little sympathy for each other's circumstances. Abraham Rosenberg, in 1913 President of the ILGWU (a union encompassing diverse nationalities though primarily Jewish and Italian), discussing declining real-estate values in a fast changing east side neighborhood, remarked: "It is true that real estate has become cheaper on account of [sic] building the new bridges, on account of [sic] the immigration of Italians and Greeks, and all kinds of nationalities, and the Jewish people who used to live there . . . *have to run away on account of* [sic] *that there are nothing but Italians there. No Jew wants to live there* [italics added]."[54]

V

Diverse neighborhoods marked by extremes of wealth and poverty were as commonplace in New York as mixed nationalities. A visit to the metropolis in the 1870's had confirmed Henry George in his belief that wealth and poverty proceeded hand in glove in the American economic and social system. The first two decades of the twentieth century brought no major transformations to New York City to challenge George's notions. It remained more than a trolley or an El ride from the tenements of the lower east side to the mansions of Fifth Avenue, from the old walkups looking out upon the tracks of the elevated to the elevator apartments overlooking the green expanses of Central Park, from the cluttered and filth-ridden streets of working-class neighborhoods to the wide and clean, tree-lined streets of the well to do. Few individuals made the transition in their lifetimes.

Visitors to New York noticed either the splendor or the misery, as impressions of the extremes crowded out those of the more modest and respectable homes of the city's middle class and well-to-do working class. Perhaps the appearance of the less attractive sector of the metropolis caused an English visitor to respond when asked if New York wasn't truly beautiful: "I have never said that Hell is ugly."[55]

Most noteworthy of the other portions of the city was Jacob Riis's famous city under the El, the area on Manhattan's east side bounded by Broadway on the west, the Brooklyn Bridge on the south, the East River on the east, and 14th Street on the north. By 1893 one and a half million human beings, of whom five of every six lived in cramped tenements, huddled together in this congested neighborhood. Observers described the section variously as the home of the pushcarts, paupers, and consumptives, or as the "horrible example of the pious moralist, and the special prey of the self-satisfied philanthropist."[56]

The neighborhood, as Roy Lubove and Moses Rischin have described it, had grown to serve the needs of a population that increased more rapidly than available housing.[57] The result, of course, was great profits for land speculators and realtors but noisome tenements for working-class families.

Despite the housing improvements detailed in Lubove's study of tenement reform, the lower east side remained a neighborhood in which saloons were neighbors to shops purveying religious objects and in which rickety wooden buildings hoary with age pressed against the rear walls of brick tenements decorated with rainbow-hued washlines. The streets remained uncleaned and the pavements hidden beneath mounds of matted debris. "Look up, look down," wrote one observer, "turn this way, turn that—here is no prospect but the unkempt and the disorderly, the slovenly and the grim; filth everywhere, trampled on the sidewalks, lying in windows, collected in the eddies of doorsteps."[58]

Still the poor and usually the newer immigrants crowded into neighborhoods similar to the lower east side. These areas, usually within walking distance of the factory, offered the working class greater opportunities for employment and essential savings on carfare. The newcomer also found the congested neighborhood of his compatriots a most congenial starting point for life in the New World.[59]

Once again, however, the immigrant's dream of the new world soured before the reality of New York life. One immigrant concluded as he trudged through crowded, dirt littered streets: "This was the boasted American freedom and opportunity—the freedom for respectable citizens to sell cabbages from hideous carts, the opportunity to live in those monstrous, dirty caves that shut out the sunshine."[60]

But what the newcomer discovered in the metropolis, while less than he expected, was also more than he had ever had or experienced previously. If in America he lacked private toilets, he had had no toilets at all in the old country; if he had no hot water, he had had no running water whatever in Europe; if he was poor, he could see opportunity all about him in New York.

The old-world illusion and the new-world reality, however, remained difficult to reconcile. Thus an immigrant girl stifled by her tedious round of work and existence cried out: "Where was the time for the free schools, where was the time for the wonderful libraries, for the luxurious museums? Where was the opportunity to rejoice in all the blessings of this free country?"[61] The shattered aspirations and the frustrations of immigrant workers made lower-class neighborhoods the battleground for trade-union gospelers, social reformers, Socialists, and Tammany politicians.

VI

The New York City Democratic Party through Tammany Hall provided essential services to the city's working class. The Hall functioned as a social and human resource as well as a political machine. Through its ubiquitous organizational establishment, Tammany furnished the necessary human cement of government and politics. It adjusted the severe laws of the statute book to the neighborhood and national peculiarities of the city, obtaining licenses for pushcart peddlars and rescuing immigrant children from the clutches of the impersonal law. It offered the community a social center and a benevolent institution—"social during the man's ordinary life, benevolent in his time of trouble." Tammany chieftains, especially Charles F. Murphy, boss from 1902 to 1924, comprehended the nature of politics in a pluralistic society and catered to diverse groups, seeking close ties with Jews, Italians, and Germans, always attempting to make room for every potential bloc of voters.[62]

Tammany was particularly well organized and effective in tenement neighborhoods where it operated as a welfare institution, establishing a miniature, private welfare state for those struggling against poverty. The needy looked to the district leader for jobs on the city payroll or permits to peddle various items; the leader secured these jobs, planned picnics and boat excursions, provided holiday food baskets for the destitute, shoes for deprived children, and even assistance with the landlord when rent was overdue. James Bronson Reynolds, the headworker at the east side's University Settlement, vividly described Tammany's grip on the insecure wage earner: "The impending threat of beggary or the poor house which hangs over the independent laborer is the power which drives so many into the arms of the political boss, who undertakes to provide an assurance of steady employment, with out-of-work benefits for the laborer's family."[63]

Tammany's twentieth-century appeal and strength remained consonant with its mid-nineteenth-century development. In the 1840's and 1850's, the Hall had championed the cause of immigrants, particularly the Catholic Irish, against Whig nativists. An alliance with Catholic newcomers became the heart of Democratic strength well into the twentieth century. Irish and Italian neighborhoods consistently returned overwhelming Democratic majorities. Republicans and later Progressives retained Whig predispositions toward nativism and Protestant morality (primarily for temperance and antigambling). Political competition failed to disturb Tammany's hold on lower-class neighborhoods. Irish politicians rose quickly to dominance within the machine and through most of the twentieth century the Hall itself maintained a Gaelic complexion.[64]

Reformers challenged Tammany Hall with mixed success. Time and again they would defeat Tammany in an election only to squander their advantage. Seth Low served as reform mayor from 1901 to 1905; then William Gaynor held office as an anomaly, a Tammany reform mayor, from 1909 to 1913; and finally, John Purroy Mitchel served as Fusion mayor from 1913 to 1917. In each instance Tammany rebounded from defeat and elected its "own" men—George B. McClellan in 1905 and John J. Hylan in 1917. Election victories illustrated the inherent strength of the metropolis' political reformers; their defeats underlined a failure to perceive Tammany's appeal as a social welfare institution. Where Tammany provided assistance, jobs, favors, and circuses for the working class, reformers promised good government, economy, and morality. Honest administration provided no substitute for machine favors to the working class. Thus though reformers won elections, they never learned that "to shatter Tammany Hall politically is not to shatter Tammany Hall socially . . . no program of mere efficiency . . . can compete with Tammany Hall in the social and human field." As Amos Pinchot wrote to Progressive Party district leaders in 1913: "So long . . . as we reformers refuse to attack the sources of Tammany's power, Tammany is perhaps a little bored with us, but, on the whole, the Tiger feels safe and happy."[65]

What the reformers failed to achieve—the liberation of the workers from the clutches of the Democratic machine—trade-unions promised. Unions provided members with some measure of job security, illness and death benefits, and other attractive and needed social services, which might render Tammany's competing services less appealing and less effective. Labor leaders and working-class politicians thus could demand favorable party platforms and appropriate legislation in return for support and whatever votes they influenced. On occasion, labor leaders attempted to lead working-class voters away from the Democratic Party. This possibility led the University Settlement's headworker to believe that "in relieving the laborer of this temptation to political serfdom, the trade-union renders an incidental civic benefit."[66] But, in most cases, New York workers, organized or not, continued to vote Democratic.

VII

If reformers failed to gain lasting political success or to achieve an alliance with the working class, they made a contribution to urban betterment through their exertions in neighborhood social settlements and also by their pragmatic cooperation with organized labor in lobbying for beneficial and protective labor legislation. Settlement house workers were probably the most effective of the metropolis' diverse reformers at the human level. They were idealistic young men and women anxious to share the experiences of the working class and to live and toil among the underprivileged. Settlement residents thus acted as a ferment, a catalyst in their communities "trying to make people realize the necessity for a different world, a better community— with parks, playgrounds, education and all cultural attainments which flavor human life."[67]

Many prominent citizens in the metropolitan community entered the world of the social settlement. The University Settlement numbered among its residents Hamilton Holt, editor of the *Independent;* Charles B. Stover, later Commissioner of Parks; Louis H. Pink, municipal advisor and housing reformer; Aaron M. Sakolski, economist and teacher; and Ernest Poole, author of the Pulitzer Prize-winning novel, *The Harbor.* Florence Kelley, Frances Perkins, and Eleanor Roosevelt also spent extended periods in the settlements, while Harry Hopkins obtained his initial contact with urban existence and social welfare needs in a lower east side settlement house. These early twentieth-century settlements served as incubators for men and women who reached political maturity during the New Deal.

Scores of these dedicated young men and women honestly hoped to understand and to better the conditions of the underpaid worker and the slum dweller. Lillian Wald, of Henry House fame, pleaded that the laborer be shown more than "a world that is . . . only work and eat and sleep." Others sought to "reduce the barrier of misunderstanding and prejudice which will always tend to raise itself between rich and poor." Reformers fought to abolish the sweatshop, and in 1902, at the instigation of Florence Kelley and Lillian Wald, the settlement houses of New York founded a Child Labor Committee to lobby for needed legislation; the following year the State Legislature passed the first adequate child labor law. When east-side families struck against high rents, settlement workers rushed to their aid and defense. In 1908, led by Miss Wald, the reformers urged state aid for the unemployed and persuaded Governor Charles Evans Hughes to appoint a commission to study the immigrant labor problem with a view to ameliorating conditions. Allied with the Consumers' League, other reform societies, and organized labor, settlement workers pressured the State Legislature to enact welfare legislation beneficial to the wage worker. In the wake of the Triangle Fire, the city's reform factions, including prominent clergymen, combined efforts and became a powerful force supporting the endeavors of the State Factory Investigating Commission and the Legislature's successful attempts to extend the scope of factory laws. New York City reformers through their diverse crusades carried the state into the vanguard of progressivism.[68]

Certain of the young people motivated by the gospel of reform were not content simply to succor the lower classes in *noblesse oblige* fashion; they insisted upon aiding the working class to help itself through the creation of effective workers' organizations. These more militant but less numerous reformers actively entered the trade-union arena or enlisted in the Socialist Party. Few captured the spirit better than Gertrude Barnum. Miss Barnum, offspring of a prominent Chicago Democratic family, passed from the University of Wisconsin to the realm of Jane Addams, Hull House, and genteel middle-class reform, and then to the rough and tumble existence of trade-union organizer for the ILGWU. She had slowly come to the realization that the conditions making social settlements and charity necessary must themselves be eradicated. The New York Women's Trade Union League represented this sentiment on an organized plane. The League, financed by wealthy citizens and staffed by volunteer reformers, encouraged trade-unionism among women workers and allowed female laborers and trade-unionists control of policy-making positions.[69] While the Barnums enlarged the reformer's mission, most reformers functioned within more traditional limits.[70]

Whether operating within established reform channels or moving in more original and radical directions, middle- and upper-class citizens concerned with the structure and tone of metropolitan society fashioned a community environment in which the working class could establish its own institutions for improvement. The omnipresence of reform and change within the urban community eased the way for the foundation of trade-unions. Concern for the plight of the working class by the city's "better" residents led them to tolerate the emergence of an independent labor movement and to assist laborers in efforts to organize trade-unions. Robert Bruere, one of the more prominent urban reformers, later became a major policy advisor to Fusion Mayor Mitchel, and Bruere utilized his position to convince the young mayor to favor trade-unionism among garment workers and transit workers.[71] But except for the singular Barnums and Brueres, middle- and upper-class concern for the less privileged seldom passed beyond sympathy and neutral assistance; reformers often feared truly independent, self-sufficient labor unions as a threat to the public welfare.

Thus, though the relatively well-to-do reformers may have descended into the gutter in order to aid those less fortunate, they made sure not to soil their clothes in the process. Jacob Riis, while overly solicitous toward the City's poorer inhabitants, represented the older, patronizing attitude toward the lower classes: "It is a dreary old truth that those who would fight for the poor must fight the poor to do it. It must be confessed that there is little enough in their past experience to inspire confidence in the sincerity of the effort to help them." Or, as another reformer frankly commented: "The strong are strong only that they may aid the weak . . . the rich are rightfully rich that they may combine and so direct the labors of the poor as to make labor more profitable to the laborers." *The Survey,* official journal of the charity societies of New York, stated the case for upper-class directed reform. The natural allies of social work are, it wrote, "the financiers and the sanitarians and the engineers and the captains of industry."[72]

In short, these reformers, anxious to preserve the fundamental capitalistic bias of American society from lower-class attack, agreed to ameliorate the working class's conditions of existence. As long as the middle and upper classes led, the laborers were allowed to share in the benefits; when labor proposed through its own organizational or political power to redistribute wealth and reorder the American social structure, reformers balked, deeming organized labor a threat to true American values.

Reformers exhibited even less understanding and tolerance toward the immigrant worker. Josephine Shaw Lowell was dismayed by the "influx of uneducated foreigners" who were lowering the American standard of living. And Walter Weyl, calling for an end to unrestricted immigration, argued that "the condition of the great mass of the working classes of this country is being depressed by unrestricted immigration as by no other cause." Other native do-gooders appeared disturbed by the Italians crowding Irish longshoremen off the docks, and by the un-American appearance of hordes of Russian-Jewish tailors in the garment trades.[73]

Only the Jewish immigrants received positive endorsement from middle-class Progressives. James Bronson Reynolds, commenting after eight years of social work experience among lower east side Jewish newcomers, said: "I can say that for the greater part, it would have been a great pity if any legislative inhibitions had prevented their coming. I feel that society is much better for their being here. Their eagerness, brightness and *fine susceptibility to Americanizing influences* are very valuable assets in our social life [italics added]."[74] A tendency by middle- and upper-class reformers to romanticize the character of the Jewish immigrant exerted singular power in drawing them to the cause of the garment workers from 1910 to 1916 during the series of bitter strikes which brought labor organization to the clothing trades.

Between the workers, immigrant and American, and the reformer a real gulf existed. The workers proved more perceptive of this void than many reformers realized, and laborers often met upper-class humanitarians with suspicion and hostility. Mayor Gaynor expressed colloquially the sentiments of many a tenement dweller:

> People come slumming and peeking in your windows, seeing how you lived and what you ate; called to see what your wife was doing; and she knew her business maybe better than they did. Their more fit place would probably have been more to stay home and take care of their own house.

Labor leaders, especially, looked askance at the reform efforts of "respectable" citizens, who appeared patronizing and critical toward independent union personnel. Trade-unionists often considered altruistic reformers eccentric and indeed made no provision for their participation in the labor movement. Many former union officials and organizers insist that reformers never had marked influence or more than nominal participation in labor's great organizing drives during the Progressive era. Union leaders preferred that the working class accomplish its own improvement and reformation.[75]

Whether or not the city's "respectable" citizens enlisted in or approved of the labor movement is beside the point; they did create the environment in which working-class organizations could function effectively; they did, in fact, on occasion provide trade-unions with material assistance and sympathy enough to turn the tide of conflict.

Within this favorable community environment, trade-union gospelers prophesied a noble future for the working class. Union spokesmen offered their followers salvation through organization, promising that trade-unions would bring job security, higher wages, and a better life. Although the labor movement's theorists agreed upon the benefits provided by unions, they fought bitterly over the best means to achieve their utopia. Let us now turn our attention to the ideology of the New York labor movement.

2.
New York Immigrants & the Gospel of Trade-unionism

DURING THE PROGRESSIVE ERA many individuals considered the labor question the "distinctive national problem." As trade-unions waged their organizational strikes and increased their memberships, they appeared to pose a distinct threat to unorganized sectors of the American community. Corporate concentration also vexed Americans but business at least was an inherently American institution. The trade-union, on the contrary, existed outside the mainstream of society and denied the national tradition of "rugged individualism."[1]

Spokesmen for labor, anxious to win sympathy for their organizational strikes, attempted to counteract antilabor propaganda and community antipathy toward working-class organization. Trade-unionists sought public favor by emphasizing traditional American values—equal opportunity and democracy. Where labor succeeded in winning sympathy, it obtained influential community support during its organizational strikes.[2] Generally speaking, however, the trade-union gospel conflicted with dominant national beliefs and values.

Labor leaders, fully aware of their movement's marginal existence, attempted to endow trade-unionism with high ethical purpose. They flavored their writings and speeches with statements expounding labor's moral mission. Conservative unionists and radical unionists in New York suppressed many of their essential differences in an effort to endow the working class with social and moral superiority.

Nationally, however, a restricted form of pragmatism dominated the

American labor movement's philosophy. Those who held positions of power within the AFL were practical, unimaginative men, whose lack of formal education or intellectual experience rendered them immune to expansive social ideas. They gratefully followed the pattern set by their leader, Samuel Gompers, who indelibly impressed his personality and ideas upon the American labor movement. During his later years Gompers had become a tenaciously conservative labor leader who confessed his inability to see where the movement he directed was heading. He thought only of immediate improvements in material conditions within a better but still capitalistic world. Gompers pledged the AFL to perpetual progress, not ultimate power and utopia.[3]

Gompers' trade-union followers, accustomed to the American myth of success through individual initiative, maintained that progress was founded upon self-interest, material desires, and piecemeal reform, not upon collective sacrifice, idealism, and revolution. They stressed the substantive aspects of the American dream, accepted capitalism as a viable economic system, and sought only to compel capitalism to function for their benefit as well as for that of the employer or *rentier*. The appeal of the Gompers-style labor leader like that of the businessman was to self-advancement—"in Carl Sandburg's phrase, to the 'dictates of the belly.' "[4]

Although Gompers' views held supremacy among most of the leaders and the largest organizations in the national labor movement, New York City was different. There, radical theories and programs exerted considerable influence, and two contending strains of thought clashed.

Leaders of the old-line craft unions, whose members had already secured many material improvements, felt little compulsion to analyze either the purposes of a labor movement or the rationale of American society. Instead, the officers of the more "aristocratic" craft unions occupied themselves with the everyday business requirements of their respective organizations and let their less fortunate union brethren theorize.

Spokesmen for struggling new unions, on the other hand, sought to justify the existence of their none too robust progeny. Their membership, commonly drawn from the less skilled groups in the city, was dominated by Russian-Jewish immigrants in the needle trades. These unions—the International Ladies' Garment Workers' Union, the Amalgamated Clothing Workers of America, the United Cloth Hat and Cap Makers' Union, and the International Fur Workers' Union—were usually more radical and militant than the firmly anchored craft unions. The desire of these immigrant trade-unionists to create a new and better world resulted in a more expansive role for the labor movement.

But radicals never monopolized the semi-industrial needle trades' unions. A functioning moderate, or conservative, opposition always existed. (Hereafter, the terms moderate and conservative will be used interchangeably to describe those labor leaders inside and outside the immigrant unions who accepted capitalism and who sought primarily to function within the existing social order.) The moderates, as would be expected, desired to limit the aims of the labor movement. Within the needle trades' unions they clashed with the radicals who believed that labor could and should revolutionize the structure of American society. Both the conservative (moderate) and the radical philosophies of labor were articulated in the course of an internal, ideological struggle within the city's newer immigrant unions. Within these unions two clearly contending conceptions of the role of trade-unionism developed.[5]

I

Conservative trade-unionism numbered among its disciples John Dyche, General Secretary-Treasurer of the ILGWU, 1904–1914, and the entire executive board of the United Garment Workers of America. Dyche, though Russian-born, lived his early adult years in England where he absorbed both the rationale of English craft unionism and antipathy to utopian programs. After coming to America in 1901, he readily adjusted to the Gompers-AFL pragmatic school of trade-unionism. His moderate policies as Secretary-Treasurer of the ILGWU won for him the respect of pure and simple unionists within the needle trades. After his defeat for re-election at the 1914 union convention, Dyche moved further away from militant class-conscious unionism. Shortly thereafter, he became a garment manufacturer and in 1923 published a scathing indictment—*Bolshevism in American Labor*—of the ILGWU's leftist leaders. Thomas A. Rickert and Benjamin A. Larger of the United Garment Workers represented respectively native American trade-unionism and an older wave of immigration. Their leadership transformed the UGWA into a loyal supporter of AFL business unionism. And their conservative, "bread and butter" leanings triggered the rebellion of militant immigrant tailors, who created in 1914 from the old UGWA shell, the new

Amalgamated Clothing Workers of America.[6] Throughout the Progressive years, the Dyches, Rickerts, and Largers challenged their socialist adversaries.

The moderate elements emphasized the primacy of immediate achievements. For them, talk of a future utopia seemed beside the point when the workingman had to contend with the harsh realities of the present. "Through conservative, conciliatory efforts," they contended, "far more can be reached than through abstract radicalism." Only the growing conservatism of the labor movement held "the promise of increasing and continuing power for organized labor." Unionism, if it accepted moderation and sanctity of contract as the twin keys to success, could gain the endorsement of the business world and the community at large.[7]

Moderates also muted references to class conflict, trying to convince workers that their material success and future progress were inextricably bound to that of their employers, that wages and profits proceeded from the joint efforts of both parties. The more prosperous an industry the greater the returns available for labor. Differences may exist as to an equitable division of the spoils, but "like the captain and the crew of a ship, whatever differences there may be between them as to treatment, both are equally interested in bringing the vessel safely into port. That is the truth we have been trying to impress upon employers and workmen alike."[8]

Conservatives suggested that the clash between capital and labor become more "civilized" than the irrepressible Marxian class war. Labor unions should not aim at the extermination of the capitalist but, rather, should convince employers "that they can just as well carry on their business under union control as without it, and that, in fact, it pays them better to agree with us, to be at peace with our organization than to fight us." Class war existed only as a weapon against recalcitrant employers; the *Ladies' Garment Worker* informed its readers,

> We openly confess we are very anxious to live in peace and have amicable relations with every employer who will recognize our Union and enter into agreements with us. Whatever the conception of the "class war" of our members may be, in actual practice it is not directed against those employers who are willing to have amicable relations with us.[9]

Moderates saw no alternative under the existing capitalistic system to obtaining in some degree the cooperation of employers. "If you succeed

[32]

in catching the employer by the throat in September, he is sure to return the compliment in the month of May." "Instead of wasting . . . energies in trying to injure each other, it is much wiser to come to an understanding."[10]

Moderates, such as Dyche, stressed the role of leadership in molding the outlook of the rank and file. Consequently he asserted that union officials should "be conservative, practical-minded men, who will stand between the employers and the union members and resolutely insist upon fair dealing on the part of both." Conservatism and skillful bargaining ability were deemed the *sine qua non* of a leadership which would restrain and control the more militant and less realistic rank and file. "The object of sane and responsible leadership should be to educate the members in such a way that they should not expect more than it is within the power of the Union to obtain for them."[11]

Middle-of-the-road labor spokesmen, in short, constantly watched for the main chance. They fully affirmed the American way of life with its emphasis on self-interest and perpetual material progress, but they agreed with the cautionary proviso issued by the President of New York Typographical Union No. 6: "Let us not hitch our wagon to a star lest we aspire too high and fall too far." Through opportunism and the securing of piecemeal concessions, moderates believed, labor would eventually obtain a share in the management of industry and equality with the employer.[12] The Webbs's slogan, the "inevitability of gradualness," seems an appropriately descriptive phrase regarding the outlook of moderates within New York City's labor movement.

Many ordinary, dues-paying union members actively supported moderate policies. Unionists, who were highly skilled and thus enjoyed job security and higher wages, were not likely to dispute pragmatic, bread-and-butter policies. Skilled workers had little desire to overturn the cart of capitalism from which they appeared to receive ample material rewards. Their union, like a good dairy farmer, should milk the cow of capitalism for all it could give without destroying its vitality.

II

Moderate voices, however, did not pre-empt the field of labor ideology. Conservative hegemony in the massive garment workers' unions, wherever and whenever it existed, was shaky. As often as not, radicals controlled executive offices in the needle trades' unions. Most of the radical spokesmen within the needle trades came to the United States directly from eastern Europe where many had served apprenticeships in the Jewish *Bund*. The abortive 1905 Russian Revolution reinforced their ranks qualitatively and quantitatively. Trained in the philosophy and practice of joint economic and political action, they frowned upon the AFL's artificial separation of the two. Raised in a radical, revolutionary environment, they disdained the AFL's conservatism. Considering a cooperative commonwealth possible in the time-worn Old World, they believed utopia a more likely possibility in the favorable climate of the New World.[13]

But the socialist utopia the needle trades radicals preached about bore a distinct resemblance to the more prosaic society sought by nonsocialist Progressive reformers. New York's Jewish socialists by 1910 had long since outgrown the revolutionary doctrines propagated by Daniel De-Leon's Socialist Labor Party, which waged total war, not just against capitalism, but also against the AFL and other so-called nonrevolutionary trade-unions. New York socialists like Morris Hillquit, Abe Cahan, and Meyer London had led the 1897–1898 rebellion against DeLeon's control of American socialism. Breaking with DeLeon, the New Yorkers later joined with Victor Berger, Max Hayes, and Eugene Debs to form the Socialist Party of America. The SPA, unlike the Socialist Labor Party, did not declare war upon the AFL; it sought instead to capture the Federation by boring from within. Moreover, the immigrant New Yorkers in most cases de-emphasized the differences between reform and revolution, Progressivism and Socialism.[14]

Unlike Daniel Bell's prototype American socialists whose inherent philosophy made it impossible for them "to relate . . . to the specific problems of social action in the here and now, give-and-take political world," New York's socialists related only too well. Unlike Bell's socialists who were "trapped in the unhappy problem of living '*in* but not *of* the world,' so they could only act, and then inadequately, as the moral but not political man in an immoral society," New York's Jewish socialists lived too fully in this world and were too much political men.[15]

Quite early, Jewish socialists learned the realities of American life. Cahan remembered that when he arrived in America he and his comrades believed "all that was necessary was to declare a social revolution and we would have a social revolution." Later, however, he and the others learned the lesson "of patience and practical achievement."[16]

Hillquit, speaking for mainstream New York socialism, amplified: "We do not expect the socialist order to be introduced by one sudden and great political cataclysm, nor . . . expect it to be established by a rabble made desperate by misery and starvation."[17] No, New York immigrant socialists by and large were not Marxist fundamentalists but were Bernstein revisionists who adjusted Marxist ideology to the American world of work-a-day reform.

The immigrant socialists, rejecting revolution and violence, saw the trade-union and the Socialist Party as the twin pillars upon which their new society would be built. Political action would bring immediate welfare legislation and eventual Socialist control of the state with public ownership of the means of production and distribution. The trade-union would win immediate concessions from employers, educate its members to the need for political action, and train them ultimately to manage the cooperative commonwealth's publicly owned industries. This revolution, if that is the word for it, would be made by a well-organized, decently paid, soundly educated proletariat acting under the leadership of intellectuals. This is the kind of socialism desired by a young female immigrant garment worker who pleaded for more socialist activity in her union. "Isn't it possible," she asked, "to make them not only trade-unions, but idealistic unions, and to make propaganda?"[18]

Despite the reform socialism expounded by most of New York's Jewish immigrant intellectuals and absorbed by their followers in the needle trades, socialists still preached the rhetoric of the apocalypse. This, more than the substance of their program, set New York's trade-union radicals apart from their more moderate opponents.

Less concerned with the work-a-day machinations of the union movement than with the inspiring thought of a new and beneficent society, the radicals appealed to the hearts and minds rather than to the stomachs and flesh of their disciples. They did not disdain appeals to the baser sentiments such as material self-interest motivating the working class, but they desired to channel self-interest into cooperative endeavors. In a sense, they dreamed of transmuting individual self-interest into a community of interests. Perhaps, they reasoned, by appealing to the nobler aspects of the laborer, the more material and mundane facets of unionism could be transcended. Trade-unionism was in their conception the dominating factor in the development of a higher view of man's duty in all of his relations to his fellow men. All their pleas and theories pointed to one conclusion—the destruction of capitalism and the establishment of the cooperative commonwealth.[19]

The militants paved their road to a new world with battles between the working class and the capitalist class. "We always are and always will be in the position of enemies in an armed truce awaiting the opportunity to strike a blow." As immigrants from the agrarian regions of southern and eastern Europe, they ordinarily experienced their initial contact with modern industrialism after their arrival in the New World. Mostly farm folk or petty traders and artisans, they proved deficient in the skills requisite for decent employment in an industrial society. They sank to the lower level of the proletariat—unskilled coal miners in Pennsylvania and West Virginia, steel workers in Pittsburgh and Gary, and sweatshop workers in New York City. To the immigrant laborers in the metropolis, the sweatshop became synonymous with capitalism, and the abolition of capitalism signified the abolition of the sweatshop.[20]

To gain their cooperative commonwealth, radicals insisted that trade-unionism needed a spiritual *élan*, a soul to its body, an idealism transcending its merely bread-and-butter purposes. Militant spokesmen sought to divorce the labor ethic from the business ethic. The socialist labor lawyer, Jacob Panken, addressing a convention of the ACWA, claimed that unionism was seeking abstract justice not material gains: "It is justice that we are beckoning. It is justice that we are aiming for. It is justice that we are striving to capture."[21]

Militants sought to broaden labor's horizons. They hoped to open the eyes of organized labor to all currents of progressive thought. Only when the movement was catholic in its interests and approach could it capture the real fire of revolution, that torch of the ultimate emancipation of the working class. May Day, in accord with this spirit of revolution, became a banner occasion for the city's more radical unionists. (To them Labor Day was a capitalist concession.) The streets around Union Square filled to overflowing on the first day of every May, as the workers gathered to hear of the impending collapse of capitalism and its replacement by the cooperative commonwealth.[22]

The radicals, basically humanitarians, justified their program as a means to paradise for all mankind. They believed that an intelligently directed labor movement offered to all humanity the cherished dream of a pure and perfect world. Militants were, in this respect, dedicated apostles of the twentieth century's millennial yet secular religion—socialism. They would usher in a new society in whose beneficent atmosphere all the ailments and tribulations of mankind would dissolve. They intended to transform the trade-union from an essentially economic institution into an agency for the complete social regeneration of alienated humanity.

Those from the lowest strata of the rank and file, those with the poorest chance of obtaining rapid material improvements, those with the most marginal social status in the New World heeded the words of idealistic visionaries. To these newly-organized workers, many of whom were unskilled, and who had just left the very depths of society, talk of increased wages and shorter hours did not promise as much as the socialist utopia. They had not yet wrested enough from capitalism to acquiesce in the system. But they were well aware of the marvelous productive potentialities of industrialism; they knew that a select few had benefited to a previously undreamed of extent from capitalism's material creations; they desired that the masses not the elite share in industrialism's marvels. So in their daily dreams, wrote one of the immigrants' labor journals, "they turned to the hopes of a brighter [socialist] future in store for the working class."[23]

On almost all facets of trade-unionism, labor's militants and moderates clashed. Politically, the radicals leaned toward the Socialist Party, whereas the moderates were either nonpartisan or, more often, ardent adherents of the Democratic Party. On the critical immigration question, moderates and militants again split, the conservative faction favoring restrictions, the radicals endorsing a liberal immigration policy. During the First World War, the militants, both before and after American entry into the conflict, outspokenly opposed involvement, whereas the moderates eventually supported President Wilson's preparedness policy and later his call for a declaration of war.[24]

III

But despite glaring dissimilarities in thought and outlook between the contending labor factions, they shared several common assumptions. Both moderates and militants endowed trade-unionism with a sanctity of purpose, an unselfishness not shared by other social classes. Both looked to the working class as the most progressive agency of the age. And both believed efficient and tight-knit organization to be the key to survival and triumph.

Labor leaders thus attempted to lend their movement a strongly religious flavor and to imbue its members with the conviction that their aspirations were virtuous and moral because they were necessary and right. They transformed the union from an instrument of power into a crusade for human dignity, which embodied all the nobler qualities of man's perpetual strivings toward a freer and more equal world. "The important thing," Jacob Panken told a union audience, "is that you and I are fighting towards a goal, towards an ideal which will give to the human race life, liberty, and happiness for all time." A bond transcending the material values implicit in modern industrial society was necessary to bring union members safely through the hungry days that marked trade-unionism's formative years.[25]

Officials also attempted to convince the rank and file that they were the advance agents of a new world whose struggle for a better life was synonymous with the spirit of the times. Joseph Schlossberg, Secretary of the ACWA, wrote: "We are living in a period pregnant with the greatest possibilities. The end of the class war is drawing near. Let us all rise to the occasion." Everywhere union leaders informed their followers that yesterday's dreams were fast becoming today's realities, that the unachievable today would be commonplace tomorrow. All in all, concluded Joseph Schlossberg, "at no time was labor so near the realization of the ideals of industrial freedom as it is today. . . . Labor is now in the very midst of the social revolution."[26]

Trade-union leaders of all persuasions argued that only the organization of the rank and file into efficient, functioning units could emancipate the working class from the thralldom of industrialism. Unions, in turn, received their greatest impetus to growth from the basic desire of men to achieve some recognition as self-respecting members of society. Fortunately for the organizers, most workers realized that no single individual could ameliorate the hardships suffered by all, but that unity and common purpose could bring common relief.

Both the mass and the elite of the labor movement sensed that the worker was merely a cog in the complicated machinery of modern industry—an automaton resembling the very machine he fed. The laborer as an individual was superfluous and could be replaced easily; thus, his only security lay in active cooperation with his machine-age fellows. "This is the age of organization and the only avenue we have to secure . . . improved conditions is by and through organization," counselled the moderate voice of the UGWA's *Weekly Bulletin*. A female trade-unionist implored workers to accept organization, industrial and political, as "*The Way Out*." The best preventive against abuse of the working class, she advised, was united action, which would abolish the notion of labor as a mere abstract commodity and transform union members into full participants in American society.[27]

What the laborer as an individual could not obtain from the employer, union organizers claimed that he would gain as a trade-union member. Organized labor's spokesmen promised to upset the prevailing autocratic patterns of industrial relations. No longer would the worker have to rely upon the employer's goodness of heart. By surrendering some of his theoretical liberty to the union and making common cause with his fellow workers, the laborer would gain a pragmatic, but more meaningful, form of liberty. "The essence of freedom," proclaimed the *Weekly Bulletin,* "is guaranteed by organization when individual action would result in subjection." A young girl, while on picket duty, revealed the same urge in simpler words: "Did you hear what the man said about organization—unionism? He's got that right. Unite! It is the workers' only salvation."[28]

Organized workers insisted that the closed or union shop was essential to a strong organization. Loyalty to the union was required in order to ensure success. Deprived of unity and loyalty the union must fail; with it, the labor movement would become infused with a new life and a truer sense of direction. *The Fur Worker* stated succinctly the case for the closed shop.

> When the members of a trade-union have by the expenditure of their own time and means created certain conditions necessary to their safety and well-being in a given industry or institution, it is morally their right and logically their duty to insist that the non-unionist who seeks to share these conditions shall first agree to share the labor and expenditure necessary to their maintenance—in other words, to insist that he shall join the union.[29]

Members considered their unions so vital that they never doubted the justice of the closed shop. Membership in unions possessing job control secured important psychological fringe benefits. It served to remove long held fears of the boss, of job insecurity, and promoted the ideal of common struggle for just rights. "This is what it means to belong to a union," thought a young girl, "you get time to straighten out your bones." Another young woman described more fully the impact of the union:

I . . . believe in the Union. It makes us stronger and it makes us happier and it makes us more interested in life and to be interested is oh, a thousand times better than to be so dead that one never sees anything but work all day and not enough money to live on. That is terrible, that is like death.[30]

Unions became the material manifestations of the dreams nourished by so many of the underprivileged, underpaid, and overworked. If the worker was to be lifted from the depths of society, he, himself, had to do the lifting with the union as lever. Reform and improvement were not to be expected from voluntary action by employers, social reformers, or even from labor legislation. "The great task," warned the *Weekly Bulletin,* "must devolve wholly upon the workers themselves, through united action." Charity, especially, added the *Ladies' Garment Worker,* was little succor to the workingman because it was "a clumsy attempt to blind the people to the glaring inequalities of extreme poverty and extreme riches," whereas the trade-union was "organized self-help and self-respect."[31]

In the aftermath of the tragic Triangle fire, when respectable middle- and upper-class citizens such as Felix Adler, Marcus Marks, Mrs. O.H.P. Belmont, and others, organized a civic committee to secure protection for the lives of sweatshop workers, Rose Schneiderman, then a young and fiery ILGWU organizer, shocked these self-satisfied community representatives by informing them that the labor movement had tried them and found them wanting. She condemned public spokesmen for offering a few measly dollars to the families of the Triangle victims yet doing nothing to prevent such tragedies. When the workers rose to alter the conditions that made life unbearable, she emphasized, the strong hand of the law beat them back into submission. The community, she continued, can no longer voice the needs of the working class, for "too much blood has been spilled. I know from my experience that it is up to the working people to save themselves. The only way they can save themselves is by a strong working-class movement."[32]

New York City's workers understood Miss Schneiderman's anguished plea for working-class organization. From 1909 to 1916, laborers all over the city, native-born and immigrant, needle trades and service trades, engaged in a series of protracted and bitter organizational strikes which affected the entire community.

3.
The Organizational Strike Comes to the Needle Trades

THE STRUGGLE IN NEW YORK CITY between capital and labor stemmed from a conflict between the demands of industrial discipline and those of industrial democracy which intensified during the Progressive era. On the one hand, the employer exhibited a justifiable concern for efficiency, economy, and the elimination of all waste; to accomplish these ends he insisted upon absolute responsibility for shop organization, strict worker discipline, and the selection of employees entirely upon the basis of efficiency and productivity. On the other hand, workers were determined that wage regulations and working conditions no longer be treated as matters of *individual* bargaining; they desired to limit the employer's exclusive control of production by interjecting the trade-union as the individual worker's "attorney-in-fact." They turned to the union for realization of industrial democracy.

Consciousness of this struggle by both capital and labor brought inevitable conflict. Julius Henry Cohen, attorney for various garment manufacturers' associations and preeminent advocate of law and order in industry, believed industrial relations patterns in the metropolis to be part of *"the inevitable movement for industrial discipline coming up one avenue and the equally inevitable movement for industrial democracy coming up another."*

Cohen, who was to play a unique role in improving labor-management relations in the metropolis, epitomized the reform spirit. Born in Brooklyn, New York, in 1873, prior to the era of mass Jewish immigration to America, Cohen was an established attorney and respected urban reformer well before becoming involved in garment industry affairs. Like other members of the older German-Jewish community, he was an assimilationist, belonging to the Ethical Cultural Society where he was influenced by the social-reform philosophy of the Society's founder, Dr. Felix Adler. As an urban reformer, Cohen served as attorney (1900–1905) for the Transit Reform Committee of 100, assisted in the prosecution of a corrupt district attorney; and investigated the Department of Street Cleaning. He also found time to amass a considerable personal fortune and to act as counsel for the New York State Chamber of Commerce and the New York Merchants' Association. This man of wealth, associate of eminent businessmen, urban reformer, and assimilated Jew nevertheless pioneered in the field of labor relations. Policies and proposals formulated by Cohen during the Progressive era became national policy 20 years later with the passage of the Wagner Labor Relations Act. Though neither a trade-union leader nor a garment manufacturer, he contributed greatly to the amelioration of industrial conflict in the needle trades.[1]

Cohen readily perceived that employers sought industrial efficiency through discipline; employees demanded "democracy on the job" through representative trade-unions; and the community attempted to protect the public interest through the establishment of "law and order in industry." In the combat between "managerial absolutism" and "industrial democracy" few clear-cut victories were won. Where organized labor triumphed, compromise resulted; where organized labor failed, the theoretical victory for discipline and efficiency did not guarantee unqualified obedience from defeated and disgruntled workers.

Further consideration of the successful and unsuccessful struggles for union organization should provide revealing comparisons and contrasts in the evolution of industrial relations. Given the basic similarities inhering in the strikes besetting New York City, comparative analysis should disclose the conditions conducive to working-class organization and the circumstances detrimental to trade-union growth.

Four factors common to all industrial conflicts in the metropolis apparently determined their resolution. These forces operated both within and outside the affected industry. Internally, the economic structure of the industry and the nature and philosophy of union leadership affected the outcome of conflict. Externally, the attitude of public-spirited citizens expressed through reform societies and the climate of opinion newspapers attempted to create brought direct and indirect pressure to bear upon strikers and employers. Community interests impelled municipal intervention in many labor disputes, and the nature of public opinion determined the city administration's role in mediating labor disputes. It should be in order to examine first the areas of successful trade-union penetration.

I

From 1909 to 1916 strikes by thousands of semiskilled and unskilled laborers disrupted the metropolitan economy. The organizational impulse was most widespread and successful among immigrant clothing workers who forged stable unions. New York needle trades' workers gained the ends—labor organization and improved working conditions— that had eluded them during the three decades from 1880 to 1909. Needle trades unions, which in 1900 and earlier had been feeble, immature labor organizations, emerged in 1910 as powerful institutions for working-class betterment.

The garment trades, as we have seen, dominated manufacturing in the metropolis and were the primary labor market for immigrants and for women who earned their livelihoods by dexterity with needle and thread. Many garment workers became better known as "Columbus tailors" because they wedded the sewing machine after reaching the land of opportunity.[2]

By 1900 the needle trades had taken on their basic character, an industry marked by the contracting system and small-scale production. Immigrant contractors perfected the section work system in which labor was minutely subdivided to utilize fully cheap, unskilled hands. The ambitious contractor assumed the major risks and responsibilities borne ordinarily by the higher cost, inside factory manufacturer. Contractors produced the garments, recruited and managed the workers, and paid the wages, taking for their profit the difference between wages and the prices offered them by inside manufacturers. Contractors became so adept at low cost production that few large manufacturers in the ladies' garment trade maintained their own heavily capitalized plants; they preferred contracting orders out to the lowest bidder. Successful contractors, in turn, often challenged the merchant-manufacturer for industrial pre-eminence. By 1900 sectors of New York's garment industry resembled a nightmare world of endless competition and terrifying business insecurity.[3]

Diversity and instability shaped all aspects of the garment industry. It had almost as many separate branches as individual shops. Men's clothing, women's clothing, fur garments, millinery, and men's caps and hats were the industry's major subtrades. And these trades were in turn subdivided into more specialized sectors.

Fashion trends and style requirements further atomized the needle trades. Men's clothing, where fashion proved subsidiary and style relatively stable, had the heaviest capital investment per worker and the largest inside workshops. But even here the small contractor was everywhere, providing cheaper production as well as a potential business challenge for the large, successful inside manufacturer. The women's sector, where fashion and style were most evanescent, was more fragmented. In the manufacture of cloaks and suits—the trade's major branch —and of higher priced dresses, style determined business success. Consequently, quantity production was out of the question and heavy capitalization in production equipment and work space an economic liability; a sudden shift in demand based upon changes in fashion could wipe out overnight an entire enterprise. It often proved better business for the manufacturer to employ directly only designers and cutters, rent only cutting rooms, and contract out the actual sewing and finishing of the garments. The vagaries of demand thus spread the competitive contracting system and business instability.

Demand factors also affected the economic structure of other parts of the women's industry. Cheaper dresses to be sold in a wider market could be copied from more expensive originals and produced in larger quantity in inside workshops where carefully supervised unskilled workers performing simple, repetitive tasks were provided with the best equipment. Housedresses and kimonos and underwear were also standardized garments, manufactured in quantity in clean, modern inside workshops, and retailed in a mass market. The millinery and fur trades, on the other hand, had to produce what high fashion demanded. Consequently, these lesser lines of production were marked by small shops, the ubiquitous contractor, and general economic insecurity.[4]

The garment industry, in its diversity, encompassed large, modern factories and sweatshops, affluent manufacturers and impecunious contractors, standardized production and specialized manufacture, and products ranging in price from the most expensive to the cheapest and in market from minuscule to mass. Hardly anywhere in America did there exist a more variegated, competitive, and unstable industry.

The unstable structure of the needle trades operated both to the advantage and the disadvantage of employees. Low capital investment requirements made entry into the industry practically unlimited for the aspiring or enterprising immigrant entrepreneur. Shoestring entrepreneurs and aspiring barons of business in their anxiety to lower costs and survive savage competition debased labor standards. But more successful manufacturers, fearing the sharp practices perfected by their shoestring competitors, became more susceptible to the demands of an organized working force. Moreover, small businesses with minimal capitalizations could not endure the rigors of industrial warfare for sustained periods. If trade-unions persisted in applying economic pressure, employers faced either bankruptcy or surrender; compromise and concession often proved the more acceptable choice. Relative ease of entry and exit from the industry, however, could weaken unions. Small employers could subvert labor organization by leaving the trade temporarily, only to return later under a different company name with a nonunion shop.

Trade-unions offered the industry inducements and advantages which some of the larger manufacturers came to recognize and sanction. A strong, well-disciplined union controlling the labor market could bring to a trade badly in need of order the benefits of industrial rationalization. A powerful union could curb the depredations wrought upon the successful giants of the trade by unfair sweatshop competitors; it could pressure into conformity the unscrupulous small manufacturer who refused to establish minimum standards of health and decency as well as the "moths of Division Street" (small-scale contractors) who by 1900 had come to dominate the trade. The union, by organizing and monopolizing the industry's labor force, could impose uniform working conditions and thus equalize competition. Here, both capital and labor perceived the mutual rewards of intelligent and pragmatic cooperation. Where capital was relatively weak, labor could intrude to implement industrial discipline and business efficiency. In Julius Henry Cohen's happy paradise of "law and order in industry" affluent manufacturers cooperated with understanding union officials to bring peace, stability, decency, and justice to the jungle of the garment trades.[5]

Disunity compounded relative employer weakness. Manufacturers in the diverse branches of the men's and women's clothing industry divided among themselves into competing trade associations, ordinarily related to the financial and business status of the member firms. Unions could therefore pursue whipsaw tactics, striking the weaker associations or small independents first, then employing concessions wrung from the small fry to pressure trade leaders into compromise or surrender; sometimes the union could and would strike the leading trade association first, gain success, and then mount intolerable pressure upon smaller organizations and independents.[6]

Despite the seeming impotence of management, in fact because of it, New York's immigrant clothing workers found neither milk nor honey in the New World. Many of these newer immigrants had been literally transplanted from the medieval European farm village to the vast metropolis of the new century, from the handicraft economy of their homelands to the factory system of the New World, from the personal ties of the Old World to the impersonal relationships of an urban America. Sometimes it appeared to them as if the stagnation of a feudal society had been exchanged for the bondage of an industrial system. For many, the promise of American life turned to dust, the riches of the New World became an illusion, and the ideal of American opportunity led to the sweatshop.

"One could never rise so early in the morning nor go to bed so late at night," wrote Jacob Riis on Manhattan's Jewish Ghetto, "that he would not hear the hum of some sewing machine," in an area he described as "a big gangway through an endless workroom where vast multitudes are forever laboring. Morning, noon, or night it makes no difference; the scene is always the same." Little wonder one immigrant cried out in despair: "We worked, worked, and our profits went into the hands of others—and should this go on forever? Why?—Why?" If they protested too vigorously, however, they were summarily discharged by employers who easily located additional immigrants to occupy vacant workbenches.[7]

Miserable working conditions led the needle crafts' workers directly into an unusually militant but ineffective labor movement. Because the sweatshop was synonymous with capitalism to the garment workers, they gratefully accepted the guidance of socialist intellectuals. Shortly after the surge of Jewish immigration to America in the 1880's, trade-unions were organized. In their first three decades, 1880–1909, however, unions were constructed on unstable foundations. The movement as it developed had ideas and aims but lacked solid organization and material resources. Meyer London, recalling the seminal days of garment unionism, remembered:

> We had unions some time ago—they existed on paper. We had agitators who were irritators only. We had a movement that moved backwards. We talked about a social revolution and had a 70-hour week! We talked about reorganizing the whole world in a day, and down under our very noses, people slaved in the sweat shops.

Trade-unions of immigrant workers appeared only to disappear; or as Abraham Cahan observed: "When our movement gave birth to a child, somehow or other, the child did not live. No sooner was it born than it died and then a new child would have to be born and the same thing would occur." The membership rolls of the ILGWU from 1900, the year of its founding, to 1910 bear eloquent witness to the ineffectiveness of the needle trades' unions. Twice, in 1905 and again in 1908, membership dropped so precipitously that ILGWU conventions considered amalgamation with the UGWA. In 1910, the year the tide turned in its favor, the ILGWU included less than half the total number of laborers in New York's women's garment industry.[8]

Several factors inhibited trade-union growth among the metropolis' garment workers. Lack of effective leadership and rank-and-file apathy perhaps proved most decisive. Workers responded dutifully to strike calls. As soon as disputes were settled and the workers' demands met, union membership evaporated; the men proved excellent strikers but poor unionists. Constantly shifting membership within union ranks also weakened organization. As one group of workers ascended the economic ladder, new immigrants, unfamiliar with labor organization, replaced them. Most immigrants, furthermore, had not migrated to the New World to doom themselves to a life of perpetual wage earning. Instead the most ambitious and talented among them (the natural union leaders) aspired to their own plentiful share of America's boundless wealth; a trade-union offered no proper prospect for aggressive individuals who dreamed of possessing their own business empires. And in the needle trades, the smallest savings combined with intense ambition sufficed if one wished to enter business as a contractor. With good fortune, success as a great inside manufacturer might follow. Men, inspired by dreams of business imperium, proved poor recruits for stable trade-unions; immigrants of talent and determination preferred business risks to trade-union emoluments.[9]

Internal conflict also retarded union organization. Early in their struggle for organization the trade-unions came under the influence of socialism. Though socialism had a beneficial impact upon the needle trades' unions, the presence of socialist agitators inevitably involved the unions in sectarian battles. Most Jewish immigrant socialists, as already pointed out, espoused the reformist variety in which immediate reforms took precedence over ultimate revolution and in which the existing trade-unions, including American Federation of Labor affiliates, worked together with the political party to bring about a socialist society. But other Jewish socialists remained loyal to the program of Daniel DeLeon and his Socialist Labor Party, which subordinated reform to revolution and the trade-union to the political party. Some of these "revolutionary" socialists turned after 1905 to the Industrial Workers of the World and its program of radical syndicalism, organizing dual unions within the needle trades. While immigrant socialists fought among themselves, the American Federation and its New York affiliate, the Central Federated Union, looked askance at the radicals in the garment trades. Torn by internal conflict and alienated by ideology from the broader American labor movement, the immigrants' trade-unions faced a dim future.[10]

Despite years of frustration and defeat, the idea of trade-unionism persisted among immigrant clothing workers. Through what Algernon Lee later described as the "Jewish workman's marvelous capacity of starving for an ideal, it survived and grew."[11] Finally, after 20 years of unceasing effort, union leaders educated workers to the value of trade-unions in "peace as well as in war." With that realization labor organization in the garment trades matured. And from 1909 to 1916, needle trades' unions entered an era of remarkable and sustained growth.

Unions grew after 1909 despite the persistence of earlier economic trends within the industry. The industry's work force by 1910 was very much what it had been in 1900; the size of workshops continued to decrease; the unions changed little in philosophy or approach. Yet from 1909 on, the garment trades were revolutionized by the spread of labor organization.

The rise of the needle trades' unions coincided with the flowering of the Progressive spirit (1910–1916) before its sublimation in Woodrow Wilson's great international crusade. Progressivism's fruition established a community environment in which workers had greater freedom to build independent labor organizations. Public-spirited reformers and citizens' groups exerted significant influence in the garment workers' organizational victories. Without community assistance labor organization in the needle trades would have come more slowly and more painfully.

Two further factors brought indigenous and capable leaders to the immigrant unions. The failure of the 1905 Russian Revolution forced many Jewish *émigrés* trained in the Russian *Bundist* and revolutionary tradition to flee to New York where they provided new leadership for the infant unions. In the winter of 1905–1906, as an east side resident recalled, idealism swept through the Jewish immigrant community. Older immigrants also began to perceive a brighter future for themselves as trade-union officials; among Jewish immigrants union office became more prestigious. More rank-and-file workers now saw future betterment in organized, collective action for higher wages and improved conditions of labor, not through escape into the ranks of contractors and manufacturers. Simultaneously, large manufacturers still vexed by sharp competition and the resulting insecurity in their trade began to conceive more clearly of employee organization as a means to stability and security. Thus by 1910, garment workers had come to realize the need for organization, leaders had come forth to serve that need, and some manufacturers looked more tolerantly upon trade-unions. Middle- and upper-class New Yorkers fortuitously appeared to serve as midwives at the birth of stable trade-unionism in the needle trades.[12]

The International Ladies' Garment Workers' Union seized command of the organizational movement in the garment industry. Founded by a handful of workers in the women's garment industry at a convention in New York in 1900, it was usually dominated by its New York locals, though it had other influential affiliates in Philadelphia, Boston, Cleveland, and Chicago. From its birth, the ILGWU functioned as a semi-industrial union; it opened membership to all workers in the industry, regardless of skill or nationality, but organized them in locals divided by sector of the trade (cloaks or dresses for example) or by job classifications (pressers, tailors, basters for example). In large cities like New York, the International encouraged the formation of joint boards, which united the separate locals under more centralized, coordinated leadership.

Throughout its early years the International had struggled with indifferent success to unite its more skilled and Americanized members who preferred conservative leaders, few strikes, and cooperation with employers with its more numerous, less skilled and immigrant members who demanded militant leaders, frequent strikes, and total class warfare. Immigrant militants chafed at the leadership of moderates like John Dyche, while more conservative Americanized cutters disapproved of the policies of a romantic socialist like Benjamin Schlesinger, union president in 1903, and again from 1914 to 1923, and 1928 to 1932. Plagued by internal dissension and external enemies, the ILGWU several times seemed on the verge of extinction.[13]

But in 1909–1910 the tide turned in its favor. The more militant immigrants, gaining ascendancy within the organization, prepared to push the ILGWU toward more direct action. And by the end of 1910 the ILGWU had waged two successful strikes for union recognition in New York that illustrated the union's tactics and strategy.

The needle trades workers united skilled and unskilled laborers, craft and industrial interests. They waged strikes on an industry-wide basis—the so-called general strike—with the more skilled workers, cutters and tailors, employing their superior bargaining power to aid their less skilled union brothers or sisters. Cutters and tailors (usually men) were the fulcrum of trade-unionism, while basters, fellers, pressers, finishers, fitters, and other specialized but unskilled laborers provided the mass and the militancy. Together they made the general, industry-wide strike effective in the needle trades decades before its appearance and triumph elsewhere in the United States. And labor leaders in the garment trades succeeded in organizing those workers—immigrants and women—deemed unorganizable by the AFL elite.[14]

II

The first indication of ILGWU resurgence came in the Fall of 1909 in the shirtwaist trade, then one of the newer branches of the women's garment industry.

Drawing its labor supply from among unmarried Jewish and Italian girls between the ages of 16 and 25, the waist trade's late entrance into the industry enabled it to bypass the sweatshop stage, while making it more susceptible to advanced methods of production associated with the large mid-town workshop. In modern shops where girls produced a relatively standardized garment, sanitary conditions and wages were distinctly superior to labor standards in older branches of the industry. Thus when labor conflict erupted girls subordinated bread-and-butter objectives to more intangible demands for self-respect and industrial justice.

The girls, despite generally adequate wages, were too often subjected to a regime of nagging, petty tyrannies, favoritism, and annoyances that degraded the workers. Fines, frequently excessive, were levied for a host of petty infractions. Employees often had to purchase their own needles and thread. Because the industry operated on a piecework basis, the employer or his agent could easily indulge in favoritism toward "cooperative" workers by awarding them larger work bundles. Superior workers allied with employers exploited novices in the trade through an oppressive apprenticeship system. Girls who had little to complain of respecting wages and hours decided to rid the trade of serious injustices and trifling tyrannies afflicting less fortunate workers. They sought, through the agency of a union, self-respect and a voice in industrial relations. The better paid and more skilled women further sought to assist their less skilled sisters. As one shirtwaist striker later commented: "This is not just a strike for self. Only by all standing together can we get better conditions for all."[15]

Neither agitation nor education by professional organizers, however, fostered unrest in the shirtwaist trade. The desire for organization and improvement came directly from the trade's workers. But once the girls acted, leaders from within both the Jewish immigrant community and the greater city provided counsel and assistance.

Discontent by the shirtwaist makers, which caught the community unawares, had been a long time in the making. Well before a general walkout disrupted the trade on November 23, 1909, employee dissatisfaction had been spreading. Spontaneous strikes erupted from shop to shop. As discontent increased, The Women's Trade Union League attempted to interject a spirit of unity and a sense of organization among the female workers.

Organized in 1903, by nonworking-class reformers like Jane Addams, Lillian Wald, and the Dreier sisters, Mary and Margaret (Mrs. Raymond Robins), the WTUL sought to arouse public sympathy for the plight of unorganized women workers, to organize those women into trade unions, and then to allow working-class female trade-unionists to make basic WTUL policy. But nonworking-class sources always provided the organization with considerable funds and numerous members.[16]

The WTUL's New York branch, which included among its leaders,

Rose Schneiderman, an immigrant garment worker, knew of the unrest in the shirtwaist trade and had already aided the girls in September, 1909 strikes against two of the largest firms in the trade: Leiserson and Company and the Triangle Waist Company. The WTUL had provided funds, a volunteer picket corps, and a means to elicit community sympathy for the strikers. It had also sought to make the ILGWU aware of the growing sentiment in favor of organization among shirtwaist makers.[17]

But the ILGWU's affiliate in the trade, Local 25, having only about 100 members and four dollars in its treasury, could not sustain the early WTUL stimulated walkouts against the Leiserson and the Triangle Companies. Organized in 1906 with about 250 members, Local 25 made no progress in the succeeding years and even declined.

Prodded by the WTUL and the discontented shirtwaist makers, the leaders of Local 25 summoned their followers—suddenly numbering in the thousands as WTUL volunteers helped sign up union members—to a special meeting on October 21, 1909, at which 400 delegates would discuss the prospects for a general strike in the trade. At this October meeting the participants planned such a strike and appointed a special committee to develop tactics and strategy.[18]

One of the first strategic decisions made by the union was to keep the girls in the trade at the forefront of the agitation and the men, mostly the more skilled workers who had originally organized Local 25, in the background. The girls, so the strike committee assumed, would be more likely to have continued WTUL assistance and public sympathy; it was also less likely that females would encounter strongarm strikebreakers or brutal, antiunion police.[19]

With Local 25 now planning a strike and the WTUL providing aid, interest in the union began to increase among shirtwaist makers. Local 25's tiny headquarters in a Clinton Street tenement could no longer contain the prospective trade-union recruits. Union leaders thus decided to strike.

In mid-November, the strike committee, formed the previous month, scheduled a mass meeting for the Cooper Union Auditorium (November 22) to discuss an industry-wide walkout. Samuel Gompers, Meyer London, Mary Dreier, President of the Women's Trade Union League, and Ernest Bohm, Secretary of the CFU, accepted invitations to speak. On the appointed evening eager young girls packed to overflowing the same Great Hall at Cooper Union where Abraham Lincoln had made his eastern debut in politics. For over two hours the excited girls listened to one dispassionate voice after another, one counsel of moderation after another. Then climactically, an ordinary working girl, one of the faceless rank and file, leaped to her feet and in a passionate outburst dissented from the placid oratory of moderation. The girl, teenage Clara Lemlich, mounted the rostrum. Disregarding the advice of her "wiser" elders, she pleaded her case in emotional Yiddish. Clara concluded her plea by demanding a general strike resolution and calling for the Jewish oath: "If I turn traitor to the cause I now pledge, may this hand wither from the arm I now raise." A thousand hands rose from the audience in unison with Miss Lemlich's.[20]

Thus the first great strike by women in American labor history was born in an atmosphere of elation. It was to mature in the midst of deprivation and cruel ordeal.

After the strike began on Thursday, November 23, 1909, it developed in two stages. The walkout's opening moments were filled with success and optimism as New York's lower east side became a seething mass of strikers and strike sympathizers. Girls by the thousands stormed the Clinton Street office to enroll in Local 25, as the union secured attractive settlements from the trade's smaller and less secure manufacturers.[21] But initial success soon gave way to disillusion. The large manufacturers refused to settle. And the strike dragged on from a pleasant late autumn to miserable mid-winter.

Originally, the strike leaders sought concessions and recognition from the Associated Dress and Waist Manufacturers' Association whose members employed most of the workers in the trade. The large firms belonging to the Association did not fear cutthroat competition. They produced standardized garments in mechanized workshops where efficiency and shop discipline effected economies of scale unmatched by their smaller competitors. To these large manufacturers absolute control of labor seemed essential to business success. As yet, they refused to share shop control with a trade-union. Despite union pressure, the Association remained obdurate.[22]

Meanwhile the smaller, non-Association employers signed agreements with Local 25. With the strike barely four days old, almost half the original strikers had returned to work with improved conditions and union contracts. As smaller manufacturers resumed production under union controls, the Association continued to be recalcitrant against the girls' primary objective, explicit union recognition.[23] Thus the walkout entered its second stage, that of a protracted siege; for three months thousands of young women walked the picket lines and suffered the tribulations—cold, hunger, bodily injury, and personal insult—which, in the first decades of the twentieth century, were part and parcel of the strikers' lot.

Freezing temperatures and snow marked the winter of 1909–1910. The severe cold weakened the will and the body of many pickets. The parent union (ILGWU) lacked the funds to disburse regular strike benefits and girls endured their winter of discontent without a source of income. Skimpy savings vanished quickly into rent and grocery bills. The strikers' slogan became: "We'd rather starve quickly than starve slow [sic]." Natural and economic elements conspired with human factors to repress the girls of Local 25.[24]

Police, judiciary, and thugs also plagued the pickets. McAlister Coleman, then a young reporter for the New York *Sun,* later remembered the strikers as mostly young girls badly mauled by "gorillas," hired by the employers, and club-swinging Tammany "cops." And Coleman described graphically what befell Clara Lemlich, one of the original strikers, in September 1909, the voice of rebellion at the Cooper Union November mass meeting, and a stalwart on the picket lines.

> The thugs rushed the line knocking Clara to her knees, striking at the pickets, opening the way for a group of frightened scabs to slip through the broken line. Fancy ladies from the Allen Street red-light district climbed out of cabs to cheer on the gorillas. There was a confused melee, scratching, screaming girls and fist-swinging men and then a patrol wagon arrived. The thugs ran off as the cops pushed Clara and two other badly beaten girls into the wagon.

When he asked himself, "Who were the shirtwaist strikers?" Coleman discovered only one answer. They were "an array of battered and bandaged prisoners." By December 22, the police had arrested 707 strikers, 19 of whom were sentenced to the workhouse and the remainder fined.[25]

Courtrooms in the city's working-class districts were filled with strikers and their fellow travelers. Regardless of the circumstances surrounding their arrests, the girls were usually convicted. A presiding magistrate, for example, proclaimed to a striker being tried for the offense of calling a strikebreaker a scab: "If these girls continue to rush around and cry 'scab' I shall convict them of disorderly conduct. There

is no word in the English language as irritating as the word 'scab.' "
Another magistrate boldly announced that despite higher courts' legali-
zation of peaceful picketing, he would forbid the right to picket.
Strikers listened contritely to judicial tirade after tirade on the sanctity
of private property, or as one judge expressed it, the wickedness of
striking against God "whose firm law is that man shall earn his bread in
the sweat of his brow." To which George Bernard Shaw replied: "Delightful. Medieval America always in the intimate personal confidence
of the Almighty."[26]

Against their natural and human adversaries the girls needed all the
support and sympathy they could muster. Established unions, the United
Hebrew Trades, the Socialist Party, and the CFU (the central organization of AFL affiliates in New York City), of course, came to their aid.
More important, however, reform-minded, influential citizens organized and directed by the WTUL brought community leadership and
financial assistance to the strikers. Earlier, as we have seen, the WTUL
had established a corps of volunteer pickets, women and girls from the
upper-middle class, to abet the strikers. And the more the police and
the judiciary harassed the girls, the more the WTUL and the reform-
oriented community rallied to the strikers' cause.[27]

Police and judicial persecution became the most potent single factor
in creating a climate of public sympathy for the girls. Guided by the
WTUL, Mrs. O.H.P. Belmont and her Political Equality League (a suf-
fragette organization) scheduled a sympathy meeting for the Hippodrome. On the evening of December 5 an audience of 8000 suffragettes,
trade-unionists, socialists, anarchists, assorted malcontents, and curiosity
seekers gathered at the huge Sixth Avenue auditorium to cheer on the
much-abused shirtwaist makers. As the New York *Times* described the
scene, the police out in riot squad force turned away an overflow crowd,
while inside "Socialism, unionism, woman suffrage and what seemed to
be something like anarchism were poured into the ears of fully 8000
persons who gathered yesterday afternoon in the Hippodrome." The
meeting, chaired by the Reverend John Howard Melish of Brooklyn's
Holy Trinity Church, won for the strikers sympathy and funds from
wealthy "fellow-travelers" also engaged in the crusade for women's
rights.[28]

Not long after, Miss Anne Morgan, niece of J.P., called a meeting at
the Colony Club, a gathering place for "The 400," where Rose Schneiderman addressed an audience of socialites on behalf of the shirtwaist

strikers. And Miss Morgan informed her wealthy friends: "The girls must be helped to organize." *Noblesse Oblige!*

Funds meant more to the strikers than sympathy, and Mrs. Belmont raised 1500 dollars and Miss Morgan 1300 dollars. Among the contributors ironically enough were the wives of publishing tycoon Frank Munsey, railroad magnate, Collis P. Huntington, and National Association of Manufacturers spokesman, John J. Emery.[29] Remarkable what sympathy girls could elicit from those who owed their fortunes to the system that exploited those very girls.

While both prominent citizens and clergymen joined in criticizing police outrages, girls recruited by the WTUL from Barnard, Vassar, and Wellesley walked the picket lines. Community efforts to aid the strikers were climaxed by an appeal initiated by Mrs. August Belmont, Miss Anne Morgan, Mrs. Charles A. Beard, and Mrs. Nathan Straus, among others, for a protest meeting at Carnegie Hall, Sunday evening, January 2, 1910. The Carnegie Hall meeting proved an immense success; the audience with one voice remonstrated against police and magisterial persecution of the strikers; placards hung throughout the hall insisted: "The workhouse is no answer to a demand for justice." And the next day the *Times* banner headline proclaimed: "The Rich Out to Aid Girl Waistmakers."[30] Public encouragement heartened weary pickets. The girls' uprising had stimulated the latent social conscience of the city's "better classes," and for the first time middle- and upper-class New Yorkers championed actively the cause of the laboring masses.

Newspaper editorials mirrored community sentiment. Editorialists retreated far enough from their usual antiunion strictures to praise the female strikers. The *Post* applauded the "effective way in which the women strikers in this city have been carrying on their fight for higher wages . . . in remarkable contrast to the mismanagement and want of resolution that characterize the average strike in the ranks of masculine labor." Popular sympathy for the girls, the editorial continued, "is a strong indication of the substantial justice of the union's demands." The *World* and the *American* shared the *Post*'s enthusiasm and respect for the shirtwaist makers. The *Times,* on the contrary, refused to concede all right and justice to the strikers, but it did admit that endorsement of the employers' position doomed large numbers of young girls to a miserable, cruel, and unjust life.[31]

While the girls and their new found allies waged the "class war" on the picket lines, union officials engaged in the painstaking process of negotiations with the manufacturers' association. Not until the strike entered its third week was any clear intimation of the union's demands presented. On December 4, Mrs. Walter Weyl, representing the WTUL, in an interview with a *Times'* reporter, stated her conception of the strikers' demands. The perceptive reporter immediately saw through Mrs. Weyl's somewhat lengthy exegesis on the girls' needs to the strike's heart—"it is the *union* thing which the strikers must have now [italics added]." Thereafter, the desire for union recognition and the closed shop remained the workers' essential objectives.[32] Wages and working conditions still proved subsidiary to the organizational impulse.

Union recognition in fact proved the crucial issue in all the era's great strikes. Actually, demands for and opposition to recognition were based upon broader employee desires and greater employer fears. To workers, union recognition was synonymous with the union or closed shop; to managers, the granting of recognition necessarily resulted in the closed shop. These terms, however, were used loosely and interchangeably in these years of experimental collective bargaining. No clear, precise definitions distinguished the union shop from the closed shop and either of those terms from simple recognition. Thus strikers in seeking recognition aspired to the closed shop (to them a union shop implied a workplace closed to nonmembers); and employers in opposing recognition desired to maintain open shop arrangements. The basic issue was simple: Would control of the work force—hiring and firing—lie with the union or with management?

Throughout December negotiations between the Union and the Associated Dress and Waist Manufacturers' Association broke on the rock of union recognition. At the opening arbitration session, December 10, the union, represented by Morris Hillquit, Socialist leader, and John Mitchel, former President of the UMWA, found the employers willing to discuss minor grievances but disinclined to consider the basic issues: union recognition and the union shop. Manufacturers demanded the unlimited right to manage their businesses without external interference (meaning the union). The union's spokesmen insisted that without an organization explicitly recognized by management "the employers will be in a position to go back on every concession they now make."[33]

During the bargaining sessions, the shirtwaist strike had spread to Philadelphia, thus exerting greater pressure upon New York's manufacturers to settle. Local producers could no longer subcontract their orders to Philadelphia clothing makers. Employers' Association agents agreed with union representatives upon a compromise, which conceded higher wages, shorter hours, and satisfaction of numerous petty grievances. Again, however, employers refused to recognize the union or to consider closed shop arrangements. Settlement hopes again collapsed.[34]

On December 27, union officials submitted the most recent employer proposals to a vote by all union members. The strikers went to the ballot box knowing that many of the girls working in non-Association shops had returned to work earlier with full union recognition. Voters therefore decisively defeated the proposed settlement, insisting upon union recognition as the sole means to preserve improvements granted under strike pressure by recalcitrant employers. After the ballots were counted, union officials acknowledged publicly that the only remaining basis for agreement would be union recognition and the establishment of a union shop.[35]

The strikers, however, had neither the financial resources nor the experience and training in organized economic action to maintain their walkout until they achieved undiluted success. Early in January union representatives approached the State Bureau of Mediation and Arbitration to request mediation of all questions in dispute between Union and Association. The Association, however, rebuffed all mediation offers which did not exclude from discussion union recognition and the union shop. The manufacturers' steadfast refusal to consider union security proposals marked the end of negotiations. Workers would not relinquish the substance of their organizational strength—the closed shop—and employers would not renounce arbitrary control over shop discipline.[36]

The strikers, after persevering from November 23, 1909 to February 13, 1910, found their resources and their desire gone. Many of the larger Association shops seized upon the girls' fading strength and waning spirit to obtain settlements excluding union recognition and the union shop. By February 1, almost the entire trade had resumed production. Finally, on Monday, February 13, the union declared the strike ended.[37]

The ILGWU organizers learned their lessons well in the shirtwaist makers' strike. In future industrial conflicts they avoided the mistakes and weaknesses revealed by the girls' walkout. Thereafter the ILGWU provided strikers with material support and the intensive attention required to sustain conflict until larger manufacturers surrendered to economic distress.

What almost immediately afterwards came to be known as "the

uprising of 20,000" illustrated that the most unlikely candidates for unionization could be united for organized economic action. Young immigrant girls possessing few skills gained, if not total victory, many concessions from their employers. Even Samuel Gompers praised the girls for laying the foundations for future progress in the garment trades. They had, he admitted, "learned the heart and soul of unionism. And when the 'tumult and shouting died' . . . it was seen that unionism would at last abide as a permanent institution in that trade." The girls themselves learned that working-class solidarity presented the most favorable avenue to equitable treatment. From their protracted battle with employers, the strikers developed a new conception of their status; alone they were helpless; together they were powerful. The conflict also revealed the weaknesses as well as the strengths of the garment trades' manufacturers. Furthermore, the dispute saw consummated a working alliance between immigrant clothing workers and socially respectable and prominent New Yorkers which would work to the union's advantage in subsequent industrial conflicts. Finally, the impact of the shirtwaist makers' rebellion reverberated throughout the needle trades.[38]

III

Less than six months after the waistmakers returned to work, the ILGWU organized another sector of the women's clothing trade with striking success. In July 1910, after careful preparations and systematic organization, some 60,000 workers,[39] primarily male, employed in the cloak and suit trade left their workbenches for picket lines. Once again needle trades' laborers sought redress of traditional grievances through labor organization and union recognition.

The cloakmakers had begun to organize their trade even while waistmakers remained on strike. In January 1910, when the cloakmakers' union included only 6000 of the 75,000 workers in the industry, union members, excited by the women's example, scheduled a series of organizational mass meetings. By April, the organizing drive brought noticeable results; on April 1, the ILGWU's General Executive Board placed a notice in the inaugural issue of its new journal declaring the occasion propitious for a strike. Increasing membership in the union had convinced the general executive board "that now is the best opportunity and best time for a big movement among the cloak and skirt makers for better conditions." International Union leaders concluded that in the unstable New York labor market, beset by the tides of immigration and the presence of diverse nationalities, organization could not be erected slowly. "Only a huge uprising can move and electrify the masses and the individuals and bring about a radical change in the conditions of labor."[40]

The general executive board proceeded to put its April notice and challenge into effect. First, male union members were each assessed one dollar for a strike fund; next, at the ILGWU's national convention, on June 10, delegates approved a resolution sanctioning a general strike during the approaching fall season in the cloak and suit trade; finally, in late June, at a wildly enthusiastic overflow meeting in Madison Square Garden, Gompers and other leaders of organized labor in America pledged their support to the impending walkout. One week later, on July 3 and 4, cloakmakers voted 18,771 to 615 to approve the general strike. Simultaneously, a committee organized earlier to negotiate in the event of a walkout released the union's demands. Recognition dominated the list. And on July 7 the strike began, as cloakmakers, responding to the union's call in an unexampled show of unity, filled Manhattan's midtown streets with pickets.[41]

Smaller manufacturers with limited capital resources, fearing economic destruction, again sought speedy settlements. Since more than 2000 employers functioned in the industry, union negotiators preferred a general, industry-wide agreement to individual contracts. The ILGWU, however, could still pressure the industry's giants by threatening to sign separate, individual agreements with smaller manufacturers.

The trades' leaders, following the shirtwaist manufacturers' example, established the Cloak, Suit and Skirt Manufacturers' Protective Association. This new employer organization immediately ridiculed union demands for recognition and the closed shop. On July 11, the Association warned the public that the union's program would "inure only to the benefit of the ambitionless, careless, and incompetent workman," not to the self-reliant, skilled workman who commands his price.

All attempts at mediation and arbitration between the cloakmakers' union and the Protective Association ruptured on the issue of union recognition. The manufacturers refused to concede recognition; strikers declined to take less.[42] There the dispute rested until the end of July when public-spirited citizens intervened.

As the strike progressed, taking its toll both upon employers and employees, the union became more amenable to signing individual agreements with smaller manufacturers. Consequently, members of the Protective Association, anxious lest they suffer irreparable business losses to their lesser competitors, edged closer to their workers' demands. Though tedious negotiations ensued during which employers initially opposed union recognition and later condemned a closed shop settlement, economic pressure relentlessly drew them closer to the union's position.

To break the prevailing stalemate on the issues of recognition and union security between Union and Protective Association, out-of-state mediators, notably A. Lincoln Filene, Boston department store owner and Progressive reformer, entered the dispute. Filene introduced his own special labor relations adviser, Louis D. Brandeis, another Progressive movement stalwart, into the negotiations. Brandeis promptly persuaded union officials to compromise their demands for the closed shop. The more militant rank and file, however, opposed arbitration if it excluded consideration of the closed shop. No agreement raising wages or reducing hours but lacking job security provisions or restrictions upon management's control of the shop satisfied the workers. Gompers' personal intervention was necessary before obdurate local workers and their leaders agreed on July 28 to enter into conference with the Protective Association.[43] Between conference and agreement, however, many an obstacle obtruded.

The conferees met little difficulty reaching an understanding concerning the strikers' specific grievances, but attempts to create enforcement machinery stymied negotiators. Union members favored, in fact insisted upon, complete job security, which could be guaranteed only through the closed shop. Manufacturers, on the other hand, considered the closed shop synonymous with surrendering shop discipline to the union. The countervailing forces of industrial democracy and industrial efficiency again clashed.[44]

Stubborn workers were urged by Abraham Cahan, editor of the *Forward,* the garment workers' Yiddish-language newspaper, to persist in their struggle for justice. Jewish workers had become accustomed to accepting advice from Cahan. More so than other Jewish immigrants of his generation, Cahan understood American society as well as the immigrant community.

After coming to the United States from Russia in 1882, Cahan tried his hand at labor organizing, preaching socialism, teaching evening school, and Russian-, Yiddish-, and English-language journalism. An aspiring novelist, he wrote well-received stories of immigrant life. But immigrants lacked the leisure and desire to read, and native Americans showed slight interest in immigrant stories. Unable to earn a livelihood or fame through his literary efforts, Cahan turned to the English-language press. He had become a close friend of Lincoln Steffens, who in 1897 placed the Jewish immigrant on the regular staff of the *Commercial Advertiser*. As a reporter, Cahan widened his perspective of American society through acquaintanceship with Jacob Riis and the brothers, Norman and Hutchins Hapgood. They introduced him to the fullness of New York life, while he guided them through the intellectual heart of the lower east side. In 1909, together with Steffens, Cahan left the *Commercial Advertiser*. With the added prestige gained from his triumphs in the Gentile world, he rejoined the immigrant community as editor of the *Forward*.

Under Cahan's guidance, the *Forward* was transformed into the voice of the Jewish Ghetto. The paper became the dominant force in Yiddish-American journalism, and by 1914 reached a circulation of 445,000. The *Forward* favored organized labor and preached a reform socialism in keeping with immigrant sentiments. To Cahan and his newspaper, Jewish workers turned for knowledge and advice. And Cahan, until his death in 1951, answered their needs.[45]

Supported by their union leaders and their newspaper, the mass of workers rejected a modified Brandeis proposal: the preferential union shop whereby employers agreed that as between union men and non-union men of equal ability the former would be hired. Brandeis' suggestion proved in 1910 too novel and untried; union officials, given past experience in American labor relations, could not conceive of an employer preferring a union to a nonunion man. Consequently, on August 3, the ILGWU concluded all joint negotiations, declaring: "The rank and file of our organization demand the closed shop. There can be no compromise on that score and if we were to accept any compromise the rank and file would not abide by our decision."[46]

While bargaining continued from July 12 to August 3, the men on the picket lines contended with problems as desperate as those that had weakened the shirtwaist makers. Unlike the girls, the cloakmakers were more often the heads of households and thus more detrimentally affected by the absence of their regular source of income. Although strike benefits were disbursed, they proved at best minimal and irregular. One teenage picket soon became painfully aware "that being on strike was more than picket-line heroics or thundering rhetoric. . . . We had to live on savings, friends, or as was the case with many of us, on miracles."[47] Those who joined the picket lines with notions of grandeur quickly lost their quixotic ideals.

The strikers, however, gained strength from several sources. Gompers and the AFL provided aid and counsel; John Lennon, an AFL vice-president, personally assisted the strikers. The workers were also encouraged by a union leadership sensitive to rank-and-file feelings and desires. Many of the International Union's officials had served their apprenticeships in the shops of New York, while local unions regularly provided aspiring and capable leaders. The presidents of the ILGWU in the era of great strikes—Abraham Rosenberg (1910–1914) and Benjamin Schlesinger (1914–1923)—demonstrated the union leadership's close relationship to the rank and file. Though quite unlike each other in appearance and character, both had shared in the hardships and dreams of the immigrant clothing worker.

Rosenberg had come to America in the 1880's and almost immediately had taken up tailoring in New York's sweatshops. The misery of the sweatshop drove him to the Knights of Labor and then to the emerging Jewish-American labor movement. Though homely, intellectually shallow, and a lackluster speaker, Rosenberg won the respect of his fellow workers who moved him up the ranks of the union hierarchy to the presidency of the International. He was never far removed in attitude or style from the cloakmakers with whom he had labored in New York's shops.

Schlesinger came to America in 1891 at the age of 15. Like Rosenberg, he soon found employment in a cloak sweatshop (in Chicago) and while still a teenager became a union organizer and soapboxer for socialism's policies and programs. He rose rapidly, first through the local and then the national union leadership, becoming in 1903, at 27 years of age, president of the ILGWU. In 1904, defeated for re-election, Schlesinger moved to New York where he became manager of the Cloakmakers Joint Board (1904–1907) and business manager of the *Forward* (1907–1912). Schlesinger, unlike Rosenberg, was tall and handsome, with ascetic features, and the look of suffering upon his face. He utilized his dramatic qualities and ill-health to play upon the sympathies of rank-and-file garment workers as well as manufacturers. Despite his domineering and irascible personality, Schlesinger commanded the loyalty of his followers.[48]

Attorneys and journalists such as Morris Hillquit, Meyer London, Abraham Cahan, and Benjamin Feigenbaum also served the cloakmakers, linking these workers to the intelligentsia, idealists, and reformers in the larger Jewish community. Both Hillquit and London fought the legal battles for the young unions. Both were Russian-Jewish immigrants, who had received good educations before leaving the Old World. Both worked at odd jobs in America to finance legal education, shared in the Ghetto's intellectual ferment, joined the Socialist Labor Party, and led the anti-Daniel DeLeon movement in New York. There similarities ended.

Hillquit, more a behind-the-scene manipulator than a public or bureaucratic personality, became Socialism's political boss, his relationship to the Party being much like that of Charles Murphy to the Democratic Party. Hillquit's public personality was enigmatic. He appeared to be a cold, calculating figure with sharp, hard features. His very acute and detached nature made him an excellent advocate in court and an attorney who built a successful practice. Garment workers and Jewish immigrants turned to Hillquit for his legal brilliance and organizational talents, not for his personal appeal or human qualities.

London, on the other hand, never manipulated the Party organization but won through his appealing personality ardent admirers within and without the Socialist camp. In 1914, 1916, and 1922 enthusiastic east side voters elected him to Congress. Lacking Hillquit's legal brilliance and sharp eye for the dollar, London never developed a lucrative law practice. But the slightly-built, small, soft-featured, and homely man conquered the hearts of the garment workers and gained for them avid supporters in the Jewish community.[49]

Strikers, supported by capable leaders and talented advisers, ably appealed to the public for support. President Rosenberg, of the ILGWU, for example, though a committed reform socialist, insisted: "The union realizes that if it is to build for the future and establish permanent relations with the employers that it must be reasonable and fair." And public-spirited New Yorkers responded to the entreaties of moderate crusaders for social justice and industrial democracy. Acting Mayor John P. Mitchel cautioned the police against interfering with strikers who employed oral persuasion or moral suasion upon strikebreakers. Mitchel, of course, directed the police to repress all violence and intimidation but he laid the responsibility for disorderly behavior on both parties to the conflict (an unusually objective position for an American public official in 1910).[50]

The city's newspapers again treated the strikers more equitably than other less fortunate workers. The *Times* engaged in the usual journalistic fulminations against union security demands, labeling the closed shop a tyranny by the minority over the majority and an infringement of American liberties. Other papers showed more moderation. The *Herald* and the *Post* calmly proposed mediation and arbitration. The *American* entreated the disputants to recognize the public interest. Even the *Times* found space to criticize cloak manufacturers, who looked down their aristocratic noses at the social gaucheries of east European Jews rising to prominence in the manufacture of ladies' cloaks. Certainly at no time did the press attempt to generate strong public resentment against the cloakmakers.[51]

As the strike persisted into late August, the entire Jewish community as well as cloakmakers and employers felt economic distress more painfully. Landlords and petty retailers in the city's Jewish districts faced a shrinking market and could no longer extend credit while the community's single largest source of employment and income remained closed. Larger manufacturers also became more fearful of their smaller competitors who were continuing to settle individually with the union. Economic discontent within the Jewish community and within the industry brought further public intervention and conciliation. Jacob H. Schiff and Louis Marshall, prominent and respected Jewish banker and attorney respectively, convinced union representatives to compromise. Both new mediators were anxious to prove to Progressive America that Jews, employers and employees, were exemplars of industrial peace and social justice. But the rank and file again refused compromise based upon the preferential union shop; they demanded instead the union shop, indicating their readiness to resist until the attainment of full job security.[52]

On the eve of a final settlement, August 28, the judiciary dealt the strikers a crushing setback. Justice Goff of the State Supreme Court, calling the strike a common-law, civil conspiracy to obtain the closed shop and thereby deny to others their constitutional right to labor on their own freely chosen terms, enjoined the union and all cloakmakers from peaceful picketing. Mayor Gaynor immediately ordered the police to disperse all pickets. Before the injunction could irremediably subvert the walkout, negotiators reached agreement.[53]

Despite the rank and file's rejection on August 26 of management's last previous offer, discussions had continued between Meyer London for the union, Julius Henry Cohen for the Protective Association, and Louis Marshall for the Jewish community. All three negotiators were eager to achieve a settlement that would bring stability and security to the garment trades. London saw in a collective bargaining agreement with the trade's leaders an arrangement which would serve as a model for the smaller manufacturers; once entrenched within the large firms, the union could build its resources to conquer the industry's pygmies. Cohen saw in the same agreement an instrument to protect the ethical manufacturers from unfair competition; the union, in return for recognition, would impose uniform wage scales upon all employers, thus eliminating differentials in the industry's basic variable cost. Marshall saw in the proposed agreement proof of the Jewish community's commitment to the American ideals of democracy and justice. And all three hoped to realize Cohen's dream of "law and order in industry." With an assist in semantics from attorney Marshall, the parties to the dispute signed a mutually acceptable agreement, largely patterned upon Brandeis' preferential union shop. Thus was born the "Protocol of Peace," a phrase designed by Marshall to save face for Union and Association.[54]

The Protocol granted the strikers higher wages, improved working conditions, and more important, union recognition. Employers were compelled to declare their belief in the union and in the ideal that all "who desire its [the union] benefits should share its burdens." Furthermore, manufacturers agreed that nonunion labor was to be hired only when union help was unavailable.[55]

The Protocol, covering all shops in the Protective Association, was among the first industry-wide collective bargaining agreements in American economic history. As such it reflected the employers' desire to utilize the union to stabilize an insecure and highly competitive trade. The agreement also recognized the public's stake in industrial disputes (a principle too often ignored in the history of industrial relations in America) by assigning impartial public representatives the balance of power on various Boards created to police, stabilize, and improve the industry. Workers surrendered the right to strike, employers relinquished the lockout. All disputes that employers and employees could not resolve peacefully were to be adjudicated by a Permanent Board of Arbitration, Louis Brandeis presiding. The Protocol, in its six years, moderated conflict within the cloak industry and functioned as a model for similar arrangements in other branches of the women's garment industry.[56]

The cloakmakers' strike proved a signal victory for the organizational impulse. The union's official journal, for example, advised members:

It is far better to strike for, and win recognition of our union, than an increase in wages, or decrease of hours, without the powerful organization needed to maintain the conditions once created. With such an organization, the possibilities of the future are unlimited.[57]

Immigrant workers again demonstrated their aptitude for organization and effective economic action. Union victory also served to expose again the structural weaknesses in the garment trades which led manufacturers to turn to the unions for the maintenance of uniform, fair standards of competition. Finally, the cloakmakers' strike re-emphasized the importance of union leadership wedded to the rank and file. And it proved the benefits of either public support or community impartiality.[58]

The cloakmakers' 1910 strike and the shirtwaist strike marked the beginning of New York's immigrant clothing workers rise from the depths of industrial despair to the pinnacles of trade-union power. The two walkouts set the pattern for subsequent industrial conflicts which transformed still unorganized branches of the women's trade, the men's clothing industry, and the fur industry. In 1912, following two years of relative industrial peace, conflict in the needle trades broke out anew and continued unabated until 1916.

4.

The Organizational
Strike Spreads

IN THE TWO YEARS IMMEDIATELY following the 1910 cloakmakers' strike the conflict in the garment trades between the proponents of industrial democracy and the supporters of industrial efficiency receded. Trade-unions evaluated past successes and considered future strategy and tactics; manufacturers debated whether they could operate their businesses profitably under the pressure of recognized but still militant trade-unions, whether they could preserve shop discipline and efficiency despite the growing assertiveness of the workers. The community, especially the reformers, bewitched and bemused by the Protocol of Peace, foresaw an era of permanent industrial peace, with the mediator replacing the striker, the arbitration table substituting for the picket line. But peace in the garment trades proved illusory and short-lived.

Large sectors of the needle trades in 1912 had neither labor organizations nor employer associations. The fur trade, the men's clothing industry, and the subsidiary women's trades all lacked rational organization. Severe competition and pressure upon wages and working conditions produced a discontented, disaffected labor force and an insecure class of employers. Thus in the spring of 1912 another and more virulent period of industrial strife struck the garment trades; within two years four general strikes afflicted the industry. In this second and more severe period of conflict, reformers within the community, through the offices of the Mayor, found themselves drawn inexorably into the vortex of industrial relations' maneuvers.

I

A furriers' general strike, beginning June 20, 1912, initiated the renewed employer-employee hostilities. In 1909 and 1910 while the waistmakers and the cloakmakers had organized themselves, the fur workers lacked solid unions. In the Fall of 1909, 80 fur workers had met in New York City to form a union in their trade. Ignored by the ILGWU, they received assistance from the United Hebrew Trades which aided the furriers to initiate an organizing campaign in the Spring of 1911. Led by Isidore Cohen, an immigrant worker,[1] the fur workers' new organization, although unaffiliated with any national trade-union or with the AFL and simply a local affiliate of the UHT, had organized 3000 workers and amassed a treasury of 3000 dollars by the following spring.

Rising membership and a financial surplus encouraged union leader Cohen to prepare for an industry-wide strike. From June 12 to June 14, 1912, fur workers balloted on the question of whether to strike for demands similar to those won two years earlier by the cloakmakers. As the voting, conducted by the UHT, proceeded more and more fur workers indicated their willingness to join the union. By the evening of the 14th 7000 men and women had voted, and that same night Hugh Frayne of the AFL installed the New York furriers' organization as Federal Local 14263, AFL.[2]

Cohen and other union leaders, preferring promptness to perfection, and now counting upon AFL as well as UHT assistance, chose June 20 as the day for their industry-wide strike. And on that day 7500 workers from 400 fur shops responded to the union's call.[3]

Manufacturers reflexively responded to the union offensive. In order to combat their employees' demands, they organized into a protective association, in this instance the Fur Manufacturers' Protective Association, which included about 300 firms. The fur manufacturers, stoutly defending shop discipline, industrial efficiency, and employer prerogatives, resolved not "to enter into any contract, agreement or secret understanding that shall or may conflict with the principle of the open shop."[4]

Once again the familiar pattern was repeated. Workers organized and struck to democratize industrial relations and employers reacted by uniting in defense of more efficient production. And again worker initiative resulted eventually in a more rational and equitable industrial environment.

After its first hectic days, the walkout became a battle of attrition. For 13 weeks, until September 8, the furriers maintained their general strike and their insistence upon union recognition. Their chances for survival, like those of all weak labor organizations lacking adequate funds, proved precarious. As financial resources evaporated, strikers were pressured for payment by grocers and landlords. The fur workers pledged not to succumb to their employers' most effective weapon: "starvation." The union thus issued an appeal to all sympathizers and friends for funds. Fortunately the response to this entreaty was generous. Despite improved finances, the pickets still contended with hostile agents of the law: police and courts.[5] Only their belief in a brighter future, especially for their children, impelled the furriers to remain steadfast throughout their long ordeal.

After two months of conflict, union and manufacturers' association had not become more conciliatory. The very duration of the strike had a sobering effect on the city's Jewish community. Leaders representing the kehillah (supposedly the governing agency for community disputes), anxious to avoid strife within their religious group and to prove the Jews first-class American citizens, attempted to bring union and employers' association together for negotiations. In mid-August Dr. Judah L. Magnes, President of the kehillah, approached the fur manufacturers in the hope of mediating the dispute.

The San Francisco-born (1876) Magnes had arrived in New York in 1906 to accept the Reform Temple Emanu-El's call. The young rabbi was much-traveled and highly educated, having earned degrees at the University of Cincinnati, the Hebrew Union College, and the University of Heidelberg. He planned to utilize his superior education and knowledge of the world to aid less fortunate Jews. Thus Magnes was active in defense associations and Zionist affairs, and in 1909 called upon New York's Jews to establish a community council (kehillah) "to wipe out invidious distinctions between East European and West European, foreigner and native, Uptown and Downtown Jew, rich and poor; and make us realize that Jews are one people with a common history and with common hopes." Before long, the handsome and eloquent young Jewish reformer, who had founded the kehillah, utilized the new organization to seek a reconciliation in the garment trades between German-Jewish capitalists and Russian-Jewish socialists.[6]

Initially the manufacturers rebuffed Dr. Magnes' peace overtures.

On August 14, the Association's attorney, Charles S. Porter, informed him: "I do not see any possibility at the present time of getting the manufacturers together in a conference with anyone representing the Labor Union. They declined most emphatically to meet Mr. London or any other Union leaders." Porter added that the employers were unanimous in their resistance to the unionization of their shops and were willing to remain inactive indefinitely. He concluded: "I regret very much that there is such a deplorable condition, but cannot think of any means whereby it can be settled at the present time."[7]

But continuing pressure from Magnes, Paul Abelson, and other influential kehillah spokesmen convinced the fur manufacturers, largely Jews, that it would be to their advantage to negotiate. Consequently, on the evening of August 20, delegates of the Union and of the Manufacturers' Association convened in secret session. Simultaneously, Gompers arrived in New York to address the strikers and to assist them in the painstaking process of collective bargaining.

In the past Gompers, and more often the AFL craft union leaders, had indicated their dislike for unskilled immigrants in general and radical ones in particular. Gompers, however, usually rushed to aid those same despised immigrants, radical or not, whenever they demonstrated an ability to strike effectively and to create stable trade-unions. He had come to the aid of the cloakmakers in 1910, he was helping the furriers now in 1912, and he would assist other garment workers and unskilled laborers in 1913 and 1916. Gompers' reason for this was simple. Although the AFL lacked the funds and the organizers to do much about the unorganized, even had it desired to do anything, Gompers realized that once the immigrants organized themselves, as they were doing, they had better be abetted by the AFL. Otherwise the new unions might go their own way, perhaps even join the IWW in its war against the American Federation of Labor. To keep newly organized immigrants within the AFL fold Gompers encouraged them in their struggles for improved conditions. But the unskilled or immigrant unionists had to hew to the AFL line of flexible craft unionism, union autonomy, and exclusive jurisdiction or forgo aid from the Federation. On this basis Gompers came to New York in the summer of 1912 to help the fur workers.

As a result of negotiations under the kehillah's auspices and with Gompers' participation, the fur workers received nearly all their demands including union recognition; only the much maligned and much resisted closed shop remained unwon.[8]

With so much already theirs, the strikers demanded additional concessions. Gompers fanned the flames of discontent, cautioning the furriers to consider carefully the proposed settlement, and, if unsatisfied, to remain out and battle for ultimate triumph. The AFL President reminded the fur workers that whatever they failed to achieve during the strike they would not gain afterwards. Once the strike ended furriers would have to concentrate upon preserving their new organization, not winning new benefits. Reinforced by Gompers' admonition and advice, the strikers refused to ballot on the proposed settlement or to return to their positions unless employers granted the Saturday half-holiday all year instead of just the first eight months. On September 7, the employers conceded this last demand and the following day the strike ended.[9]

The strike settlement, however, only thrust the kehillah more deeply into trade affairs. Both parties to the conflict were inexperienced in the intricacies of organizational techniques. They constantly complained about and excoriated each other, while working to expand the membership of their respective organizations by bringing independent workers and manufacturers into the Union and the Association fold. In their attempts to achieve industrial stability, Union and Association took their problems and grievances to the kehillah's industrial relations committee which sought to preserve the peace.[10]

Two years later, in 1914, upon the expiration of the original agreement, Abelson and Magnes, representing the kehillah, agreed to underwrite any new settlement reached between the Union and the Associated Fur Manufacturers. Magnes had dreams of making the Jewish community's arrangement for industrial peace in the fur trade a model for other industries. Dr. Magnes proved so eager for a new agreement that when some members of the Associated Manufacturers were recalcitrant, he prepared an open letter to the public placing complete responsibility for any impasse upon the employers alone. Magnes wrote:

Should the outcome of this regrettable situation lead to a conflict between workers and the employers in the fur industry in the city, the responsibility for this lamentable situation must, and will be placed, squarely upon the shoulders of a small group of employers, who, contrary to the best judgment of the most responsible employers in the industry, prefer strife and chaos to order and peace.[11]

Throughout the summer of 1914 Magnes pressured the manufacturers. He informed them that if they desired the kehillah's Committee on Industrial Relations to guarantee a trade agreement, manufacturers had to accede to enforcement machinery entirely acceptable to Abelson and Magnes. Thus when agreement was finally reached, both the Union and the Association selected Magnes as Chairman of the Conference Committee, informing him: "We hope this change will make the moral support and advice, which you and your Committee of Industrial Relations can render, of even greater service to the Industry."[12]

The furriers' 1912 strike and the ensuing negotiations foreshadowed future events in the needle trades. While the strike in the fur industry affected a relatively small number of workers and had its major impact on the Jewish community, impending industrial disputes were to engage many thousands of laborers and to concern the entire metropolitan community. Subsequent strikes again saw an active and influential Magnes at work; but he and the kehillah were upstaged by non-Jewish social reformers and by Mayor John Purroy Mitchel. In fact, in 1915–1916, Mayor Mitchel became the leading figure in negotiations between garment manufacturers and union officials. His intervention demonstrated middle-class Progressivism's realization that industrial disputes concerned the public as well as the disputants. Mitchel thus reflected aggressively, if not always wisely, the community's increasing awareness of the ramifications of industrial warfare.

II

In the early months (January–March) of 1913, garment workers struck four sectors of their industry, repeating their earlier successful organizing tactics. On December 30, 1912, men's tailors, organized by the UGWA, initiated a general strike in the men's coat and suit industry. The ILGWU, recognizing the propitiousness of the moment, called out 15,000 white goods workers on January 8, 1913, 15,000 wrapper and kimono workers the following day, and 35,000 shirtwaist operators a week later (January 16). Thus, by the third week of January, 1913, nearly 150,000 workers from allied trades marched the picket lines in the most tumultuous and explosive labor disturbances of the era in the needle trades. To a prominent old-line socialist and union leader, Joseph Schlossberg, the 1913 strikes were a veritable revolution, for "in times of revolution thousands of people are converted to the cause, many times the number that years of organization would bring. This is the time of revolution on the economic field."[13] The occasion for the strikes had been set, however, by previous developments within the ranks of the unions and the manufacturers.

Like the cloakmakers strike of 1910, the first of the new walkouts climaxed a well-prepared organization campaign. As early as May 31, 1912, the UGWA had begun an aggressive organizing drive among the men's tailors in New York. Strong sentiment had been brewing among the tailors for several years because of growing conviction that trade conditions, though not worsening, were hardening. As militancy increased among the tailors, UGWA leaders decided to mollify the New York workers before the situation passed beyond control of International officials. Rank-and-file desires and International Union politics combined, on December 18, 1912, to lay the foundation for an overwhelming favorable vote (35,786 to 2,322) on the general strike issue. The enthusiasm of the tailors led union officials to select December 30 as the date for the walkout in order to act before ardor cooled and caution replaced militancy.[14]

While strike agitation among men's tailors heightened, labor organizers in the women's trade were also busy. Although the cloakmakers had maintained their organizational strength in the years since 1910, the shirtwaist makers (Local 25) had lost much of their membership, and other branches of the trade remained relatively unorganized. Ineffective labor organization characterized the trades where young girls recently arrived in the country formed the bulk of the labor force. These trades included, in addition to the shirtwaist trade, women's underwear, kimonos and housedresses, and children's wear. Wages were low for the inexperienced girls working in a surplus labor market within an industry where strong competition and intense pressure on wage rates prevailed. Narrow profit margins and nagging insecurity caused employers to charge their workers for electric power, needles, thread, and other necessary work supplies. The girls had been provided by the WTUL with a skeleton labor organization; but in 1911 there were probably no more than 1000 organized employees at work in all these trades.[15]

Then, in the spring of 1911, the tragic Triangle Fire generated militancy among the girls. The fire, taking the lives of more than 100 shirtwaist makers, proved a turning point in the organization of the women's trades. Conditions had always been harsh, perhaps even intolerable; now that girls perceived the imminence of physical danger, the breaking point was reached. The fire also etched indelibly upon the public mind the picture of an industry brutalizing its employees. Thus during the strikes, the community offered the girls much needed assistance.

From the fall of 1911 to the winter of 1912–1913, demands for a general strike echoed across the industry. The ILGWU executive board, however, bided its time. It waited for an opportune moment before permitting inexperienced girls to strike. Word of the approaching upheaval in the men's clothing trade put an organizational campaign among female workers in a more attractive light. In preparation for a general walkout among the girls the ILGWU at its 1912 national convention authorized New York organizers and officials to spread actively the gospel of unionism. And in December, 1912, on the eve of the men's strike, a local organizer pleaded with his union's general executive board:

> I do not see any future for these people, or any way of improving their conditions, unless by means of a general strike. I feel confident that should such a strike be called, it will terminate very speedily and successfully. The nature of the trade is such that employers will not be in a position to carry on a fight very long.

The GEB impressed by the logic of this entreaty made plans at its December session to inaugurate the oft-demanded organizing drive which, in the first weeks of January, 1913, took the form of three separate yet related general strikes.[16]

In both the men's trade and the women's trade the weaknesses of the employers provided the basis for settlements attractive to the disputants. Generally the employers tended to split among themselves. The highly capitalized firms having more to lose from conflict and competition prepared to bargain more readily with trade-unions. The manufacturers of men's clothing, for example, divided into three separate trade associations; the Allied Clothing Trades (makers of higher-grade clothing) comprised more than 200 manufacturers and employed about one fifth of the workers in the trade; the United Merchants and Manufacturers' Association ranked second in wealth and in size of member concerns; and, at the bottom, the United Association of Clothing Contractors, composed of more than 2000 concerns and claiming to employ over three quarters of the workers and to manufacture half the total volume of the entire trade. The three major associations split in their approach to organized labor, and internal dissension ultimately led the employers toward negotiations with the union.

In the women's trades, on the other hand, employers generally favored working-class organization in order to rationalize and stabilize a disorganized industry. In fact, the shirtwaist makers' strike actually witnessed cooperation between labor and management for a mutually desired objective, the strengthening of their respective organizations—the Union and the Associated Dress and Waist Manufacturers' Association. Even before the calling of the general strike, the *Women's Wear Daily,* a trade journal, reported that with the ranks of the union and the employers' organization swelling,

> it is believed that the time will soon arrive when the two can get together and plan the protocol system, which the manufacturers appear to favor. It is known that there have been several conferences between representatives of the manufacturers and the International Ladies' Garment Workers' Union with a view to planning the details, but the stumbling block in the way of a definite arbitration before a strike seemed to be the inadequate number on both sides. When the two organizations are representative of the trade, then, it is said, little difficulty will exist in arranging a settlement.[17]

Julius Henry Cohen, advocate of "law and order in industry," served as attorney for many of the employer associations and advised them to recognize the union in order to gain economic security and justice. The workers in the white goods and kimono and wrapper trades faced employers who, in most cases, existed on a shoestring. These manufacturers, counseled by Cohen, accepted the protocol device to establish common industrial standards and thus eliminate the unscrupulous sweatshop competitors. Recognition grew that "a strong organization of the employers, and a strong union are necessary, each working to strengthen the other."[18]

III

Of the four separate yet related general strikes, that of the men's garment workers proved the longest and most acrimonious. Not only did the conflict engender enmity between boss and worker, it also shattered the solidarity of the union. The dispute developed into a struggle pursued simultaneously on two fronts: one with the primary objective of organizing workers to end onerous conditions of labor; the other against the cautious and conservative officialdom of the UGWA.

Founded in 1891 the United Garment Workers built its early membership among American-born workers in small towns and rural districts where they produced overalls and work clothes which could be marketed largely on the basis of the union label. By the time it began to organize immigrant tailors in New York, Chicago, and other large cities, the UGWA's leaders, American-born or Americanized immigrant, were fixed in their beliefs and tactics; like so many other American craft unionists, President Rickert and Secretary Larger sought to protect their followers' status by obtaining immigration restriction, avoiding strikes, and emphasizing union labels. None of this sat well with urban immigrant tailors who favored immigration, produced garments worn by nonworkers, and who saw the strike as the best single means to improve their existence. In 1910 delegates representing New York tailors who claimed that UGWA officers neglected the interests of immigrant workers went to their union's national convention to plead for a voice on the UGWA's general executive board. But the convention majority declined the immigrant tailors' demand, leaving the most important source of new union members unrepresented on the organization's policy-making board. Just such action by the UGWA establishment led one of New York's immigrant spokesmen to characterize the history of the union from its founding in 1891 to 1914 as "the story of corruption, betrayal, sold strikes, broken faith, crushed hope."[19]

Much of the intensified acerbity and longevity associated with the men's strike can be traced directly to the duality of the conflict. Immigrant workers fought both hostile employers and unsympathetic national union leaders.

The men's strike also provoked an immediate reaction from the business community. The New York Chamber of Commerce, fearing violence and harm to a key sector of the metropolitan economy, intervened unsuccessfully. The Chamber proposed to the union and the manufacturers that strikers return to work under sanitary conditions pending an impartial investigation of wages, hours, and working conditions in comparison with other competitive markets. Strike leaders immediately rejected the Chamber's proposal. Its offer simply awarded the workers compliance with state sanitary requirements without any promise of either ultimate improvements in wages or union recognition. In short, the manufacturers would retain the services of their entire working force for the busy season, while the strike's momentum would be, if not halted, deflected.[20] The Chamber's abortive attempt at conciliation presaged a protracted struggle. The following day the union announced the beginning of mass picketing to secure immediate wage increases, reduced hours, and *union recognition.*[21]

The manufacturers split on basic issues. All employer groups agreed that New York wages were the highest anywhere in the trade and that union recognition was out of the question. The wealthier and more affluent clothiers in the Allied Clothing Trades, however, refused to negotiate with the union under any conditions. The United Merchants and Manufacturers' Association, advised by Julius Henry Cohen, agreed to treat with union representatives. Cohen compared the President of the Allied Clothing Trades to Mr. Baer of anthracite coal notoriety and similar labor baiters, declaring that the United Association "is not opposed to any organization, either of employers or employees. It wants to preserve the clothing industry of New York. It believes it cannot be preserved by a continuous state of warfare."[22]

The men's trade proved difficult to organize. Strikers represented a dozen or more different nationalities. Jews formed the largest segment (over half the total number); Italians composed about one third of the labor force, and Germans, Poles, Russians, and native Americans, among others, comprised the remainder. Difficult as it was to unify heterogeneous workers, the International's officials, more Americanized or even of native birth and representing the most skilled and nonurban areas of the industry, showed scant sympathy for the problems and aspirations of New York's immigrant workers. The leading manufacturers in the industry represented an older generation of Americanized German Jews with secure status in the community, untroubled by problems of social marginality and thus less amenable to the pressure of the Jewish community or of general community organizations. Further, they operated in a relatively standardized industry which included heavily capitalized firms better able than their feeble counterparts in the women's trade to withstand the strain of a strike or other production disruptions. The men's trade was also more decentralized than the women's, and New York's manufacturers encountered vigorous competition from other clothing centers. They could not possibly accede to union demands that might undermine their competitive position in the national market.[23] Diversity and disunity among the workers and the social and economic strength of the leading employers portended a protracted struggle in which strikers required external, nonworking-class aid for success.

The walkout resembled the previous struggles of cloakmakers and furriers. If the strikers suffered neither from hunger nor from exposure to a savage New York winter, they waged the typical war of the picket line; clashes with strikebreakers, thugs, and police occurred almost daily. Despite the employers' insistence that the union inspired violence, the strike, in the testimony of one respected eyewitness, "was on the whole conducted with no great disorder or breach of the peace; and in view of the numbers involved, the amount of violence committed was small."[24] But police and judiciary continued to treat strikers as the sole instigators of violence and disorder. The strikers protested against police interference and judicial injunctions banning peaceful picketing. On January 13, they organized a mass protest parade of 85,000 workers.[25] Once again police and judicial interference with the strike probably worked to the pickets' advantage.

Civic groups rushed to aid poor, immigrant workers struggling against affluent, well-organized employers and civil authorities. Radical and labor organizations also assisted. The *Call,* the Socialist Party, and the United Hebrew Trades promptly provided aid. On January 14, a number of ministers and public-spirited citizens, including Canon George W. Douglas of St. John the Divine, Dr. Henry E. Cobb of Marble Collegiate Church, and William J. Schiefflin, wealthy importer and philanthropist, addressed a strikers' mass meeting. A week later the combined churches and synagogues of Brooklyn scheduled a public rally to win new allies for the strikers. The Reverend John Howard Melish, featured speaker at the rally, declared: "We want to help the employee secure his rights to a living wage and a fair day's work, and sanitary and human conditions. We will not be content until there is industrial peace, which is based on industrial justice." Previously the Reverend Mr. Melish had obtained a promise from Mayor Gaynor that the police would not interfere unlawfully with pickets and would not be permitted to favor either side.[26]

In the third week of January a citizen's committee established by prominent civic leader, R. Fulton Cutting, and including among its members Cleveland H. Dodge, Rabbi Stephen S. Wise, Dr. Felix Adler, and Dr. Henry Moscowitz, criticized the employers. In its first official policy statement the Committee insisted:

We can see no just reason why any groups of employers should fail to recognize the right of work people to organize in order to present their case to their employers and to the public through their chosen representatives. Least of all should any employers ignore the fair and reasonable demand of the public for conciliation, mediation and arbitration.[27]

The city's press when it chose to comment editorially on the strike was exceedingly attentive to the workers' plight and critical of the employers' intransigence. The New York *Times* refused to criticize severely the strikers at any point and saved its editorial wrath for the manufacturers who, the paper wrote, "should be more intelligent than their workmen [and upon whom] . . . it was . . . incumbent to see the light and walk in it." At the same time, the *Times* applauded the strikers for conducting their walkout "with remarkable judgment, with a minimum of violence and inflammatory speech-making, and with the manifestation in most instances of a desire to conduct negotiations peaceably toward a proper settlement."[28] The *Times* suggested that the dispute be ended by the signing of a Protocol covering the entire men's clothing industry. The *World* also called for a Protocol agreement, asking: "Why prolong it [the strike] needlessly when it is to the advantage of both parties that it end?"[29] And the *Tribune* demanded that the employers arbitrate in order to ward off the spread of extreme radicalism among still moderate workers.[30]

Pressures from public, pulpit, and press caused manufacturers to respond more amicably to the union. On January 21, the Clothing Contractors' Association, speaking for itself and for the United Merchant and Manufacturers' Association, consented to enter into conference with the UGWA. The conference, once in session, apparently made rapid progress. Compromise and good intentions reigned. Thomas Rickert, President of the UGWA, declared that his organization was amenable to certain concessions; Julius Henry Cohen, representing the employers, confidently proclaimed the imminence of a definitive settlement because the negotiators had already agreed to arbitrate outstanding differences. Immediate concessions on wages and hours remained the only hurdle to overcome before strikers returned to work, pending arbitration of more basic grievances and issues.[31]

At first such optimism appeared justified. On January 27, negotiators announced final terms for termination of the strike. Both union and employers concurred in recognizing their interdependent status—the manufacturers and contractors recognized the necessity for a strong union; the union admitted the right of the manufacturers to establish an employers' association; and both parties agreed that no stable settlement could be completed in the heat of battle. So it was decided to award workers immediate concessions, while additional conferences and arbitration proceedings disposed definitively of the trade's intricate and complex economic problems. The manufacturers agreed, at the suggestion of Charles L. Bernheimer of the Chamber of Commerce, to concede the workers temporary reductions in hours as well as wage increases. All other matters in dispute were to go before a three-man board of arbitration—one member to be appointed by the union, one by the manufacturers, and the third to represent the public and be appointed by the AFL in conjunction with Cohen.[32]

The agreement, however, instead of restoring peace to the industry introduced a new and more virulent phase of industrial conflict. Where previously the dispute had been the traditional employer-employee conflict, it now became a civil war within labor's ranks. The Joint Executive Board of the metropolitan New York locals almost unanimously rejected the agreement negotiated by their International Union officials; the dissidents insisted upon continuation of the strike until all demands were won. While International officials debated with local strike leaders, the mass of workers who had not yet voiced their desires wielded the balance of power. Thus the UGWA leadership attempted to convince the rank and file of the exceptional advantages inherent in the proposed settlement. They hailed the agreement as one that would result in "permanent peace in the men's clothing industry similar to that which exists in the women's clothing industry." The mass of strikers, however, disputed this optimistic prophecy and instead chose to remain out until even shorter hours, higher wages, and immediate *union recognition* were granted.[33]

Although the strikers had declined what many respected individuals deemed a reasonable settlement to engage in internecine warfare, New York tailors retained important and necessary sources of aid. Left-wing labor and political organizations led by the ILGWU, the Socialist Party, and the *Forward* continued to provide moral and financial support.[34] Even the city's clergy maintained their endorsement of the now recalcitrant strikers. And State Assemblyman Meyer Greenberg of Manhattan, an east side Tammany Democrat, introduced a resolution in the state assembly demanding an investigation of private detectives and strikebreakers in the employ of men's garment manufacturers.[35]

The tailors, thus fortified in their resolve, pressed their demands upon reluctant employers. By mid-February, numerous smaller firms, feeling the economic pinch, had acceded to workers' requests, signing contracts conceding union recognition and total wage and hour demands. The resumption of production by the trade's smaller firms threatened the security of the larger businesses, and on February 28, the three largest associations of clothing manufacturers submitted revised settlement terms to the union. President Rickert, representing the UGWA's general executive board, promptly accepted the revisions; his fellow officials waxed ecstatic in praise of the proposed settlement. The strikers were to return immediately to their former positions pending impartial investigation of the hours issue by a commission composed of R. Fulton Cutting, Marcus M. Marks, and Dr. Judah L. Magnes—their recommendations to be binding and final. In addition, the tailors gained an immediate wage increase, sanitary conditions, abolition of sub-contracting, and a promise of nondiscrimination in the re-employment of strikers. With this new and apparently advantageous agreement in hand even the Socialist *Forward* urged the men to return to their jobs. All parties took for granted the conflict's end. Julius Henry Cohen wrote to Dr. Magnes: "Permit me to congratulate you upon your most successful work in bringing about peace in the clothing industry."[36]

But rank-and-file strikers again arrayed themselves to the left of their more cautious leaders. Militant action by the tailors belied the UGWA executive board's proclamation ending the walkout. Workers, once more enraged by policies promulgated by their erstwhile officials, exploded in protest. The men had concluded that the Union's International leadership was far too conservative and ready to compromise essential issues to the disadvantage of the membership. The latest agreement, for example, had omitted both union recognition and the closed shop. Tailors doubted their ability to enforce compliance with the remainder of the settlement without a recognized union to guard against employer chicanery.[37]

Taking matters into their own hands, the tailors met on March 2, together with the Socialist Party, the Cloakmakers' Union, and the Workmen's Circle to select a committee of five to confer jointly with UGWA officials and the three arbitrators named in the February 28 proposal. Thus rank-and-file workers were striking against both their employers and their international union, and were negotiating simultaneously with both. The tailors' Committee of Five, which included

Fiorello La Guardia, Jacob Panken, Meyer London, and John Dyche, was to inform Rickert and his associates of the strikers' temper and the justice of their demands.[38] The Committee was balanced carefully to represent various interests: La Guardia, the Italian nationality tailors; Panken and London, the Jewish Socialist workers; Dyche, the more conservative business unionists.

Rickert and the UGWA leaders, however, refused to listen to the New Yorkers' case. The International continued to urge the metropolis' tailors to accept the agreement, and on March 7, Rickert officially declared the strike's end. He also enlisted the support of Mayor Gaynor, whom he authorized to order the police to disperse all remaining pickets.[39]

Before the beleaguered strikers agreed to vacate the picket lines, they won, through their persistence, further concessions. Negotiations between the Committee of Five, the UGWA leaders, and the three arbitrators resulted on March 11, 1913, in a new agreement which provided for gradual reductions of work to the 48-hour level and Meyer London's appointment to the Arbitration Commission in place of Cutting, thus implicitly recognizing the union. Finally, on March 12, 1913, 72 days after the strike's commencement, industrial peace returned to the men's garment industry.[40]

While the walkout brought improved conditions of employment, shorter hours, and higher wages to the tailors, its significance was deeper. By 1913, to rootless Jewish and Italian immigrants the union had become the embodiment of unity and organization which transformed the industrial worker into more than a replaceable cog in the machinery of industry. The strike instilled in the tailors conscious awareness of the economic and moral strength provided by disciplined working-class organization, and proved beyond doubt that not only were immigrants organizable, but they understood clearly the rationale of trade-unionism.

The strike again involved the kehillah deeply in industrial relations and from the settlement in March, 1913 through the summer of 1914 both union and employers appealed to Magnes to preserve peace in the industry. As a result in June, 1914, the kehillah's Commission on the Clothing Trades averted a threatened lockout and eventually arranged a Protocol-type agreement which it underwrote.[41] Finally, the 1913 walkout rendered the impasse between the Jewish and Italian immigrant workers in New York and their cautious, business-oriented, Americanized officials irremediable.

IV

While the tailors carried their extended struggle to an ultimately successful conclusion, the girls on strike in the women's trade, free of internal dissension, gained success more fully and more promptly. Within a week of the men's walkout, over 30,000 white goods, wrapper, and kimono workers had joined the picket lines.

Not only were the girls united, but they enlisted unprecedented community support. The strikers were little more than girls in short dresses. "They are," one observer felt, "the youngest, the most ignorant, the poorest and most unskilled group of women workers who have ever struck in this country." Although the girls, lacking skill and economic power, labored under the vilest conditions, systematic organization of such an unstable labor force had in the past proved impossible.[42]

The girls' appearance on the picket lines amid police, strikebreakers, and thugs created an unusual amount of overt community sympathy for the strikers' cause. The WTUL, in what was fast becoming typical strategy, assumed the lead in organizing amorphous public support in the interest of the girls. Members of the League operated six of seven strike halls, served on picket lines, collected funds (1000 dollars of the League's own limited resources and 6000 dollars from special solicitations), and defended the more unfortunate girls in court. Other sympathizers enthusiastically joined the pigtail crusade. Coeds from Barnard and Wellesley, marching with the pickets, did their share for industrial justice, while Fola La Follette, a daughter of "Fighting Bob," acted as peripatetic orator, circulating among the strikers as a morale builder. The irrepressible Theodore Roosevelt, in fitting manner, supplied the final touch. In melodramatic fashion, he took one of his by then familiar whirlwind tours through the strikers' haunts. Repelled by what he witnessed of the living conditions of these "future mothers" of America, Roosevelt sounded the trumpet for yet another moral crusade.[43] Public, pulpit, and press again provided immeasurable assistance for striking garment workers.

During the course of the white goods and kimono workers' walkouts, shirtwaist workers and employers engaged in a brief, successful, and collusive strike. In this dispute, unlike other bitter industrial conflicts of the early twentieth century, labor and management cooperated for a common aim—to strengthen their own respective organizations, the Union and the Associated Dress and Waist Manufacturers' Association.

Conferences between ILGWU officials and the Employers' Association had begun in November, 1912, and lasted for seven weeks. Employers, during the conferences, agreed to concede their employees' demands if the union organized at least 80 percent of the trade, thus equalizing labor standards for all manufacturers. Cutthroat competition meant that working conditions could not be improved piecemeal. Only a strong union controlling the labor market could guarantee uniformity and protect the established, respectable employer from fly-by-night, sweatshop competition. The union consequently consented to a general strike in the trade to demonstrate its effective control over the workers.[44]

On January 15, the union called this general strike to prove its power. Two days later, employer and union representatives adopted a tentative protocol for submission to strikers for a vote. The next day, January 18, the new Protocol for the dress and waist industry was officially signed. The agreement, similar in all basic respects to the 1910 cloakmakers' Protocol, brought reduced hours, increased wages, and union recognition.[45]

At the same time, the other girls terminated their more protracted and noncollusive strikes with Protocol agreements. On February 11, one month after their walkout's start, the Wrapper, Kimono, and House Dress Makers' Union signed an agreement patterned after the 1910 Protocol with the Employers' Association. The girls obtained a shorter working week, a wage increase, the preferential union shop, and the abolition of payment for power and machinery. And, most important, both parties to the settlement "recognize[d] the value . . . of an organization representing the workers in the industry, and of an organization representing the employers."[46] The white goods workers also settled their dispute through the instrument of a Protocol, but only after an initial misunderstanding during which the girls voted against an arrangement failing to provide the preferential shop. The employers, however, immediately acquiesced on the job security issue. On February 18, a clause was inserted in the original agreement in which the manufacturers concurred "that those who enjoy the benefits of the union shall share in its burdens . . ." and that both parties recognize that "a strong organization of the employers and a strong union are necessary, each working to strengthen the other."[47] Thus employers and workers in the two trades accepted union recognition and the preferential shop in order to establish common standards and rid the garment industry of unscrupulous sweatshop operators.

1913 marked the conclusion of the initial wave of organizational strikes. In January, 1910, there had been less than 75,000 organized garment workers; by March, 1913, there were, on paper, more than 200,000 organized clothing workers in New York City. Through militant action, men and women had attempted to achieve a socially conservative objective: the integration of marginal immigrants more fully into American society. Uprooted from their old-world homes, families, and friends and disenchanted with the impersonality and insecurity of metropolitan life, immigrant workers turned to their new unions for amelioration of immediate circumstances and the creation of a more fruitful future. Unions promised immigrant workers the material benefits and economic power which would enable them to prepare their children to attain the American dream and social status that had forever escaped first-generation newcomers.

Although the initial surge of organization was apparently complete by March, 1913, many unresolved problems persisted. From 1913 to 1915 the garment unions endured a period of stress and strain, culminating, in 1916, in a final uprising which solidified the structure of immature and insecure unions. The issues arising in the men's and women's garment industries derived from different sources: the men's tailors had organized a dual union independent of the UGWA and the AFL; employers and employees in the cloak, suit, and dress trades were confused by the intricacies of their experimental Protocols.[48]

5.
The Collapse
of Protocolism

THE PROTOCOLS, RATHER THAN establishing permanent peace in the garment industry, created an armed truce in which unions and employers' associations jockeyed for advantage and ultimate power. In the cloak and suit trade, workers and bosses contested the meaning and implementation of the Protocol. Workers, theoretically shorn of the right to strike, felt, at times, impotent to protect their vital interests and security in the shop. Manufacturers, sworn to bargain with the union faithfully and to forswear antiunion activities, felt themselves unable to maintain proper shop discipline and productive efficiency. Occasionally militants in both camps disrupted the peace. Then only the impartial Boards of Grievances and Arbitration preserved the limited peace, quickly mediating any rupture in the armed truce.

I

Throughout 1912 and 1913, militant east side women's tailors disputed the employers' right to discharge workers and threatened to destroy the Protocol of Peace. Certain local union officials, in violation of the 1910 agreement, attempted to play the various manufacturers' associations against each other. Finally, the President and the Secretary-Treasurer of the ILGWU, Abraham Rosenberg and John Dyche respectively, hastened to assure the Cloak, Suit and Skirt Manufacturers' Association that local union leaders "do not in the least express the opinions of the responsible leaders in our organization, but rather voice the sentiments of irresponsible and irreconcilable elements in our organization." The ILGWU officials cautioned the New York rank and file not to employ the right to strike without the permission of the International office or they would face severe retaliatory measures.[1]

The dispute among local union leadership, International officials, and employers over the right to discharge and the right to hire continued on into the spring of 1916. Isaac Hourwich, scholar and intellectual, upon becoming the New York Joint Board's Chief Clerk, the union's responsible agent on the various Protocol boards, assumed the leadership of the rank-and-file workers in their battle against employers and International Union officials. Hourwich became the tailors' hero as he castigated the conservatism and "class collaboration" of the ILGWU's officialdom, while demanding for the rank and file the right to strike freely in order to win the class war. Internal differences seemed about to split the women's garment workers into warring camps.[2] International officials exerted stronger control over metropolitan locals but only at the cost of great grass roots disaffection and discontent.

Even tight discipline from above failed to resolve the basic issues in dispute between workers and bosses. The Union's attorney, Meyer London, lamented the unfinished business ahead, and the Association's counsel, J. H. Cohen, reviled the prevailing industrial anarchy. Only Chairman Louis Brandeis of the Board of Arbitration persisted in his optimism, complimenting manufacturers and workers for desiring to implement the Protocol. Though impressed with the difficulties existing, he concluded: "It is the accomplishments rather than the failures which impress me."[3] Before long, however, the failures overwhelmed the accomplishments, causing the collapse of Protocolism.

Similar problems vexed administrators of the Protocol in the dress trade. The union's power to control workers in the industry in order to maintain uniform standards of competition and the employer's right to discharge inefficient employees were the points at issue. J. H. Cohen, speaking for management, while insisting that the union must control the trade's entire labor force, refused to admit that employers had an obligation to insure or maintain union membership, either through a dues checkoff or by allowing business agents to collect dues in the shop. Brandeis, in fact, had to remind the manufacturers that the "whole agreement rest[ed] upon the assumption, that it is to the interest of both, that this Association should be strong, and that the Union should be strong." More disturbing to the workers, however, was Cohen's insistence that the employer's responsibility for turning out his product entailed

> orderliness and a spirit of discipline in the shop that will enable the manufacturer to perform the duty to the people to whom he assumes obligation. Now, when the shop chairman whose business it is to see that the orderly procedure for the redress of grievances is carried out, deliberately refuses to tell the girls what they are obliged to do, and herself violates the rule, what else is there for the manufacturers to do except discharge her, in order to maintain the discipline of the shop.[4]

Again the conflicting principles of industrial efficiency and industrial democracy met head on.

By 1915 bitterness between employers and employees had become endemic. Wildcat strikes, not sanctioned by International Union headquarters, continued to disrupt production and shop efficiency. Aggressive employers, despite Association denials to the contrary, continued to implement arbitrary work policies which generated spontaneous strikes. Workers complained of unjustified discharges; employers criticized unauthorized shop strikes. Anarchy apparently prevailed in spite of the elaborate Protocol peace machinery.

New York's rank-and-file cloakmakers, contending that the Protocol had paralyzed their option to strike and to defend themselves, urged immediate action; they were restrained only by the moderate and cautious counsel of their International leaders. Employers, on the other hand, complained of the Protocol's failure to eliminate anarchic competitive conditions and the marginal operator who undermined the security and stability of an entire industry. The Union, however, proved more masterful than manufacturers in strategy and tactics.

As early as January 8, 1915, the industry's trade paper, the *Women's Wear Daily,* reported that the manufacturers desired "to eliminate the radical element which thinks it can dictate to us how we shall conduct our business. If we do not win now it is good-bye to the cloak and suit industry of New York. Under conditions as they are at present, the situation is an impossible one." Thus, the Manufacturers' Protective Association decided the time was proper to break with the Union and the Protocol.[5]

While the employers appeared as the aggressors and disturbers of the industrial peace, the ILGWU proclaimed its "desire that all difficulties shall be adjusted by reason and agreement, rather than by an appeal to force." Despite the Union's plea for peace, the manufacturers on May 17, 1915 notified the ILGWU of their intention to abrogate the Protocol and to sever all relations with the Union. The ILGWU responded with further pleas for industrial harmony, but made it clear that responsibility for any overt conflict rested with the employers.[6] There matters remained until early summer. Each side continued to accuse the other of having destroyed the spirit of the Protocol and industrial peace.

As labor relations deteriorated and the Union prepared to marshal its forces, it had apparently won the battle for community sympathy and support. Newspapers, regardless of whether they convicted the Union or the Association of breaking the peace, united in their insistence upon the restoration of the Protocol and the resurrection of permanent peace in the trade.[7] Sensing the drift of public opinion, union leaders joined to the general strike threat the promise of further peaceful negotiations.[8] The employers, under community censure and pressure, grudgingly consented to arbitration.

On June 28, Mayor John P. Mitchel, urging employers and employees to act in the public interest, wrote to both the Union and the Manufacturers' Association requesting them to appear before a council of conciliation composed of disinterested and neutral parties, with any unresolved questions to be submitted to a board of arbitration. Both the Union and the Association immediately accepted the Mayor's offer. Mitchel promptly appointed six conciliators, and set July 13 for the initial sessions of the Mayor's Council of Conciliation.[9]

Mitchel brought to his handling of labor disputes the Progressive reformer's desire to serve the public interest. The Mayor had made reform his way of life. Born in Fordham, New York in 1879, Mitchel inherited from his mother an aversion to Tammany Hall. By the age of 30, he had gained sufficient reputation as an attorney and municipal reformer to be elected anti-Tammany President of the Board of Aldermen. In 1913 Mitchel, after waging a successful campaign as a Fusion candidate, became at 34 the youngest Mayor in New York's history. Though youthful, vigorous, and dedicated to serving the urban community impartially, his appearance as the cultivated gentleman in politics did not appeal to the voters. Mitchel's inability to reach the working-class masses cost him re-election in 1917. As Mayor, he had proved too progressive for organization Republicans and too gentlemanly and efficient for Democrats and workers. Though Mitchel personified "too much Fifth Avenue, too little First Avenue," he supported consistently the workingman's right to organize independent trade-unions and was more friendly to the union cause than were Tammany Mayors.[10]

The Mayor's Council met continuously for ten days, recommending on July 23 that the workers receive wage increases, the old Protocol machinery be re-established, and strikes and lockouts again be forbidden for the new agreement's two-year life. On July 28 the Chairman of the Association, Charles Heineman, while commending the Mayor for his mediation, refused to commit the manufacturers to acceptance of the Council's proposals. Benjamin Schlesinger, ILGWU President, however, applauded the Council's recommendations as fair and just to both sides. He announced that the Union "would accept the Council's conclusions without reserve." The Union again placed responsibility for any conflict upon the manufacturers; thus Schlesinger argued: "We feel that the cloakmakers have exhausted every honorable means to bring about an amicable understanding with their employers by peaceful methods, and if the effort should fail at the last moment, the responsibility rests wholly with the employers."[11]

Manufacturers were under constant community pressure to accept the Council's recommendations. Joseph Marcus, President of the Bank of the United States and a leader in the business community, wrote to Mayor Mitchel: "The economic welfare of this community . . . demands that there be no conflict . . . and that you will not cease your efforts until a working agreement is put in force between the employers and employees in the cloak industry." And the metropolitan press immediately praised the Council's recommendations, criticizing the employers for their procrastination and intransigence.[12] Not until public sentiment and official municipal pressure intensified did the Protective Association accede to the Council's terms.

The Mayor's Council of Conciliation attempted to meet squarely the essential issue at stake, the reconciliation of industrial efficiency with the fundamental human rights of the workers. It recommended that the workers not sacrifice industrial efficiency to their needs: "For how can it be to their best interest to destroy the business on which they depend for a living, nor may efficiency be declared paramount to the human rights of the workers, for how in the long run can the industrial efficiency of a country be maintained if the human values of its workers are diminished or destroyed? The delicate adjustment required to reconcile the two principles named must be made. Peace and progress depend upon complete loyalty in the effort to reconcile them."[13]

Despite the Council's attempt to reconcile industrial efficiency with industrial democracy, the agreement of July, 1915, allowed employers the right to hire and fire freely, whereas the union could not strike in order to forestall discrimination against union members or to protect union security. Another cruel strike was to be waged before this issue was resolved.

The ILGWU leaders learned two important lessons from the 1915 dispute. First, that thereafter the City Administration would recognize the principle that "labor struggles are not private feuds, but they are matters of public concern, that the public . . . has a right and has a duty to interfere and to regulate the relations between employers and workers, if possible." Second, labor officials discovered further proof "that calmness and moderation in word and deed are a prerequisite to gaining public opinion." Consequently, "when the Union adopts such methods and is backed by organized strength, it is impossible for employers to resist its wishes."[14] In the future as in the past, comprehension of these two principles of twentieth-century industrial relations was to stand the garment workers in good stead.

II

Early in 1916 conflict erupted anew in the women's garment industry. On February 8 the Waistmakers' Union called a general strike of its 40,000 members in the dress and waist trade to prove again its actual control of the industry's labor force and thus to exact a more favorable contract from the employers' association. The primary aim of the strike was to equalize conditions in the entire industry and bring independent manufacturers in line with Association standards. And on February 12 the Union, having proved its strength, signed a new agreement including both Association and independent shops.[15]

Simultaneously, employers and workers in the children's wear industry and the house dress and kimono trade averted a bitter strike only through the intervention of Mayor Mitchel. Mitchel, again representing the community's interest in industrial disputes, offered the services of his Council of Conciliation to the disputants. He wrote in response to a manufacturer's request for aid: "I am greatly concerned to secure in the interests of the public, the settlement of industrial disputes by methods of negotiation, conciliation, and arbitration, rather than through the method of the strike. The strike, though it may be at times justifiable, is at best costly to the workers, to the employers, and not infrequently results in violence and public disorder." Both the union and the manufacturers accepted arbitration by the Mayor's Conciliation Committee, thus establishing a precedent to be employed in the more bitter and protracted cloakmakers' strike later that same year.[16]

III

Within less than a year of the signing of the 1915 agreement in the cloak and suit industry, labor-management relations had again reached the breaking point. Workers, disenchanted with the 1915 settlement, claimed, not without some justice, that employers persisted in interpreting the preferential shop in a manner discriminatory to the union. And employers gave their workers more than ample grounds for such suspicions: In March, 1916 the Manufacturers' Association unilaterally abrogated the 1915 conciliation agreement, and on April 18, the trade paper reported that the manufacturers' intention was "to bring about a condition of affairs which will compel the ILGWU to sue for peace. . . . To smash the yoke of the labor body is how the trade generally views the contemplated lockout of April 29." The paper also stated that the manufacturers would not accept less than the open shop in its fullest sense.[17]

Union officials, however, again proved more masterful tacticians and strategists than their entrepreneurial opponents. Both union leaders and the rank and file desired to end the 1915 agreement without alienating the community; their employers, by abrogating the agreement unilaterally, became the victims of public censure and inadvertently did their workers a good turn.

When rumor of the impending lockout became public knowledge late in April, Mayor Mitchel, asserting the community's concern with the approaching industrial conflict, promptly sought to mediate the differences. On April 24 Mitchel asked the Union and the Association to meet with his council of conciliation, and on April 25 he requested Brandeis' aid in terminating the dispute. Mitchel was determined to do everything in his power to avert a conflict, but he was convinced of the employers' culpability for they had rejected out-of-hand the council's last proposal. The manufacturers, having already appeared the aggressors in their quarrel with the union, next refused absolutely the Mayor's mediation offer though they were quite willing to meet with him informally. While Mitchel publicly assumed a friendly attitude toward the employers, privately he had already decided they were entirely at fault for the impending conflict. In a private memo, Mitchel explained the cloak manufacturers' disregard of public opinion and the community's welfare. The employers, he noted, considered themselves potent enough to gain their own selfish ends even while ignoring the general welfare. Thus Mitchel considered issuing a public statement blaming the manufacturers for the collapse of industrial peace. The Mayor reasoned that, as a result of the subsequent public pressure brought upon the employers, "it is quite probable that the electrification of the community and of the association following this dramatic incident, may serve to clear the atmosphere."[18] The manufacturers' woeful strategy permitted the Mayor to utilize community censure against the Association in his efforts to settle the dispute.

Before Mitchel could avert the conflict, a lockout and a general strike followed in quick succession. On April 28 the Cloak and Suit Manufacturers' Association locked out approximately 25,000 workers in 409 Association shops. The union speedily joined the issue. Fearing that employers in the Association would subcontract their orders to non-member shops still operating, the ILGWU on May 3 proclaimed a general strike affecting workers in all the city's cloak and suit shops. The resultant walkout was the largest in the women's garment industry since 1910; it also proved to be the most protracted; and it demonstrated most clearly the union's working alliance with public, press, and pulpit.[19]

The strikers began their combination lockout-walkout in a spirit of gaiety and elation. This soon gave way to misery and irritability. As the strike progressed over its 14-week course, the strikers' changing attitude and altered condition were poignantly described in an open letter by a group of east side doctors: "We have seen babies die because their parents had no money for a doctor. . . . We have seen men suffer because they had no carfare to go to a hospital. . . . Money is the only medicine that can save them."[20]

With no immediate settlement in sight because of the manufacturers' intransigence and the union's militancy, ILGWU leaders searched for support in the community. The union, realizing from past experience the prominent role exerted by public opinion in labor disputes, started a systematic courting of civic organizations. Its primary tactic was to heap complete responsibility for the raging conflict upon the manufacturers. The union, so its tale went, had sought peace and impartial public adjudication; the employers, in reply, had declared industrial war. And the Protective Association by its very policies and Mayor Mitchel through his public and private statements lent weight to the union's contention.[21]

As in their earlier strikes, the garment workers again received a favorable response from the community. On May 18 the Executive Committee of the National Consumers' League censured the manufacturers and demanded, in the public interest, an immediate settlement. The following week, at a meeting arranged by the Women's City Club, delegates representing nearly all the metropolis' women's civic organizations publicly denigrated the attitudes and policies of the garment "bosses." Shortly thereafter, a group of Columbia University faculty members, in an open letter addressed to the community, accused the Employers' Association of attempting to smash the union at an advantageous moment. The letter condemned the lockout as "little less than a calamity." And as May passed into June further endorsement and aid came to the strikers.[22]

Soon intangible pledges of community sympathy were transformed into organization support and material assistance. In late June prominent New Yorkers, including Mrs. Benjamin Guggenheim, Mrs. Learned Hand, Mrs. Willard Straight, Miss Ruth Morgan, and Jacob Schiff, established a Citizen's Committee for the Locked-out Cloak and Suit Makers. The Committee labored to increase popular sympathy and financial aid for the strikers by placing advertisements in all the city's newspapers soliciting contributions for a special strike fund.[23] The WTUL again rendered yeoman service, raising over 30,000 dollars in support of strike services such as free milk and medical care. Even Helen Keller employed her singular prestige to gain public favor for the strikers. The mounting endorsements and growing monetary contributions were all needed to preserve the spirit and body of the pickets before the walkout terminated.[24]

The press also departed from its traditional hostility toward organized labor. Immediately after the strike's beginning, many of the editorial pages unsparingly castigated the employers' arrogance.[25] As the strike progressed, the papers condemned employers for failing to arbitrate; they demanded a revised Protocol. When the strikers pleaded for financial aid, newspaper editorials requested contributions for the ILGWU's strike fund.[26] Only the carriage-trade journal, the *Sun,* remained antipathetic to the workers' cause.[27]

Morris Hillquit, the union's legal adviser, was among the first to credit community censure of the employers with a role in union victory. He believed that endorsement of the strikers by civic organizations and New York's newspapers compelled manufacturers to concede more fully to the cloakmakers' demands. "It was," Hillquit commented, "in the last analysis, the ever-increasing presence of public opinion which forced the employers of this industry into a fair settlement."[28] Community pressure upon garment manufacturers was revealed most lucidly in the long series of negotiations, lasting from early June to early August, conducted by Mayor Mitchel.

Throughout June and early July, while the Protective Association refused to bargain with the union or to accept the Mayor's intervention, Mitchel acted as intermediary in tedious bargaining between the union and two newly-formed independent manufacturers' associations. Unlike the Protective Association, these new employer organizations proved willing to accede to public arbitration and were even solicitous of Mitchel's advice. In this case, however, the union was skeptical of bargaining under the Mayor's auspices. The union feared that a settlement with the two independent associations returning strikers to their jobs before agreement was reached with the Protective Association would allow the latter organization to subcontract its orders to operating shops and thus subvert and counteract the strike indefinitely. Thus, the ILGWU refused to deal with the new organizations unless there were explicit guarantees against subcontracting for the Protective Association. The union's negotiators demanded assurances of the character and business background of the independents' member firms. Mitchel proved a shrewd mediator. He comprehended at once the union's position and refused to jump carelessly at the opportunity to negotiate. Mitchel preferred a solution which would guarantee job security and industrial stability to the blind public favor which would be showered upon him if he arranged an easily-achieved settlement.[29]

The Mayor followed a policy outlined by his special assistant, Paul C. Wilson:

The Union should not be asked to walk into a blind alley. Once negotiations at any time have been commenced, the spirit of the workers is likely to be broken so far as the strike is concerned. The mere announcement that negotiations of any kind are on foot would convey the impression [falsely] that the Protective Association had come to terms. . . . It seems to me [Wilson] that the Union's position is sound on this matter."[30]

Consequently, Mitchel, while acting as a public servant attempting to serve the community welfare through mediation of industrial disputes, owing to the ILGWU's strategy, also served as a union spokesman in negotiations with the manufacturers.

Mitchel continued to exert pressure upon the Protective Association to arbitrate. By July 10, he appeared to have accomplished his objective. Bilateral negotiations opened in the Mayor's office. But his efforts became involved and confused with similar attempts by Manhattan Borough President Marcus M. Marks, who also sought to mediate the dispute. The Association employed the resulting confusion to bow out of talks gracefully.[31]

Continued failures to bring the disputants together caused members of the Council of Conciliation to petition for the appointment of a special Presidential commission to investigate the New York impasse and suggest remedies.[32]

Ultimately, unrelenting public pressure upon the manufacturers resulted on July 20 in the resumption of bargaining between the Union and the Protective Association. The new round of negotiations within two days brought a preliminary agreement increasing wages, reducing hours, awarding union recognition, retaining the preferential shop, and guaranteeing the right to strike against discriminatory layoffs and arbitrary shop policies. Apparently anesthetized by their startling success, the rank and file rejected the proposals over minor questions of contract terminology. Finally, after two weeks of additional efforts by Hillquit and Schlesinger to moderate worker militancy, the strikers on August 4 overwhelmingly approved an agreement similar in all basic respects to that of July 22.[33]

Mayor Mitchel and his metropolitan community had served the ILGWU cloakmakers exceedingly well. The Protective Association, faced by a hostile Mayor, an aroused public, a critical clergy, and a condemnatory press, acquiesced generally to the union's demands. The Association surrendered completely the claims which had impelled the lockout in the first place: the open shop and unrestricted shop discipline. No sooner was the agreement signed and sealed than the Mayor divorced himself from negotiations with the recently formed independent associations, deferring to the ILGWU which had a clear power advantage over the infant employer organizations.[34]

The 1916 agreement marked a new era in the union's history. Under the 1910 Protocol various boards and impartial public chairmen, social workers, and philanthropists nursed the workers. In 1916, owing to the earlier assistance of public-spirited citizens motivated by the Progressive impulse, the union felt competent to stand on its own feet and to transfer ultimate power into its own hands. By rejecting the Protocol and perpetual industrial peace, the workers regained the option to strike and the will to rely on their own organization rather than upon outside boards and impartial arbitrators. In that sense, the community impulse which had done so much to bring success to the garment workers was rebuffed by rank-and-file workers.

The new agreement, the union believed, would strengthen the rank and file's conviction in the efficacy of united action, loyalty to intelligent leadership, and solidarity in shop and union. Therefore the 1916 ILGWU national convention proclaimed that the organization no longer required the artificial stimulant of elaborate public machinery; the union had matured and was "capable of taking care of the workers' interests without the benevolent protection of the employers."[35] The cloakmakers' experience illustrated *the working class' willingness when weak to accept middle-class reform assistance but when strong its desire to protect and defend independently its own interests.*

IV

The immigrant garment workers of New York City had, by the end of 1916, amply demonstrated their talent for organization and effective labor activity. Through their organizing efforts and strikes, the needle trades' unions added 200,000 members to organized labor's ranks. In the words of Perlman and Taft; "it was in clothing where the union advance [before the First World War] . . . was a spectacular conquest of a new province for industrial government based on union recognition."[36] The garment workers in their conquest were undoubtedly the beneficiaries of the reform impulse. Members of the clergy, solid citizens, social reformers, and a municipal administration representing the urban revolt against the old-line political machine provided needle trades' workers with the necessary measure of community backing to win recognition from divided and insecure employers. In December, 1916 the organizational phase in the history of the garment workers had for a time come to an end. Thereafter garment union history would center on the preservation of union solidarity and organization of the industry's backwaters.

In their organizational endeavors the garment workers had seized a singular opportunity. They benefited from community assistance and from the felt needs of garment manufacturers. Immigrant needle trades' workers utilized their own unique brand of trade-unionism—idealistic yet pragmatic, militant yet moderate—to secure recognition and gains from stability-conscious manufacturers who hoped that labor unions could do for the garment industry what the combination movement had done for America's basic industries.

The needle trades' unions in their internal structure and in their philosophy were doubly fortunate. The workers produced their own brand of indigenous leadership directly from the shops, and labor baiters could never successfully or honestly accuse "nefarious, interloping agitators" of fomenting discord among contented clothing workers. Local labor leaders, who commonly labored alongside their followers, handled much of the agitation and organization stirring the garment trades. When International Union officials directed local endeavors, they, too, were usually New Yorkers, men or women only recently risen from the ranks. Most of the union officials and labor organizers also spoke the language (Yiddish) of the rank and file and as coreligionists were able to surmount many cultural and ethnic barriers facing the typical AFL organizer.

The waistmakers, for example, had initiated their 1909 strike without the basic instruments of economic warfare—a stable union, a strike fund, and trained organizers and leaders. The strike call itself had been partially the result of an impassioned plea for action in Yiddish by Clara Lemlich, a teenage unionist, and it had been adopted in an atmosphere charged with emotion. And the subsequent walkout was marked more by rank-and-file militancy than by authority and direction from above.

In 1910, the cloakmakers combined the rank-and-file participation of the waistmakers with more careful planning and more experienced and intelligent leadership. The 1913 strikes also illustrated clearly the importance of local leadership and its proximity to the rank and file. The women's walkouts were organized and directed, in part, by women like Rose Schneiderman and Pauline Newman, themselves immigrants risen from the sewing machine to positions of influence within the ILGWU and the WTUL. The men's tailors in 1913 repudiated their national leadership and established their own local committee to negotiate simultaneously with national union officials and New York employers. And even before they combined with Chicago tailors to found the ACWA, New Yorkers had developed their own autonomous local organization—the Brotherhood of Tailors—led by immigrants. Thus by 1916 the city's needle trades' unions had produced leaders who, by their own past experiences, could communicate easily with and win the devotion of the mass of workers.

The unions' philosophy, a combination of old-world millennialism and new-world idealism, suffused members with a glowing picture of a new world to be. During their long sieges on the picket lines, the garment workers could look forward to more than shorter hours and higher wages; they could think of themselves as dedicated apostles and prophets of a new society in whose beneficent atmosphere all the ailments and tribulations of humanity would dissolve. For workers walking picket lines in the heat of summer and frost of winter, without income, without strike benefits, dreams served as well as material considerations to maintain ebbing spirits, and the needle trades' unions offered their members a socialist *élan* and dream absent among the more job-conscious conservative unions.

Clothing workers, however, did not rely upon socialist dogma. Instead, they constantly indicated to the community "that while being militant in theory . . . they could remain pacific in practice."[37] Union leaders never disdained signing cooperative agreements with employers nor were they above consorting agreeably with capitalists if both parties benefited mutually. Thus victorious strikes generally resulted in advantageous terms for the workers, while, to some extent, pacifying the employers. Because of the unions' willingness to compromise, the great garment industry disputes never resulted in a heritage of hatred comparable to that of the steel and mine organizing drives of the same era.

Although pulpit, press, and public created the community environment within which the unions could operate most effectively, disagreement exists as to whether union strategy attracted the community's favor, or whether contact with the respectable reform elements tempered labor leaders' attitudes and altered their strategic conceptions. Hyman Berman maintains that the activities of social reformers widened the horizons of labor, induced union officials to curb their dogmatic Marxist assumptions, and compelled them to consider more fully the welfare of the community.[38] The debate, however, partakes somewhat of the controversy over the chicken and the egg. Participation by socially respectable individuals and municipal officials, notably the Mayor, in labor disputes on behalf of the workers undoubtedly influenced the attitudes of needle trades' unionists. But the sympathy of the community could not have been attracted originally unless the garment workers had captured the public's fancy and attention. Revolutionary socialism, radicalism, and violence would have turned away the community and interaction would never have followed.

Union leaders comprehended the function of public opinion and community pressure in labor disputes. They realized that calmness and moderation in action as well as in word were essential for popular support. And they knew full well that small-scale employers could not resist the demands of organized labor backed by organized public opinion. Further, the plight of the Jewish immigrant in America caught the imagination of settlement workers, who during the white goods' strike of 1913, moved from the world of the settlement to the world of organized labor. Together with the WTUL, Theodore Roosevelt, Louis Brandeis, Louis Marshall, Henry Moscowitz, and others aided the immigrant workers in time of direst need. The poor, wretched, and despised immigrants, particularly the young girls and women, seeking the material rewards of American life were accorded a full measure of sympathy by those who had already sampled the good things in the New World.

But clothing workers also understood that community assistance was worthless without effective working-class organization. Workers and their leaders had often been disillusioned by the failure of reformers to improve working conditions when trade-unions were bypassed. The settlement ending the 1916 strike and annulling the Protocol system indicated organized labor's desire to free itself from overdependence on its social superiors. In short, what the community could give, it could also take. Consequently, the needle trades' workers concentrated on perfecting their own organization for the inevitable moment when community endorsement and aid would be unavailable.

Most important to the success of the garment workers, however, was the clothing industry's economic structure. Small-scale business ventures with minimal capitalization failed to endure the rigors of industrial warfare for sustained periods. And unions could bring to the trade the benefits of rational organization and business discipline. Many of the wealthier and more successful garment manufacturers thus looked to the unions to equalize standards in the industry, erase cutthroat competition, and bring stability to a disordered business world. Julius Henry Cohen, leading attorney for the dominant manufacturers' associations before the rupture of the Protocol system, assumed the lead in arguing for employer recognition of strong unions. He argued that only negotiations or collective bargaining between powerful organizations which respected each other could lead to "law and order in industry." Economic necessity caused both capital and labor to perceive the advantages of intelligent and pragmatic cooperation. And the relative weakness of the employers in relation to the needle trades' unions made possible reconciliation in the garment industry between the demands for industrial efficiency and for industrial justice or democracy.[39]

The clothing workers thus capitalized on factors unavailable to other American laborers. Other working-class organizations, however, at the same time, in the same city, not favored by such a fortuitous conjunction of circumstances failed in similarly motivated organizational strikes. Public service employees and private industry workers outside the garment trades pursued a chimera in their search for unionization. Their failures provide historical chapters as illuminating as those describing the garment workers' success, and it is to the unsuccessful strikes that we should now turn.

6.
The Organizational Strike Fails in the Nongarment Trades

ALTHOUGH INDUSTRIAL CONFLICT in the needle trades dominated metropolitan labor relations in terms of public interest, working-class rebellion against autocratic patterns of labor relations developed on other industrial fronts. Powerful established craft unions further whittled away at the employers' prerogatives; elsewhere unorganized workers asserted themselves in an effort to establish trade-unions and improve working conditions. But failure rather than success marked the organizational strikes of nongarment workers. And labor's defeats must be analyzed as fully as its victories.

While the garment workers had achieved internal unity by 1916, and the established craft unions continued to inch forward, important areas remained untouched by labor organization. Here were fertile grounds for the labor organizer. Workers on a far-flung urban transit network, service employees in numerous fancy culinary establishments, and teamsters performing multifarious services for the city's residents were in 1910 largely unorganized. By the second decade of the century the drive toward industrial democracy impelled these very workers to strike for greater security and economic power through organization.

From 1910 to 1916 discontent in public service trades and municipal agencies brought protracted and violent industrial conflicts. Three times, once in the fall of 1910, again in the winter of 1910–1911, and finally in the fall of 1911, the Teamsters' Union conducted walkouts among express company drivers and city sanitation workers. Adherents of the Waiters' and Bartenders' Union walked the picket lines in the spring of 1912 and again in the winter of 1913. And climactically in the late summer of 1916 industrial warfare culminated in a transit strike which threatened the metropolis with the much-feared and oft-maligned city-wide general strike. The timing of the above industrial conflicts was related closely to the strikes in the needle trades. This fact reinforces the hypothesis that the organizational impulse motivating New York's working class emanated from a common urban environment enlivened by reform ferment.

Unlike the strikes in the garment industry which affected small, private business enterprises and concerned the community only indirectly, the walkouts by teamsters, waiters, and transit workers involved long-established, public and private enterprises serving the public directly. In each case, the conflict had a direct impact upon the interests and welfare of the urban community. And the strikers found their struggles for union recognition and improved working conditions subject to the scrutiny of public judgment. Industrial strife in semimonopolistic and monopolistic private and public enterprises tended to inflict hardship upon neutral parties. Such distress might turn the public and the municipal authorities against the strikers' cause. Consequently in all the labor disputes to be discussed below, the community's stake in the ultimate disposition of the conflict was voiced emphatically by Mayors William F. Gaynor and John P. Mitchel.

Gaynor was a maverick in life and politics. Born and raised in upstate New York in extreme rural poverty, Gaynor was educated for the priesthood by the Christian Brothers, who sent him on missions to the Isthmus of Panama, Mexico, and San Francisco. While in San Francisco he abandoned the order, renounced Catholicism, and decided to return to the East. After teaching in the Boston public schools and studying law in Utica, New York, in the late 1870's he settled in Flatbush, Brooklyn, where he established a law practice. Gaynor quickly developed a local reputation as a reformer and opponent of political machines, which in 1893 won him election to the Brooklyn Supreme Court, an office he held until 1909. As a judge, Gaynor was widely respected and proved more solicitous of labor and welfare legislation than most American jurists.

Tammany, in 1909 anxious to refurbish its reputation, selected Gaynor as mayoralty candidate on a platform favoring municipal construc-

[104]

tion of the subways. And Gaynor was the lone member of his ticket to win. As Mayor he battled and defeated his Tammany patrons, winning admiration from reform Democrats who pushed him as Democratic gubernatorial and presidential timber. But in 1911 an assassin's bullet ended Gaynor's political career, though not his life. Though blunt, hot tempered, and pitiless to all opponents, he was one of New York's outstanding mayors, and he demonstrated that even Tammany on occasion bowed to the spirit of reform.[1]

As might well be expected of a reform mayor, Gaynor took an advanced view of labor relations: "Labor has as much right to organize as capital has. What would be the condition of labor to-day had it never organized and asserted its rights?" On still another occasion he supplemented these brief thoughts on the rights of the workingman. "I think that if workmen are not properly paid or are made to work long hours, or are mistreated, they have a right to strike. Labor has as much right to combine for its protection as capital has to combine for its protection."[2]

Good intentions on the part of city officials intervening in labor disputes, however, did not guarantee sophisticated or successful mediation. Mayors Gaynor and Mitchel were not always equal to bargaining with highly capitalized, well-managed private businesses knowing what they wanted and how to get it. Neutral mediation in industrial conflicts thus proved a feeble and, at times, an ill-advised approach, particularly when one party to the dispute was inherently stronger than the other. Unfortunately for New York's reform mayors this was precisely the case in the transportation industries where teamsters and transit workers rebelled. Furthermore, theoretical official espousal of labor's right to organize and to strike did not extend in practice to municipal agencies. Sanitation workers, much to their sorrow and loss, learned this hard lesson. Thus walkouts against public and semipublic concerns began with hope, were marked initially by unrestrained enthusiasm, and ultimately left in their wake pessimism and defeat.

I

Express drivers (those employed by the Adams Express Company, the American Express Company, the United States Express Company, and the Wells-Fargo Company) were in 1910 the first nongarment workers to seek unionization. Teamsters in the express trade at that time worked as many as 17 hours daily for wages averaging only five to ten dollars weekly. Although employment conditions had always been harsh, the expressmen lacked a history of past efforts at union organization. But in the atmosphere of the Progressive era with reform spreading and working-class organizing activity seemingly ascendant, the drivers proved responsive. One driver succinctly expressed his co-workers' impression of their employers' management autocracy: "Bosses are the best union men there are. They drive us and put the screws to us till we get our backs to the wall. Then we have to organize and fight to live."[3]

By October, 1910 when the needle trades' unions had concluded their first successful organizing campaigns, the expressmen were prepared to strike. Late in the third week of the month, Jersey City drivers left their wagons. Within days, a spontaneous sympathetic strike developed east of the Hudson. By Friday, October 28, Adams and American Express Company men had joined the walkout. Short hours later, drivers from the United States, National, and Wells-Fargo companies followed suit. No sooner were the men on the streets than the Teamsters' Union and the CFU offered them the support and counsel of organized labor.[4]

The strikers in the express trade, unlike those in the garment industry, encountered a resourceful, substantially capitalized, and united opposition. Only 13 express companies operated in the entire nation. Those affected by the New York strike were nation-wide concerns with offices and business operations scattered across the United States; the New York market represented only a small part of their total business and economic activity. The companies shared business histories dating back to the mid-nineteenth century and were the descendants of the major transportation concerns which had emerged during the railroad age (1850–1893). The Adams Express Company operated over 100 steam railroads, electric lines, and steamboat and stage lines; four of its seven directors served on the management of the nation's leading railways. The American Express Company, with assets in 1898 of over 5,300,000 dollars, operated multifarious transportation facilities, and in 1909, 3,-000,000 dollars worth of its outstanding shares were owned by the New York Central and Hudson River Railroad. Its Board of Directors included some of the most influential men in the state of New York (Lewis Cass Ledyard, Francis F. Flagg, and William H. Seward) who also served as directors of other great corporations. The United States Express Company had extensive transportation holdings, and its Board of Directors included the Chairman of the Adams Express Board and a director of the American Express Company as well as representatives of other substantial American corporations. Wells-Fargo demonstrated a comparable interlocking corporate relationship; its Board of Directors was strongly represented by Erie Railroad executives and the Harriman railroad empire, with E. H. Harriman himself sitting on the Board.[5]

Thus the fledgling Teamsters' local in the express trade, lacking an experienced membership, a union treasury, indigenous union leaders, and a coherent philosophy, challenged employers representing established, multimillion dollar corporate interests. Not only did management represent immense capital resources, but it was united in interests and policies by an intricate system of interlocking corporate directorships. Everything the strikers lacked the companies possessed: long experience in supervising large enterprises and managing diverse labor forces, almost unlimited financial resources, outstanding executive leadership, and a philosophy of labor relations inherited from the Gilded Age. They in fact symbolized the worst and the best which that much denigrated age had to offer. Their labor relations philosophy was simple and stark. Property rights were absolute! Management could not share its prerogatives and responsibilities (to shareholders) with hired employees. The only right the worker held was to work or not to work as he chose individually. Concerted working-class action interfered illegally with the rights of private property. And finally they believed with George F. Baer of the Reading Railroad and anthracite coal strike notoriety that

> the rights and interests of the laboring man will be protected and cared for—not by labor agitators, but by the Christian men to whom God in His infinite wisdom has given the control of the property interests of the country.[6]

The strikers, divided among themselves as to tactics, strategy, and objectives, came to rely upon Mayor Gaynor's influence with management. To trade-unionists bargaining with concentrated capital, municipal intervention proved a frail reed.

From the express strike's beginning the companies employed tactics calculated to appear reasonable and moderate, while they simultaneously weakened the strikers' will to resist. As early as October 29, 1910, the companies, conceding the walkout's effect, agreed to confer with representatives of the Teamsters' International Union. Management, however, emphasizing its Spencerian commitment to absolute freedom of contract, consented to negotiate with its own employees solely on an individual basis. While choosing to confer with Teamster Union officials on undisclosed matters and to negotiate with their own dissatisfied employees on an individual basis, the companies on the supposition that they would receive police protection also began to import and hire strikebreakers.[7] They thus conducted bargaining sessions with the union as window dressing for the benefit of good community relations. If deliveries could be made despite the strike, little reason existed to make concessions to the strikers or even to negotiate with them in good faith.

The police, in fact, played a dual role: originally, they acted as mounted escorts for strikebreaking drivers; when scabs became scarce, some officers of the law themselves took to driving wagons. Strikers, aroused and frustrated by management's effective tactics, proved less than innocent bystanders. Animosity toward the police flared into overt violence. To forestall further turmoil and damage to the strikers' cause, an International Union official, Valentine P. Hoffman, led a drivers' committee to the Mayor's office to protest police partiality. Mayor Gaynor accepted the protest as just if true, and he cautioned the Police Commissioner to keep the force absolutely neutral. The police, Gaynor advised, should only be put in wagons to protect drivers from actual violence; their driving wagons would be enough to provoke public disorder. The Commissioner endeavored to comply with the Mayor's request.[8] The express companies, however, attempted to continue deliveries for merchants and department stores. In doing so they provoked the further violence feared by Gaynor without moving the wagons effectively.

Eruptions of violence and the interruption to wholesale and retail businesses as well as the breakdown in home deliveries bred powerful public sentiment urging mediation of the strike. On October 31, the National Civic Federation requested from the strikers a list of their grievances and demands to serve as a basis for arranging a peace conference between employees and employers. The following day the State Bureau of Mediation proposed settlement terms which became the basis for additional negotiations between the disputants. Strike leaders in responding to the Civic Federation's request had placed union recognition at the top of their list of demands. The State Bureau of Mediation's proposal, however, omitted the issue of recognition, offered no immediate improvement in wages or in conditions of labor, and returned the men to work on prestrike terms pending future arbitration.[9]

Management, certain of the success of its strategy, hesitated to consider even the State Bureau's limited terms because they implied recognition of employee negotiating committees. Although the State's suggestion failed to satisfy the strikers' essential objective—union recognition—the strike leaders, unsure of their tactics, allowed Mayor Gaynor on the basis of the above proposals to pressure them into continued bargaining with management. But before negotiations resumed, the conflict took a strange twist.[10]

After consenting to renewed bargaining with management, the Teamsters' Union, without prior warning, raised the possibility of a sympathetic walkout. Union officials, immediately upon receipt of the State Bureau's recommendations, formulated a new and more complete set of demands stressing union recognition, the union shop, and an immediate wage increase. With the new terms in mind the New York Joint Council of Teamsters empowered organizer William Ashton and International Vice-President V. P. Hoffman to call, if necessary, a general strike of the metropolis' 45,000 organized teamsters.

The sympathetic strike threat was to serve two ends. First and foremost, the Joint Council wished to persuade Gaynor to order police from express wagons; secondly, the union leaders hoped to impress management and the community with the raw economic power of labor united. In short, the Teamsters were seeking their ends by threatening to disrupt essential municipal and private services. Union leaders, confused as to the best tactical course, conciliated Mayor Gaynor on the one hand and on the other hand tried to coerce the companies and the community.[11]

On the surface the Union's confused strategy appeared successful. Gaynor had ordered the police to desist from driving or directing express vehicles; the express companies had authorized the Conciliation Committee of the National Civic Federation to initiate hearings through the good offices of the Mayor. Actually, as described above, Gaynor had already ordered the police to remain scrupulously neutral, and management had always been willing to negotiate because it was certain that union recognition was not a negotiable or arbitrable issue. The general strike threat in truth only succeeded in alienating the community and the Mayor from the strikers' cause.

While the Teamsters delayed the sympathetic strike, peace conferences opened on Thursday, November 3, between representatives of each of the affected firms and two employees (union officials were excluded) from each company. Although International Teamster officials were absent from the conferences, the substance of the proceedings was immediately relayed to the city's Teamster Executive Council for discussion and decision. The strikers had entered the sessions insisting upon both union recognition and the union shop. Although the drivers still believed that they had the full support of other Teamsters in employing the sympathetic strike as a last resort, union leaders, notably central organizer William Ashton, now cautioned against precipitous action. With Gaynor and the State Mediation Bureau applying the requisite pressure on the disputants on the one hand and on the other holding the union recognition issue in abeyance, they combined forces to influence management to discuss employee grievances and demands.[12]

Management quickly turned the negotiations to its own advantage. The companies simply refused to entertain the issue of union recognition. Therefore the State Bureau, as a sop to the expressmen while not vitiating the essential management position, proposed that employers agree not to discriminate against their workers because of union membership. Thus instead of positive union protection, the strikers were offered an employer disclaimer affidavit. The companies were also led to understand that they would retain complete freedom to hire and discharge employees. The mediators worked unceasingly to attract management's consent to watered-down terms. And on November 4, the union accepted the mediators' minimal proposals which were then forwarded to management for consideration. On November 5, the express firms informed Mayor Gaynor that they would re-employ the strikers upon individual application without discrimination.

The Union, however, could not consent to management's promise of nondiscrimination in re-employment unless the employers promised explicitly not to penalize a striker or any other driver for union membership. Correspondence between Gaynor and company officials indicates that the companies apparently intended to discriminate against union members. As the Mayor wrote to Frank H. Platt, President of the United States Express Company, the men could not accept his offer to be taken back "without discrimination against any because of having left the service." The clause, Gaynor reminded Platt, left open discrimination on all grounds including union membership. Gaynor suggested to Platt that, if the companies did not intend to discriminate against union men, they should say so and why, and if that were the case, they should pledge that they would not discriminate for any cause "except having used physical violence during the strike." But Gaynor added that the companies appeared unwilling to accept his suggestion and he warned Platt that the men would not return to work only to be discharged for joining a union. Mayor Gaynor concluded his remarks by emphasizing his basic impartiality and his overriding concern for the public interest. "I do not want to enter into the dispute on this head and have only used my good offices to prevent the merchants and people of this city from being further annoyed by this strike."[13]

Before management ultimately acceded to Gaynor's request and labor's concessions, Samuel Gompers stirred the dying embers of discontent. During a brief stay in New York relating to the strike, Gompers counselled the strikers not to return to work on the companies' terms. He characterized the employers' peace proposals as the shadow not the substance of victory. To Gompers it was absolutely out of the question for labor militants to concede the removal from arbitration of an issue so basic as union recognition. (Actually, the strikers had already conceded the point entirely.) Gompers warned: "I would not advise the strikers to accept the express companies' offer. The men can get such conditions at any time. . . . The important thing is recognition of the union."[14]

The expressmen had no intention of surrendering their union. An interested observer from the United Mine Workers of America captured the sentiment prevailing among the city's strikers: "At no time has there been such a spirit of revolt and a desire for organized solidarity in the various industries of the city than [sic] there is at present."[15]

Unfortunately for the strikers and, partially owing to their poor tactics, their efforts to secure more equitable job treatment met an unfavorable response from the press. Since the companies had the resources to hire innumerable strikebreakers and to protect them with private police when city police became unavailable and also had every intention of continuing deliveries despite the walkout, violence resulted.[16] And the newspapers employed every suspicion and occasion of violence to brand the strikers as irresponsible individuals engaged in an unjust, publicly deleterious dispute. In typical American journalistic fashion, the press twisted the usual chaos associated with industrial disputes into incipient anarchy and imminent social revolution.

No sooner were the men on the streets than the *Times* charged strike lawlessness. "Sympathy with the grievances of workingmen does not extend," the paper warned, "to breakers of the laws and disturbers of the peace." Almost simultaneously, the *Post* cautioned strike leaders to "see to it that their cause is not identified in the public mind with law-lessness and brutality." Even the usually moderate *World* warned the strikers to consider the public interest; it offered its advice not for the drivers or the companies but for the public "that suffered. . . . It is intol-erable that a great public utility should be interrupted while a private quarrel is fought out with lamentable and needless loss of life and property."[17] Such manifestations of public disfavor did not augur well for the strikers. Unlike the garment workers, the express drivers en-listed no committees of respectable, private citizens to defend their rights.

Without community support the expressmen were compelled to repudiate their basic objectives. By November 8, the New York Mer-chants' Association (the community organization most immediately affected by the strike), in an open letter to the express companies, em-phasized that the drivers were no longer demanding union recognition but only re-employment. Consequently the sole barrier to an acceptable settlement was management's failure to acquiesce in its employees' re-quest that no expressman be discharged because of membership in a trade-union. On these terms, the Merchant's Association urged the em-ployers to treat with their men. State Deputy Commissioner of Labor William C. Rogers seconded the merchants' appeal. He also conceded to the companies complete freedom of contract in hiring employees. Both intermediaries agreed that the strike could be ended if the firms involved refused to re-employ only those convicted of violence or other illegal behavior. Furthermore, as Mayor Gaynor pointed out to the com-panies, workers had reduced their demands to two: reduced working hours from 12–16 hours daily down to 11 hours, with overtime pay, and union recognition. The firms had previously assured the Mayor that no problem existed regarding the settlement of wages and hours, and at his request, the men had withdrawn their demand for union recog-nition and agreed to return to work prior to a definitive settlement of the wages and hours question. Thus Gaynor insisted the strike should have been ended.[18]

But, surprisingly, the companies refused Gaynor's recommendations. They insisted instead that they "should be free to reject or discharge anyone on the ground that he had joined the union." They rejected "what is called the 'open shop.'" Hence, Gaynor angrily informed a corporation attorney: "I say again that there is not the slightest excuse for the continuance of this strike by the companies."[19]

The companies' determination to retreat not one inch proved masterful strategy. Strike leaders, encountering an adamant and resourceful opposition, first equivocated and then in a public announcement postponed indefinitely the threatened general strike. From doubt to surrender was a short step. On November 10, the express companies, in a long and vitriolic diatribe criticizing their workers' demands, inserted a solitary clause stating there would be no discrimination simply because of union membership. The Mayor subsequently isolated from the context of an otherwise antagonistic communication this one singularly moderate clause as the basis for a negotiated "compromise." Gaynor through separate conferences with company and union officials next elicited joint approval of the following terms: "We are willing to take back our employees who are on strike, whether or not they have joined a union, reserving the right, however, to decline to take back any of them, whether they be members of a union or not, who may have committed or incited acts of violence and hostility toward us." Consideration of wages and hours was delayed until after the men returned to work; old standards continued in effect until December 1.[20]

On Thursday evening, November 10, the strikers approved the meager terms—no union recognition, no immediate reduction in hours or rise in wages. Teamster Union officials attempted to save face by proclaiming falsely: "We got recognition of the union in the promises of the companies to take all men back regardless of whether or not they have joined the union." Thus it was slight wonder that the diluted settlement elicited worker approval. After an unforseen delay caused by recalcitrant Jersey City drivers was terminated successfully, William Ashton declared the walkout officially ended.[21]

The strikers returned to work with neither union recognition nor material improvements. Prominent municipal spokesmen, however, believed the settlement equitable. Mayor Gaynor, obviously an impartial party primarily concerned with protecting the community's interest, wrote to Ashton: "You were always in favor of an honorable settlement, and the settlement made is certainly honorable to all concerned." And John V. Hylan, later to become Mayor of New York, congratulated Gaynor for settling the strike in a manner satisfactory to employers, employees, and the public.[22]

Even after agreeing to the Mayor's terms express company management attempted to pursue what Gaynor called a "closed shop" policy, barring all union men. Gaynor again found himself forced to intercede with the American Express Company and the Adams Express Company to obtain the re-employment of some of the strikers. The companies had attempted to interpret the clause in the November 10 agreement reading "acts of violence and hostility" toward the companies as "acts of violence *or* hostility," thus permitting them to remove union men as obviously hostile to company policy and proper discipline. Gaynor had to warn the companies to obey the terms of the agreement and accede to the general understanding of the nondiscrimination clause which protected the jobs of union members unless convicted of violence.[23] Union members in fact were to find themselves subjected to a host of discriminations. And the Socialist newspaper, the *Call*, drew a moral from the strike which the drivers would have done well to heed: "The workers must at all times depend upon themselves and the strength of their own organization, and upon nothing else. The organization must be simplified and perfected."[24]

The suspicion and fear of violence which had done so much to alienate community support from the strikers and had worked to the companies' advantage later proved to have been much inflated and distorted. By December 7, when the past could be weighed more coolly, Gaynor informed the Commissioner of Police: "The information I had from your department that there was little or no violence by the express company employees on strike, notwithstanding loose and mischievous statements to the contrary from day to day, has been verified by the companies themselves."[25] But community fear of working-class rebellion and direct action, justified or unjustified, was to do much in the future to undermine union activities and organizational strikes.

The agreement of November, 1910 proved a feeble instrument upon which to erect industrial peace. Within four months of its signing industrial warfare again disrupted the express trade. By early March, 1911 disgruntled union drivers were again talking strike in order to obtain explicit union recognition and job security. On March 11 grumbled threats became reality; some 1100 drivers and helpers employed by the Adams Express Company refused to report for work that day unless the company abolished its gross discrimination against union men.

Statements issued by contending parties portended a bitter battle. The strikers, finally incensed at the substance and subsequent implementation of the November settlement arranged by Gaynor and the Civic Federation, proclaimed: "We have had one lesson from politicians and we will now keep them out of our fight for bread and butter and for the right to belong to an organization." Adams Company officials countered by insisting upon the open shop principle, declaring the strike's objective to be the closed shop, and promising to combat the walkout ceaselessly.[26]

On this occasion employers were in a stronger strategic position than they had been four months earlier. The first strike had caused them to pay greater attention to their labor relations. Thus in the interim company unions had been formed. Employers, reinforced in attitude by their previous success and by new labor relations policies, intended to brook no opposition from their workers. Management, better prepared for conflict the second time, received endorsement from some of their own employees as well as from the Mayor. Drivers employed by the American Express Company who had been organized into a loose company union adopted a resolution criticizing the actions of the Adams' Company employees. Gaynor, in a letter to William Ashton, quondam Teamster organizer and strike leader, suggested that the Adams Company strikers appoint a committee of three to discuss their grievances with the Mayor, and in the meantime, return to work immediately. Gaynor promised to consider such grievances carefully and, if substantial, to present them to the company which had promised rectification of any injustice. If done promptly, he insisted, the strike could be settled to everyone's satisfaction. In a concluding compliment to Ashton, the Mayor added: "I wrote this to you because I found you to be a man of intelligence and moderation in the former strike."[27]

The strikers declined to fall into the old trap by returning to work prior to the settlement of grievances. They considered their demands— re-employment of all strikers at their former position, free access for business agents and union committees on company premises at all times, and outlawing of company unions and clubs—to be reasonable and statesmanlike.

The company naturally took a different view. "We are offering nothing to these men except permission to return to their jobs under the old conditions. We will confer with them if they come to us as employees, but not as representatives of the union. *We will not recognize the union, and we have nothing to arbitrate.* This is decisive and final" [italic added].[28] Management and labor both pledged not to concede.

When the strikers disregarded Gaynor's advice, he threatened to employ all the means at his disposal to break a "criminal, brutal, and inexcusable strike." And despite the drivers' more obviously truculent spirit, Ashton once more trod the path to surrender. On the basis of Gaynor's mediation, he ordered an end to the walkout.[29]

At the conclusion of the first week of their walkout, the Adams Company workers found themselves beset on all sides by opposition.[30] The drivers promptly perceived their own sad predicament. It was difficult enough for them to contend with express companies, but the highest officials of their own unions apparently had rebuffed them unnecessarily. Union leaders had become so moderate in their policy declarations that they won encomiums both from Gaynor and from avowedly antiunion employers.

On March 20 Gaynor informed Ashton that the strike was frivolous, unjustified, and destined to fail after causing commerce and the community great loss. And it would only injure labor's image. The Mayor advised the Teamster officials that the strikers' grievances were jejune. The company could not be expected, he stressed, to re-employ men convicted of violence. Gaynor added that the Adams Company was prepared to make arrangements for the collection of union dues on company premises but that the strikers' grievance regarding the company union seemed incredible. "In my judgment the District Attorney ought to take charge of the matter. It may well be a criminal offense to conspire to coerce anybody in any such way as this."[31]

By March 21, the beginning of the end was at hand. The Joint District Council of the Teamsters' Unions of Greater New York appointed a committee to call upon Gaynor requesting him to mediate the dispute. On March 22, the Mayor pronounced his predisposed verdict: Drivers would return to the job on March 23; the company would not have to re-employ the ringleaders of a wholly unjustifiable strike. When the strikers reported to work on the morning of March 23, management exacted the final pound of flesh: only one-half the men were re-employed and the other half had their names placed on a waiting list (the ringleaders almost outnumbered the followers).[32]

Thus the first significant union attempts to reach unorganized workers outside the ranks of the garment industry came to naught. Inexperienced, ill-led workers proved no match for heavily capitalized, astutely directed business establishments. Community aid also proved of little assistance in equalizing the imbalance in economic power and leadership quality. Neutral and impartial intervention by concerned city authorities, notably the Mayor, apparently aided intransigent capital, which already dominated the primary positions of economic and legal power.

The pattern that governed the two express strikes marked similar endeavors by unskilled and semiskilled workers to gain bargaining power and concessions from large enterprises. Time and again strikers suffered from a hostile press, vacillation within their own ranks, and a lack of support from reformers. Internal dissension led to retreat; external opposition to defeat.

II

The Teamsters for the third time, in November, 1911, struck against substantial, determined opposition. On November 8, after Mayor Gaynor had refused their demand for the abolition of night work, teamsters employed in the Street Cleaning Department of the Municipal Government failed to appear for work. On this occasion the walkout was crushed within two weeks.

The sanitation strike culminated a protracted controversy. Since an abortive strike by its employees in 1907, the Sanitation Department had utilized detectives from the Ascher and the Pinkerton Agencies to keep workers under surveillance. By January, 1910, order and control appeared restored and the Department decided to discontinue the use of outside detective agencies. It resolved to employ a few special departmental men for surveillance.[33] Then, in April, 1911, the Department instituted on a limited scale a new work schedule—night work for all employees. The discontent and disorder which the Commissioner of Sanitation thought he had ended through the use of private detectives was revived.

On June 19, 1911, night labor, apparently a proven success, became general departmental policy. At that time, the sanitation workers believed night work to be a temporary summer expedient. As early as July, however, strike talk among sanitation workers became common enough to reach the Commissioner and the Mayor. Commissioner William Edwards advised the Mayor that night labor in the hot summer months had been advantageous both for the men and for their horses. Gaynor, in reply, warned Edwards to be stringent regarding departmental rules. The Mayor felt that any discontent was the work of a few malcontents fomenting a strike. It had to be met, he felt, by removing the names of any strikers permanently from the departmental role. "The city pays its employees well and treats them well, but the city will know how to protect itself against any effort of coercion." Gaynor even implied that, if necessary to crush a strike, civil service regulations could be waived. Edwards transmitted the Mayor's message to Ashton and another Teamsters' Union delegate who had come to protest night work. The city as employer thus proved no different from most private businesses; city authorities, too, sought autocratic control of their work force and themselves judged the contentment and desires of employees.[34]

As night labor persisted well into the fall, employee discontent gathered steam. On November 3, a committee from Teamsters' Union, Local 658, made an oral request to the departmental commissioner for the restoration of day work. The committee was told that its request would receive the Mayor's immediate attention. But on Sunday evening, November 5, workers seized the initiative, voting to strike if night work were not abolished. Gaynor promptly accepted the challenge. He declared publicly his intention to punish severely all strikers.[35]

Unlike the other major labor conflicts of the era the sanitation workers did not walk off the job to achieve organization and union recognition. Their grievances were more tangible, their demands more limited in nature. Their fate nevertheless proved worse than that of the express drivers.

Night labor (8 P.M. to 4 A.M.) had brought the workers grave discomforts and threatened to bring even more. Accidents and injuries rose because of the difficulties in locating and lifting heavy loads in the autumn darkness. Winter snow and ice would add further discomfort and danger. Work naturally proceeded at a reduced pace. Since the working day was incomplete until all garbage had been removed, the allotted eight-hour day jumped to ten. Finally at six or seven in the morning, the weary toiler would straggle home to his bed in a tenement in the noisiest and most congested part of the city. Furthermore, gratuities collected by the men during the course of a day's work helped make a meager salary adequate. Night work curtailed the prospect of tips. The sanitation workers therefore struck to restore previous job conditions.[36]

From its onset, violence marred the strike. Commissioner Edwards had promptly discharged all strikers and employed in their place professional scabs (noncivil service employees) under police protection. As more and more strikebreakers entered the city at the Administration's behest, rioting ensued. Limited warfare erupted between union sympathizers and their scab and police adversaries. Irish rain (bricks) poured down from tenement rooftops upon the guardians of the law. Police records cited 26 injuries, four serious and one fatal, as a result of strike violence. With scabs and union men engaged in incessant conflict, garbage disposal was disrupted. In tenement districts street traffic ploughed through piles of stinking refuse. By the end of the strike's first week, the city was literally in a state of bedlam with Sanitation Department stables transformed into pseudomilitary barracks housing an army of scabs.[37]

The press, disturbed by civil disorder, condemned the walkout. "Those who work for the 5,000,000 of New York," proclaimed the *World,* "should learn and long remember that public officials must not strike." The *Tribune* seconded this opinion, adding that "such an act by members of a government service is tantamount to mutiny, insubordination, and anarchy." Other newspapers echoed these views. Force was hailed as the only effective response to an outrageous breach of community welfare. The city's press was generally unanimous in demanding coercion against the strikers. The police, the *Herald* urged, "should be instructed to use their nightsticks on all who interfere . . . and if necessary ask questions later." "If necessary," the *Times* recommended, "the whole National Guard must be called into action to protect the men at work." The cry for aggressive action carried all up and down the newspaper offices along Park Row and further uptown.[38]

Mayor Gaynor took to heart journalistic strictures for stringent action. Shortly before the strike had begun, Gaynor wrote to Edwards that he should permit the men to strike but then insure that they never return to city employment. "If they think they can make the city conform to their dictation they will find themselves grievously mistaken. Use the contract system to hire laborers if necessary." The following day Edwards reported that all but 100 men had left work but that the Department had already contracted for 5409 men whom Police Commissioner Waldo guaranteed would receive full protection.[39]

On November 11, when Ashton, speaking for the strikers, proposed the abolition of night work and the resumption of duties by the strikers pending complete arbitration by a nonpartisan committee, Gaynor delayed his answer only two days. He then offered the strikers little; he refused to speak to or to see either Ashton or a representative from the State Bureau of Mediation. Gaynor publicly vowed to crush the rebellion. To citizens disturbed by the city government's role as strikebreaker and employer of scab labor, the Mayor replied in sophist fashion.

He insisted that the city was not breaking a strike because "the city employees who quit are out of the city service and are not to be taken back." Therefore, the city had simply hired replacements. When Marcus M. Marks tendered his good offices in an attempt to mediate the dispute, Gaynor replied that Marks' assistance would be accepted only to aid in the procurement of strikebreakers. "We need help in no other respect. This city will not be put in the humiliating position of allowing its employees to dictate how the public business shall be conducted."[40] Even the Board of Aldermen, controlled and dominated by Tammany, supposedly the workingman's friend, refused assistance to the strikers.[41]

Once again Teamsters' Union officials followed a strategy composed of equal parts sham bravado and vacillation. At a mass meeting on Monday evening, November 13, called by the Socialist Party to arouse sympathy for the strikers, Edward Gould, President of the Teamsters' District Council, and Ashton threatened "a tie-up of everything on wheels" immediately unless Gaynor granted the drivers' demands within 24 hours. But the next afternoon, November 14, the Teamsters Joint Council of Greater New York, at a special meeting, decided against any sympathetic walkout. Union leaders subsequently devised various compromise proposals all of which undermined or negated the threat of mass walkouts.[42]

Deserted by their leaders and countered by an intractable municipal administration, the street cleaners continued their losing struggle. The odds, however, proved too decisive for the small group of ill-equipped trade-unionists to surmount.[43]

By November 14, the Sanitation Department had been completely restaffed. Gaynor, on the basis of emergency conditions, had received from the Civil Service Commission a waiver of requirements for employment in the Sanitation Department. And the Commissioner informed the Mayor that no further need existed for the hiring of new men. "I expect in a short time to have the driving force of the Department entirely reorganized with new men." The Mayor in fact had to criticize Edwards for his temerity in informing the press that he had successfully hired 4000 strikebreakers. Gaynor advised his Commissioner: "The work of reorganization should be done quietly and not through the newspapers." Furthermore, use of the term strikebreakers "has a very unpleasant sound to many just people."[44]

To add insult to injury Commissioner Edwards ordered the strikers to appear in his office on Monday, November 20 to show cause why they should not be dropped from the civil service list. As a result of the Commissioner's *in camera* hearings, 1,872 men were dismissed from public service (a few were later reinstated). Edwards also announced that union members or labor agitators remaining in the Department would not be tolerated.[45]

The sanitation strike should have provided labor with several instructive lessons. It proved that membership in a labor union was fruitless unless the organization possessed actual power. In the sense that the walkout was intended to breathe life into an almost emasculated union local, it could be termed an organizational strike. But the only result of the garbage driver's uprising was the utter destruction of a weak labor union. The strike's outcome further indicated that labor organized within a municipal agency could not rely upon Tammany support. Although the Tiger may have been the "ally" of the working-man, at least on the precinct level where its alms were readily available, it knew surer ways to obtain working-class votes than by catering to the whims of "anarchic" laborers. Finally, organized labor learned that the Progressive era's tolerance toward labor organizations and the right to strike stopped short at public employees; a Mayor, for example, who had defended in theory the right of workers to organize and to strike, in practice utilized all his powers to crush a strike by city employees.[46]

III

The organizational impulse next struck the city's hotel and restaurant trade. From early May through June 1912, the more exclusive dining places in the city frequently found themselves without kitchen and dining room help. By May 30, hotels such as the Plaza, the Astor, the St. Regis, the Waldorf-Astoria, and the Prince George were preparing to establish a special employers' association to combat the recently organized Hotel Workers' International Union.[47]

Employee discontent and strike action had caught the hotel and restaurant managers by surprise. In 1911, few of the 75,000 cooks and waiters working in the hotel trade and fancy restaurant trade belonged to an effective labor organization. The Hotel and Restaurant Employees and Bartenders International Union had approximately 2,000 members in New York City, mostly bartenders in neighborhood taverns. Union officials commonly claimed that the better-class New York dining spots were beyond organization. John Bookjans, editor of the union's journal, characterized his organization in New York as "but an insignificant, small islet within an ocean of unorganized territory."[48]

What passed for a waiters' union was a tight-knit, aristocratic craft organization that used closed membership books and high initiation fees to exclude the hordes of depressed workers toiling in the expanding luxury establishments. The two groups in the same trade could not meet on common ground. The ins and outs literally spoke different languages. The outs, ruthlessly exploited by the larger hotels, saw small hope for the future in the clannish waiters' union.[49]

Working-class discontent, so contagious within the city's confines, did not bypass the unorganized hotel and restaurant workers. The International Waiters and Bartenders Union perceived the mounting unrest in New York and laid plans to establish a new waiters' branch, Local 5. Problems, however, immediately beset the organizers. Aristocratic, old Local 1 erected one barrier after another to intramural competition; organizers from International Union headquarters, unfamiliar with the luxury trade and with the mores of the various nationality groups employed there, appeared lost and bewildered. Organizing remained more ephemeral than substantial until the spring of 1912 when a "prophet" appeared. Joseph Elster, a disaffected organizer for the new Local 5, proceeded to foster a dual union. Breaking with International Union officials, he shepherded his followers into a rival hotel employees' union then in the process of organization by the IWW. Thus began a tumultuous and ill-fated alliance between waiters and Wobblies.[50]

The Industrial Workers of the World in the spring of 1912 were at a peak of organizational strength and fervor. Founded in Chicago in June, 1905, by a strangely assorted collection of radical trade-unionists, political socialists, and utopian reformers, the IWW declared itself a class-conscious, revolutionary labor organization which intended through persistent class warfare to destroy American capitalism. Sectarian squabbles, however, vitiated whatever radical appeal the IWW had had at birth.

But after 1908 when Western workers came to dominate the organization, the IWW assumed the character and style which it brought to New York's hotel workers in 1912: emphasis on direct action, sabotage, and violence suffused rhetoric. For four years, 1908–1911, the Wobblies waged free speech fights and sporadic strikes filled with much sound and fury but ending with little to show in the way of organizational growth. Then, in January, 1912, dramatically, even sensationally, the IWW gained control of a spontaneous walkout by 20,000 ill-paid immigrant textile workers in Lawrence, Massachusetts, and carried the strike through to a victorious conclusion.

Suddenly, in March 1912, the IWW seemed to be a real labor organization; not only did it preach revolution, but it also won higher wages; not only did it publish newspapers, produce soapboxers, and issue manifestos, but it also organized workers. And its leaders at Lawrence—Elizabeth Gurley Flynn, William D. Haywood, Joseph J. Ettor, Arturo Giovanitti—became national celebrities. Moreover, these four colorful, charismatic personalities considered New York their home and returned there from Lawrence anxious to find new followers as loyal and resourceful as had been Lawrence's textile workers.[51] They were to find their new recruits among New York's hotel workers.

Hotel workers, seething with unrest by 1912, had already begun to take matters into their own hands when the IWW, never inhibited in its rhetoric and ever ready to lead crusades of the dispossessed, created the Hotel Workers' International Union. Big Bill Haywood, stressing the urgency for working-class solidarity, arrived in town to urge the desirability of a strike against fashionable restaurants and hotels. By May 31, at least 1,800 workers were on the picket lines, and exclusive hotels and dining establishments faced their first major labor difficulties. During June many upper-class New Yorkers had unexpected difficulty locating dining tables set with silver service and featuring continental cuisine.[52]

Hotel men, however, at no time intended to recognize or treat with an organization of their employees. F. A. Reed, President of the Hotel Men's Association, threatened to close every hotel represented in his Association before conceding union demands. Another Association spokesman argued that union recognition was simply impossible, that employers had absolutely no intention of submitting to the dictation of an outside organization. Hotel men presented a united front in refusing to bargain with employees, strikers, or the union. Employing to the fullest their considerable capital resources and their manifold connections with the world of big business, the hotel managers recruited large numbers of Negro strikebreakers (volunteer workers also appeared from Columbia and other local colleges and universities). The hostlers' association to weaken further the strikers' morale simultaneously announced immediate and also prospective wage rises for loyal employees.[53]

Management's strategy again proved too effective for inexperienced strikers lacking indigenous leaders or material resources.

The local press agreed with management's right to control completely, even autocratically, its employees. "It is inconceivable," the *Herald* maintained, "that any properly managed establishment could afford to do anything that would place the control of its servants in the hands of an irresponsible union."[54]

The strikers at first remained unimpressed with their bosses' recalcitrance and strength. Receiving support from the Socialist Party and the *Call,* strikers prepared for a long conflict. Despite incessant harassment by police and judiciary and lowering morale, leaders as late as June 12 proclaimed union recognition the only guarantee for improved working conditions.[55] Thus union and management staked out their respective claims: the latter contending for the open shop, the former for union recognition.

Management's tactical offer to concede all demands except union recognition drove the final nail into the strike's coffin. The waiters, lacking financial resources, a clear philosophy of action, and effective leaders, retreated before their bosses' modified policy. For more than a week— from June 14 to June 25—union members debated the wisdom of accepting a settlement that omitted union recognition. While the more militant unionists argued against submission to management's terms, the bulk of the undisciplined strikers broke ranks and drifted back to their old jobs. Ultimately, with their ranks depleted and their resources exhausted, the union members, on June 25, voted to halt their fruitless strike. They accepted defeat. Nonunion waiters returned to work; the more loyal trade-unionists found instead of jobs an industry-wide blacklist.[56]

During a second effort to organize the hotel and restaurant trade, the coalition of waiters and Wobblies disintegrated. The IWW was not an organization to take failure philosophically. It should have come as no surprise to management and the city, when, on New Year's eve 1913, the Hotel Workers' Industrial Union announced a general strike. The second strike by waiters coincided with the January, 1913, upheaval in the needle trades. The new walkout, fortunately for the hotel managers, never attained industry-wide dimensions. Nevertheless it proved a distinct sore to management. Frequently and without warning, in IWW style, waiters left their jobs and dining establishments found themselves unable to serve impatient patrons.[57]

This time the IWW utilized Joseph J. Ettor and Arturo Giovanitti, famous for their role at Lawrence, Massachusetts and recently acquitted of a murder charge growing out of the textile workers' strike. Once in New York they seized upon every opportunity to urge on the strikers. Ettor, in particular, offered unsettling advice. "If you are compelled to go back to work, under conditions that are not satisfactory," he counselled, "go back with the determination to stick together and with your minds made up it is the unsafest proposition in the world *for the capitalists to eat food prepared by members of your union*" [italics added].[58]

Ettor's rhetoric set the tone for the entire strike fiasco—talk rather than action. Sinister but unintended threats were substituted for strategy and tactics. Elizabeth Gurley Flynn, ardent Wobbly and later equally ardent Marxist, continually proclaimed the general strike which never came. The rhetoric of the IWW may have misled many an unsuspecting New Yorker but it had no perceptible impact on hotel managers. The latter wisely made little effort to combat a general walkout. Their strategy worked. On January 31, the ethereal general strike was no more. Once again while militants marched and leaders orated, the mass of waiters and cooks either never left their jobs or rapidly drifted back to work.[59]

The waiters' experience confirmed what teamsters had already discovered. Strikers unsupported by indigenous, experienced labor leaders and lacking internal solidarity and direction could not succeed against well-organized, united, and affluent adversaries. Furthermore, middle-class reform endorsement and assistance did strikers much good. And the very alliance of waiters and Wobblies, utilizing IWW methods and agitators, spelled doom for the waiters' walkout. Wobblies were anathema to the "respectable" community. And in this case respectable reformers had no pigtailed girls, worn-out women, or ascetic looking male Jewish immigrants upon whom to shower their sympathy. Moreover, the waiters' strike often inconvenienced just those wealthy, middle- and upper-class reformers who had assisted the garment workers but now found sympathy hard to come by for strikers who interfered with the rituals of hotel living or fashionable dining out.

The unsuccessful walkouts staged by teamsters and waiters foreshadowed the era's most notable and eventful labor dispute. In the fall of 1916 organized labor threatened a city-wide general strike. Newspaper headlines during the last two weeks of September, 1916, warned the community of the imminence of an industrial Armageddon. The press estimated that between 200,000 and 500,000 strikers were about to tie up the arteries of metropolitan commerce and life. Stories detailed in full the awful crisis to be faced by the city's inhabitants the day the wheels of industry ground to a halt. The ugly visage of social revolution, many New Yorkers honestly feared, was rearing its head at the gateway to the American nation.

7.
The General Strike Fiasco

THE ERUPTION IN 1916 OF A MINOR labor-management dispute on the city's transit lines generated the era's greatest industrial crisis. Workers combined economic grievances with their more primary objective of achieving union recognition and self-administered job security in what became a violent, protracted and nearly unmanageable dispute. Management, pursuing policies it considered enlightened and which foreshadowed the welfare capitalism of the 1920's, claimed unilateral control over its workers. The community took umbrage at powerful private parties—trade-unions and corporations—disregarding the public welfare for their own selfish aims. Community spokesmen thus attempted to resolve the labor conflict in the public interest. And municipal intervention in a labor dispute between unequally matched adversaries revealed inherent weaknesses in the Progressive or middle-class approach to industrial relations, and why the organizing efforts outside the garment trades were doomed to failure.

I

New York City's transit workers generally received lower wages than employees of comparable municipal transportation systems. They worked long hours (10 to 16 daily) and the strain imposed on them by metropolitan traffic often endangered the public. Management's unrelieved autocracy added to the indignity of deplorable working conditions. The Interborough Rapid Transit Company's (hereafter IRT) work regulations, for example, provided as grounds for dismissal any employee complaint or any failure to discharge exactly and immediately any of an endless list of rules in the regulations' book. As one worker complained: "I wouldn't mind working at the rates as they stand if things were run fairly. But they're not and *the only defense we have is to stick together*. You can see what chance one man has against the boss and all his spotters and investigators" [italics added].[1]

With the working class throughout the city exhibiting dissatisfaction with prevailing patterns of job organization and discipline, it was small wonder that the organizational impulse struck the transit workers. The *New Republic* ably captured the climate of opinion among transit employees. The revolt, it wrote, "came because the intense dissatisfaction with conditions had provided the cohesive cement of group action. The men had exhausted the possibilities of individual effort. There remained only the power of combination."[2]

The transit workers fought powerful opponents. The metropolitan transportation companies represented concentrated capital. The two largest, the IRT and the New York Railways Company (actually under the same management and common ownership), had in 1917 total assets of 230,000,000 and 90,000,000 dollars respectively. While New York Railways suffered an absolute income loss as a result of the 1916 strike, the IRT actually improved its earnings position in the fiscal year during which the conflict occurred. August Belmont and Cornelius Vanderbilt dominated the Board of Directors of both the IRT and the New York Railways Company. At a conference with union representatives, Frank Hedley, Vice-President and General Manager of both companies, conceded: "I don't know of a single member of the Board of Directors . . . who is in New York at the present time. I don't know exactly where they are but they will be found wherever the members of the four hundred congregate in the summer time."[3] Concentrated capital and united management proved more than a match for novice trade-unionists.

Although the transit workers had a long history of strikes and other attempts to organize, they had achieved neither strike victories nor any lasting form of union organization. Walkouts usually ended, particularly the short but bitter 1905 strike, with the workers' organizational strength and morale weaker and with management in firmer control of its labor force. Between the 1905 and the 1916 debacles, the workers failed to produce any leaders. Thus, in 1916, strike leadership was supplied largely by agents of the Amalgamated Association of Street Car and Railway Employees (hereafter the Amalgamated) who had neither close ties to the local workers nor roots in the New York community. Management, on the other hand, between 1905 and 1916 had begun to develop and introduce a labor relations program based upon a primitive form of welfare capitalism.

The company executives, Theodore P. Shonts, President, and Frank Hedley, Vice-President and General Manager, personified the realities behind the Horatio Alger myth. Both came from middle-class backgrounds, the proper ethnic groups—Shonts of old Pennsylvania Dutch transplanted to Iowa origins; Hedley of Anglo-Saxon roots (born in Kent, England)—the right religion, and the necessary politics, Republicanism. Both also reached adolescence and manhood in the age of unfettered enterprise which produced the "Robber Barons." And both were typical of the entrepreneurs who first pioneered in paternalistic company welfare programs.

Shonts, after graduating from college and studying law, married the daughter of his boss, a prominent Iowa attorney, politician, and railroad promoter and organizer. Thereafter, Shonts rose rapidly on the executive ladder of the American railroad world, serving at various times as president of five Mississippi Valley railroads. His reputation for diligence and efficiency in management brought him in 1905 presidential appointment as chairman of the second Isthmian Canal Commission, from which he resigned in 1907. In that year, Shonts accepted the presidency of the IRT, a newly-effected consolidation of subway, elevated, and surface lines.

Hedley also started early in the railroad world. His uncle had designed and built England's first locomotive traction engine. After Hedley's arrival in the United States, he worked as a machinist on the New York Central and the Erie Railroads. In 1903, he joined the IRT and by 1908 had become Vice-President and General Manager, positions he held until 1919. In 1914 he assumed the same positions with the New York Railways Company. And in 1919 he succeeded Shonts to the presidency of both companies. Like Shonts, Hedley was noted for managerial efficiency, improvements in urban transportation, and hostility to independent trade-unions.[4]

By 1916 both the IRT and the New York Railways Company maintained elaborate but limited and paternalistic welfare programs. From 1897 to April 1, 1914, the New York Railways Company had had a voluntary employee welfare system to which workers contributed small monthly payments (membership dues in a so-called association) which management administered. The voluntary association through its dues provided small pensions for long-term employees, sunshine committees, recreational activities, lunch counters, and free transportation for workers' families. While voluntary, the association was entirely dependent upon support and facilities donated by management.[5]

In April, 1914 when Shonts and Hedley also assumed control of the Railways Company, they decided to rationalize and extend the rudimentary company welfare program. Company officials, announcing the creation of a new Welfare Department, expressed their ultimate objective: "more perfect cooperation between employees and officials." As Shonts informed his employees: "The more prosperous the company becomes the more it will have with which to do for the benefit of employees and the public." In good Horatio Alger fashion, he promised his men immediate advancement and eventual high success if they took the proper attitudes, respected their superiors, and worked harder and better than others. To command the continued loyalty of its laborers, the Company opened a line of company grocery stores for which it suggested the men should be thankful. And transit company executives also demanded from their workers a show of gratitude for the many dinners, athletic events, and concerts arranged to improve the men physically and mentally in the interests of greater labor efficiency. In line with his program of "enlightened" labor relations, President Shonts announced on December 28, 1915, wage increases for all IRT and New York Railways Company employees to take effect January 2, 1916, plus five-dollar gold pieces for the great mass of workers.[6]

The IRT simultaneously instituted a comparable program. On April 1, 1914, its welfare director notified the men that a Voluntary Relief Department would lend needy employees up to 50 dollars without interest on the basis of payroll deductions. As with the Railways Company, the IRT financed the bulk of its welfare policies from employee contributions, which the company managed without review. In 1916, however, obviously in response to rising discontent, the IRT combined a company subsidized pension plan with its announced wage increases. The pension program illustrated management's autocratic attitudes; for what it gave with one hand, it removed with the other. A corporation with total assets of nearly 250,000,000 dollars, the IRT provided that annual appropriations for pensions should not exceed 50,000 dollars, and if demands exceeded funds, pension rates would be cut conclusively without appeal; further, persons receiving sickness or accident relief from any other source would receive only the difference as a pension (obviously a penalty for the provident). Finally, the Company's specially created pension board would decide definitively eligibility for benefits and make, without right of appeal, all the governing rules and regulations. For the most part, the workers provided the funds which supported the benefits while the Company established the procedures and controlled disbursement. And the Company officials held out the promise of the greatest reward to the "employee in any department accomplishing more work and doing it better than any other chap."[7] In brief, the intent of welfare capitalism on the transit lines was to insure employee loyalty to an arbitrary management through amorphous promises of advancement.

II

Welfare capitalism failed in both its immediate aims. Before management could discipline the entire labor force, it was forced to apply more forceful measures. Coercion had to be utilized to ensure employee commitment to the Alger success rhetoric. A full month before overt conflict erupted on the city's transit lines, employees complained to a state legislative investigating committee of management's policies and practices. The men were particularly displeased by their employers' insistence upon unchecked power of discharge and the existence of an elaborate spy system; only in Russia, they claimed, would such a system of tyranny be tolerated.[8] By July 26, protests had become action.

Late in July, William V. Fitzgerald, an organizer for the Amalgamated, had called workers out on the trolley lines in the city of Yonkers just north of the Bronx line. Fitzgerald, however, had more expansive aims in mind. To him, Yonkers was a diversion, New York City the primary target. And by Wednesday, July 26, Fitzgerald had successfully urged 1,100 Bronx trolley operators to quit work. Immediately thereafter, W. D. Mahon, President of the Amalgamated, arrived in New York to establish central headquarters from which to direct accelerating strike activity.

Mahon came to New York with a reputation as a successful and respected union organizer. A native of Ohio, he had worked as a street-car driver in Columbus in the 1880's, where he helped organize the local union and served as an elected official. He was one of the original organizers of the Amalgamated in 1892, and the next year was elected president of the national union. Mahon also edited the union's official journal, *Motorman and Conductor.* He quickly won attention from labor and nonlabor sources, serving as a member of the executive committee of the National Civic Federation, as a judge on Michigan reform Governor Hazen Pingree's State Court of Arbitration, as a member of Woodrow Wilson's Industrial Relations Commission, and on numerous special committees of the AFL. All Mahon's national positions and prestige, however, did him little good in New York. As a relative outsider, he never commanded the full loyalty of the transit workers; as a labor leader, he gained only the enmity of the Shonts and the Hedleys.[9]

Mahon's presence signified the conflict's spread. On Saturday evening, July 29, 3,200 employees of the Third Avenue Transit Lines voted unanimously to strike. By the following Monday, Third Avenue trolleys were at a standstill. Still union officials remained unsatisfied. They sensed the general discontent present on all transit lines. Fitzgerald promised to organize workers on every transit company in the city and its vicinity, with the elevated and subway men not to be ignored. He moved throughout the city warning workers that as individuals "you amount to nothing when it comes to raising your wages or lowering your hours. Why, you haven't even a name—only a number."[10]

Management immediately responded to labor's offensive. Frank Hedley warned all New York Railways' employees that outside labor agitators would cause hardship to the men's families and to the public. He informed the workers that the company had arranged for their personal protection against union coercion. Finally, Hedley called upon all loyal employees, desirous of holding their jobs, to beware of meddlers and agitators. In a more positive move to keep the men on the job and the union off, New York Railways and the IRT announced wage increases to take effect July 1 and August 1 respectively.[11] While those two companies sought to ward off union organizers, the Third Avenue Lines' operations had been halted and negotiations compelled.

Mayor John P. Mitchel, believing the dispute to be of direct public concern, sought to exert impartial municipal influence in the interest of a quick settlement. On Tuesday, August 1, he called representatives of the Third Avenue Line and the Amalgamated into conference. This first attempt at impartial mediation proved short-lived. Though the union accepted the Mayor's intervention, the company refused to bargain with its employees when represented by a union.[12]

Union officials and organizers countered company hostility by threatening to tie up the arteries of the New York Railways Company. At this early stage of the conflict union leaders pursued wiser and more effective tactics than management. Mahon, speaking for the Amalgamated, informed Mayor Mitchel of the New York Railways' employees' demands for better conditions and union recognition. The union president agreed to participate in any action or discussion Mitchel desired. He also consented not to present union demands to the company before the Mayor could use his good offices to bring about peace. But since the company failed to respond to Mitchel's overtures, the union presented its own demands to management. Union leaders warned that if no answer was forthcoming by Friday, August 4, the men would meet that evening to decide upon appropriate action. But Mahon maintained his hope that the Mayor could arrange a mutually acceptable agreement.[13]

While Amalgamated officials cooperated with municipal authorities, company spokesmen refused mayoral intercession and demanded the freedom to deal arbitrarily with employees. The New York Railways Company officials argued that working conditions were satisfactory, that the men had not given any union the authority to present demands on their behalf, and that 94 percent of the company's employees remained loyal and believed relations between employers and men could be settled within the family without outside interference. President Shonts, in a letter to Mayor Mitchel, assured the Mayor of employee loyalty to management and requested adequate and immediate police protection against the violence and destruction which inevitably accompanied strikes. The following day Shonts attempted to link Mahon and the Amalgamated to Tom Mooney, the San Francisco Preparedness Day bombing, and violence across the length and breadth of the land.[14] In short, management declined to negotiate with union representatives; it acceded to municipal intervention only if it meant police protection to break the strike.

On the eve of their threatened general strike, trolley workers presented a united front and commanded community support. The AFL, the State Federation of Labor, and the CFU provided the strikers with encouragement and endorsement. The Chairman of the Public Service Commission, Oscar Straus, on August 4 issued a statement accusing Frederick W. Whitridge, President of the Third Avenue Railroad, of precipitating the original dispute. On the same day, the Merchants' Association of New York demanded that, in the public interest, the transit companies meet with the Mayor and their employees' representatives. Editorial opinion regarding the initial walkouts also put the strikers in a favorable light. While the companies supplied the newspapers with a steady flow of full-page advertisements intended to becloud the basic issues, editorial opinion remained moderate and impartial. Striking laborers, as usual, garnered their accustomed share of press criticism, but editorial criticism of traction company executives was remarkable for its severity.[15]

In the prevailing spirit of things, Mayor Mitchel formulated settlement terms amenable to the union and also reflecting middle-class Progressivism's basic attitudes toward labor relations and organized labor. Mitchel noted on August 4 that with a climax approaching both sides should recognize that "in this crisis, the public interest is paramount." The public would not tolerate arbitrary action by either labor or management. The Mayor then enunciated principles axiomatic to the "present situation" and to all industrial disputes. First, employees have the right to organize and companies have no right to refuse to confer with or to recognize such organizations. "If stockholders may organize and insist upon dealing with employers through corporate officials, who can deny the same right to employees?" The cry of alien agitators is patently absurd, Mitchel observed, for companies have gone to other cities and states for officials. Second, while "the right to organize is a fundamental civic right," the union may not exclude others or insist upon the closed shop. "These are *public* utilities and the labor organizations have no more right to exclude a man who refuses to join than the companies have to discharge or refuse to employ a man who does join." Mitchel urged the disputants to drop all claims conflicting with his two essential nonarbitratable principles, and he suggested a joint conference or arbitration to settle all other points in dispute. "Any person, company, or organization that refuses to recognize the rights of the public in this situation and brings about arbitrarily a suspension of transportation or forces others to do so, merits the severe condemnation which will be heaped upon him."[16] In this instance the warning was aimed at the New York Railways Company executives who had refused to negotiate with the union or with the Mayor. Mitchel's principles also became the basis for the settlement of the August 4 strike.

Thus the vote to strike by New York Railways' workers on the evening of August 4 came under propitious circumstances. With the Public Service Commissioner, a large part of the press, the Merchants' Association, and the Mayor aligned against them, transit company executives beat a strategic retreat. They allowed the Mayor to arrange a settlement respecting the workers' right to organize. But the actual process of negotiation raised further disturbing and time-consuming problems. Only mutual concessions upon the emphatic urging of the Mayor prevented the peace conferences from resulting in renewed warfare.

On the evening of August 5, Mayor Mitchel met with Public Service Commission Chairman Oscar Straus in White Plains where they agreed to cooperate in securing a strike settlement based on the Mayor's August 4 memo. Mitchel and Straus worked well together, for the Commissioner shared the Mayor's reform attitudes. Straus, the well-educated scion of a wealthy German-Jewish immigrant family, was, like Mitchel, averse to party loyalty. A conservative, Cleveland Gold Democrat, Straus broke with his party in 1896 to support McKinley and gold. Like many McKinley backers, he became a Roosevelt Progressive, serving as Roosevelt's Secretary of Commerce and Labor from 1906 to 1909, and running for Governor of New York on the Progressive Party ticket in 1912. In 1915 Republican Governor Charles Whitman appointed Straus Chairman of the Public Service Commission, a position which thrust him into the midst of the transit strike. His association with Jewish welfare and community agencies brought him an awareness of the problems faced by the lower classes. Thus Straus like Mitchel sought to aid the strikers, while at the same time serving the public interest.[17]

Mitchel and Straus conceded the strikers' legal and moral right to organize; the company was enjoined from interfering with organizing efforts either by discharge or by intimidation; the men would be guaranteed the right to bargain collectively with management through their own freely elected *committees of actual company employees;* and if management received such committees, the workers would waive the question of explicit union recognition. All material questions concerning wages and working conditions were to be arbitrated after the strike ended.

On Sunday, August 6, the Mayor submitted these peace terms to the union's representatives (W. D. Mahon, Louis Fridiger, union attorney, William B. Fitzgerald, and Hugh Frayne, AFL representative) and to the company's agents at separate meetings. Shonts and his attorney had refused to sit with union officials. After four hours of continuous conference, Shonts agreed to recommend as a basis for settlement the Mayor's proposals to his Board of Directors.[18] Before the Board ratified the recommendations and the union accepted them, Shonts attempted to subvert the concessions and the rights offered the strikers.

President Shonts, in his report to the Board of Directors, altered slightly but significantly Mayor Mitchel's terms. Shonts included in his personal report the following: a guarantee by the union not to coerce employees who declined to organize; explicit refusal to recognize any union or "outside" employee organization; and a clause granting the management, in the interest of public safety and public service, absolute control (not subject to arbitration) of employees in all matters relating to efficiency. When Mahon surprisingly accepted Shonts' four revisions, the President of the New York Railways proceeded to demand further concessions. He insisted that the company would deal with committees of the men only if they "shall be truly representative of the employees as a whole (shall be citizens of New York State and have resided in New York City for five years prior to the date of this agreement)" and that committee elections be supervised by four inspectors including a company agent and a representative of the unorganized workers. Mitchel, however, convinced Shonts to delete his two latest proposals. And Mahon and the Amalgamated consented to terminate the strike on the basis of the Mayor's original terms and Shonts' later revisions concerning union coercion and company efficiency.[19] Although Shonts, under community and Mayoral pressure, eventually omitted his more extreme demands, they had more truly reflected management's attitudes. Commitment at heart to these principles of employer autocracy portended further conflict.

The Board of Directors, in conceding its employees' right to organize, also hedged. The Board warned that membership by transit workers in a labor organization with interests in other cities and not responsible solely to the local community was contrary to the best interest of New York City transportation. It also promised to wean men away from any outside organization (the Amalgamated) by advising their employees that in the long run affairs would be better if all matters were settled without external intervention. The company would make its alternative to the union's settlement so attractive "that no one will want to deviate from it."[20] Management's determination to weaken the union moved the conflict into a new and more virulent stage.

Meanwhile the decision of the Mayor and Commissioner Straus to underwrite the agreement of August 6, and Mitchel's judicious intervention on behalf of the community brought applause from prominent New Yorkers. A New York *World* editor, for example, congratulated the Mayor on his "peaceful termination of the most serious labor problem that ever concerned New York."[21] Mitchel's role as settlement guarantor and labor relations mediator on the transit lines was in fact just beginning.

III

After their early concessions the transit companies counterattacked. Company executives assumed that workers once back on the job were unlikely to tolerate a union-initiated resumption of hostilities. Although at first no direct assaults were made upon the Amalgamated, spies were in evidence at union organizational and policy meetings, the company informed its employees that no union had been recognized, and, in the future, they would be best served by accepting a new company labor relations plan. On August 12, the New York Railways Company announced the creation of a management sponsored representation system. Company unions were quickly created to alienate the workers from the Amalgamated. The Company had never intended allowing its employees to hold union elections unchallenged; it procrastinated in the rehiring of the more active union leaders and strikers. New York Railways officials continued to maintain that the "best interests of New York would be served if our employees dealt directly with the company, without reference to outside organizations having no such responsibility to this community as we and our employees have." Management concluded that company unions demonstrated that "the adjustment of grievances is better left to the employees' own organization without the interposition of any outside body." And at meetings with officials of the Amalgamated, company representatives refused to rehire the fired men or to desist from establishing a company union through company sponsored elections. Management, however, offered to allow Straus and Mitchel to arbitrate differences.[22]

Management's decision to go to arbitration was not entirely a matter of free choice. The Company had proved incorrect in its estimate of the union's strength after work resumed. The men, although back on the job, promised to strike again if their demands were not met. A walkout seemed imminent; the workers had had their fill of company speeches and notices warning them not to join the union. The *New Republic,* speaking for the middle-class Progressive segment of the local community, emphasized management's infidelity. "The entire attitude of the company is replete with bad faith, and indicates a determination to undermine the union by any means." The Amalgamated continued to emphasize moderation rather than militancy and thus to remain in the good graces of the public.[23]

Only Mayor Mitchel's intervention averted a resumption of hostilities. After a conference in the Mayor's office on Monday, August 21, the heads of the New York Railways Company promised to reinstate immediately all men previously discharged for participating in the strike. The union, still in a conciliatory mood, conceded management's right to hire and fire men provided fair hearings were held in protested discharges. The Mayor, however, refused to restrict the company's activities on behalf of a company union. Mitchel failed to see coercion or intimidation in management promises to treat loyal employees more satisfactorily. He argued that as long as the employers did not hold out specific financial inducements "you cannot properly object to the company arguing with their men not to join the union. . . . Let us have it clearly understood that both sides have a right to argue, persuade, and induce."[24] Given management's financial resources, its high-powered attorneys, and its nearly unchallenged right to hire and fire, the Mayor's neutrality offered the New York Railways Company free rein to continue its labor-baiting policies.

IV

Although Shonts and his fellow executives had been compelled to negotiate with their employees on the city's surface transit lines, they resisted organizing attempts by elevated and subway workers. While trolley operators were striking, laborers on the IRT's subways complained of "the tyrannical abuses practiced upon the employees of this company." While the management of the New York Railways Company was attempting to vitiate the settlement of August 6 by holding company elections and establishing company unions, Shonts, as President of the IRT, had instituted a similar policy, establishing the Brotherhood of IRT Employers to maintain management-labor "harmony."[25]

Three days after Mayor Mitchel's second attempt at mediation (August 21), subway workers transmitted demands for union recognition to President Shonts of the IRT. But IRT officials, speaking through their subsidiary concern, New York Railways, refused to concede any element of union recognition. Vice-President Hedley emphasized the "we do not recognize the Association [Amalgamated]." While the Amalgamated's organizers continued to impress the community with their moderation and cooperativeness, management persisted in circulating among IRT employees an individual labor contract. The contract, labeled by its opponents a master-servant agreement, forbade the signer to join any labor organization not recognized by the employer. All workers who signed the individual contract were promised immediate wage increases as their reward for forswearing union organization. The Amalgamated responded to management's new tactic by criticizing the Shonts-Hedley strategy of "yellow-dog" contracts as an infringement of the August 6 agreement guaranteeing workers the right to organize without interference, intimidation, or coercion. The union's leaders empowered organizer Fitzgerald to call a strike if the contracts were not withdrawn from circulation.[26]

Management's intractability could have but one result—industrial warfare. The IRT General-Manager Hedley warned the Amalgamated: "We intend to run our roads, and the public can rest assured that we are ready to run them." He added that even if court action proved necessary, all employees would be held to signed contracts. William Fitzgerald, for the union, replied simply and to the point: "I don't see how we can avoid a strike on the Interborough Rapid Transit Company's lines— subways, elevated, and streetcars."[27]

Even before the strike began, management had made intensive preparations for defense and ultimate victory. On September 4, Shonts informed Mayor Mitchel of the impending strike by a "minority seeking to dominate the great majority." He requested police protection before disorder occurred and denied the community essential services. Shonts assured the Mayor that the IRT, given adequate protection, could provide uninterrupted service and thus respect its obligation to the public. The following day he cautioned IRT employees that only those who remained on the job would obtain the higher wages and improved conditions promised in the "yellow-dog" contracts. Shonts next informed the community, through daily paid newspaper advertisements, of the IRT's notable welfare capitalism and its pattern of regular wage increases, both of which had won the affection of the loyal majority of employees. He gulled the public with a simplified explanation of a complicated conflict: "There is nothing involved in this controversy except the right of employees . . . to form their own brotherhood and the right of the company and the members of the brotherhood to enter into contracts respecting rates of pay and hours of labor."

Although both Shonts and Hedley were the governing officers of New York Railways and as such had entered into the agreement of August 6 respecting the workers' right to organize freely, they sought to dissociate the IRT from that agreement by substituting the letter for the spirit of the agreement. In management's purview, "the whole situation grows out of the attempt of the Amalgamated . . . to force employees . . . to join their organization."[28] It was questionable, however, whether organized labor in truth had violated the letter of the August 6 settlement.

Just before the second IRT walkout which spread to other transit companies, Hedley admitted at a meeting with union officials that transit executives had contemplated issuing individual contracts to New York Railways' employees. In response to a question from the union's attorney, Hedley stated that the Board of Directors decided individual contracts would not violate the August 6 agreement because "under the Constitution of the country . . . if a man wants to enter into a contract with another man, he can do so." If the Supreme Court could employ Spencer to infringe organized labor's rights, why not management!

As the New York Railways Company had already prepared proofs of the new "yellow-dog" contract, the Amalgamated concluded its conferences with company officials and threatened a sympathetic strike with IRT men. Fitzgerald, emphasizing management's seeming destruction of the spirit of the initial settlement, announced that employees of both the Third Avenue Lines and the New York Railways Company, despite their legal contracts, would strike in sympathy with their fellow workers.[29]

The Amalgamated's decision to violate a formal, binding contract created innumerable and finally insuperable difficulties. The community, although aware of numerous examples of management's duplicity and breach of faith, could not understand labor's willingness to break written contracts. New York's citizens in common with countless other Americans valued the formal provisions of the law above the human spirit.

While union officials negotiated with representatives of the New York Railways and the Third Avenue Lines, the IRT's organized workers had voted on September 6 to strike. The following morning streetcar traffic on IRT facilities was practically halted, and the els and subways operated only under irregular schedules. Workers had decided to challenge their employers' determination to go to the "mat with this thing and fight it out to a finish, even if we have to discharge every man in our employ and hire new ones."[30]

In the brief interval before the strike spread from the IRT to other lines, the press treated the Amalgamated fairly despite the union's failure to cultivate community sympathy. Mildness in this instance resulted more from management's obtuseness than from union strategy or genius. Except for the *Times* which minced no words in castigating the strikers, the papers proved generally tolerant. The "yellow-dog" contracts and Shonts' efforts to vitiate the collective bargaining process were viewed by the *World* as the key to the dispute. "There would be no danger of a traction strike," the paper concluded, "if the Interborough did not want a strike." The *Herald* labelled Mr. Hedley of the IRT a professional union hater, observing that "here was a deliberate attempt to drive the unions out of the street car employment in this city." "Neither side," observed the *Tribune,* "has shown any regard for the public . . . they are selfishly pursuing what they deem to be their own interests at the expense of the people." The *Post* criticized the disputants for disrupting the comfort of the public but added that the company's position "was to do what right-minded men felt from the start to be unjustifiable, and . . . appears . . . to be unthinkable."[31] Press sympathy, however, proved short-lived. The Amalgamated alienated press and community by unfolding a strategy of sympathetic and general strikes.

By Sunday, September 10, the strike on the IRT had spread to the trolley lines of the New York Railways and the Third Avenue Transit Company. Events appeared to be reaching a serious impasse. Frank Morrison, an AFL Vice-President, fearing the worst, cabled Gompers asking him to hurry to New York in order to confer with Secretary Ernest Bohm of the CFU. Gompers arrived in time to attend a conference (September 10) of representatives of organized labor in the city and the state which recommended "a sympathetic strike of all organized wage earners in their jurisdiction in support of the contention of the street railway men for the right to organize." Gompers, conscious of the basic issues involved in the dispute, advised concerted action though refusing to endorse a full-scale general strike.[32]

Management seized upon labor's unusually militant position to turn the community against the Amalgamated. President Whitridge of the Third Avenue Company, speaking of the union's violation of the August 6 settlement, called his workers "members of a secret society, bound to obey the orders of a master." He considered the Amalgamated to be a promoter of disorder and disloyalty, a violator of contracts, and a public nuisance. That the company executive's attitude was shared by responsible members of the urban community was illustrated in the volume and tone of the correspondence on the strike received by Mayor Mitchel.[33]

The workers, however, would not return to work until they had their union. "We want the Union now. We know what would happen to us if we would go back without the Union."[34] Thus rumors of an impending general strike continued to saturate the atmosphere and embitter community sentiments.

The Public Service Commission, hoping to terminate the conflict before it intensified, submitted four recommendations for a settlement. Individual, nonunion contracts as well as the union charge of fraud and coercion directed against IRT executives were to be arbitrated. While peace conferences proceeded between the contending parties, strikers were to return to the job. Shonts and the IRT, however, refused the Commission's peace tender. Employers instead declared their intention never to arbitrate the strike and never to re-employ a single striker.[35]

Both sides continued to appeal to the Mayor for assistance. On September 15 the Amalgamated indicated to Mitchel its desire to end the walkout peacefully through the mediation of Mitchel and Straus in the interest of the public. But union spokesmen stressed that the conflict could not be terminated unless the men returned to work with their union. Only the union, they argued, could offer the workers protection and security against arbitrary employer discharge and discrimination. Simultaneously, IRT company officials led by the corporation's general attorney had an audience with Mitchel during which they presented their own case. The IRT Brotherhood (the company union) representatives claimed that the majority of the workers approved both the individual, "yellow-dog" contracts and the company union. They appealed to the Mayor for additional police protection to aid them in their struggle against outside agitators and "alien" organizers.[36] Thus the battle lines were clearly drawn.

While the contenders appealed to the Mayor, the CFU on Friday, September 15, by unanimous vote ratified its earlier recommendation endorsing a general sympathetic strike. The vote, however, was meaningless unless local unions and their parent internationals approved the general strike decision. In theory, the transit workers' right to organize without management interference had become symbolic of labor's solidarity; in practice, despite community misconceptions, working-class solidarity proved chimerical.[37]

With the strike situation taking a turn for the worse, Mayor Mitchel conferred with leaders of organized labor on the role of the police and the threatened general strike. At this September 18 conference general strike talk dominated the discussions. Hugh Frayne warned the Mayor that the scene was fraught with danger and great sentiment existed for a sympathetic walkout. He also informed Mitchel that since the IRT directors controlled many other New York industries, their utilization of "yellow-dog" contracts appeared to be part of a more general conspiracy against trade-unionism. Thus all labor was uniting in self-defense. Frayne, emphasizing his own moderation, deplored the possibility of a general strike but insisted, "if there is nothing else that we can do in order to protect the rights of our men, we may be forced to do that whether we want or not." President T. V. O'Connor of the Longshoremen's Union echoed Frayne's warning, adding that his own men were becoming harder to control. All the labor delegates present at the meeting pleaded with the Mayor to use his influence to bring the IRT officials to terms.

Organized labor's spokesmen, although threatening the general strike, indicated their clear preference for negotiation and arbitration. They advised Mitchel that he had until Thursday, September 21, to settle the strike. The Mayor sympathized with the union men and agreed with them that the issues in dispute since August 30 should be arbitrated. Mitchel, however, was at a loss to deal with management representatives who refused resolutely to arbitrate on the basis of the original August 6 agreement, which recognized the principle of liberty on both sides.[38]

While labor postponed the general strike pending Mayor Mitchel's further intervention, Shonts quashed all remaining hopes for an early *rapprochement*. On Monday, September 18, Shonts, speaking for the IRT's directors, refused to confer on any terms with the Mayor if representatives of the Amalgamated attended. "Under no conditions," he emphasized, "will I deal with the unions. . . . I am unalterably opposed to any such arrangement, and I tell you now emphatically that I won't participate."³⁹ Shonts' harsh words simply aggravated an already grievous impasse.

On September 20 Shonts dogmatically turned down suggestions by Mayor Mitchel and Chairman Straus that he deal with striking workers on a collective basis. Shonts informed the Mayor and the Commissioner that the IRT strike was broken and thus negotiations were unnecessary; furthermore, he would deal with the New York Railways strikers only on an individual basis since they had broken the August 6 agreement and their binding contract with the company. Shonts also admitted that General Manager Hedley's promise to allow IRT workers to organize freely had been made only for purposes of conference, was not binding or guaranteed by Mitchel and Straus, and had served its purpose. Mitchel, on the basis of Shonts' intractability, concluded that mediation "is impossible . . . if the Company . . . will not deal collectively with the men who are on strike. As long as that position is taken, it is futile for us to be making abortive attempts at mediation."⁴⁰ The company executives thus had mastered both the Amalgamated and the Mayor, causing the union to rely upon Mitchel's intervention and Mitchel to concede his impotence. Consequently, the general strike as labor's weapon of last resort threatened the community.

Mitchel, in order to forestall the implementation of a general strike, agreed to meet again with organized labor's representatives on September 21. (Shortly before the union men appeared in the Mayor's office, Mitchel and a Citizen's Committee on the Traction Strike, which had been formed to urge Shonts to arbitrate, agreed that an impasse had been reached.)⁴¹

The labor leaders, led by their elder statesman, Samuel Gompers, implored Mitchel to aid them in dealing with deceitful employers. Gompers impressed the Mayor with management's desire and efforts to undermine and destroy the spirit of the earlier agreements by establishing company unions to interfere with the normal development of *bona fide* workers' organizations. If company unions were not intended to circumvent the Amalgamated, Gompers asked, why were they not formed prior to the first strike? He also criticized the autocratic attitudes of Shonts and Hedley and reminded Mitchel that only management's stubbornness and disregard of essential human rights fostered sympathetic strike talk. Gompers, seeking to place the complete onus for the impasse upon

Shonts and Hedley, warned that if management did not alter its inhuman approach, "there is going to be trouble, but I have no power to do anything." He pleaded with Mitchel and Straus to compel company executives to change their policies. Though the AFL leader implored the Amalgamated's members to stand for their rights like men, he cautioned them to operate within the law, thus in large degree adulterating the general strike threat. In conclusion, the assembled labor spokesmen advised the Mayor that the strikers were not yet hungry enough to surrender and return to work without their union.[42]

The Amalgamated's mixture of threat and equivocation only served to becloud management's guilt. Public servants tended to value statute law more highly than moral commitments. The companies had only violated their sworn word; but as Straus commented: "I only regret that the men [Amalgamated members] have made it so difficult, if not impossible, for us to carry our views by reason of their breaking contracts which we so strongly recommended to them they should not break."[43] As the Public Service Commissioner's attitude indicated, management rather than labor had a fuller and more perceptive comprehension of the limitations of municipal intervention in a labor dispute, particularly when statute law favored concentrated capital.

Organized labor in its endeavor to protect the right to organize ignored the community's hostile reaction to contract breaches and sympathetic strikes. No sooner did the Mayor's conference of September 21 end in failure than organized labor appeared ready to implement its dire threats. On Friday, September 22, the Greater New York Labor Conference, consisting of the CFU, the Central Labor Union of Brooklyn, the UHT, and the Building Trades Council, issued a proclamation calling for a general suspension of work[44] in all trades in Greater New York and vicinity to take effect Wednesday morning, September 27. The CFU, acting alone, immediately voiced approval.[45]

Before the general walkout began, all union locals had to ratify the labor council's proclamation. To this end, the Cloakmakers, the largest single local in the area, planned a mass meeting for Saturday, September 23 to "renew their pledge of class loyalty to the brave strikers." This and similar sessions held by ILGWU affiliates resulted in the appointment of a committee to observe the response to the general strike by other organized trades. Only if the response proved positive would the ILGWU call out its own locals. Hugh Frayne insisted, for public consumption, that the morning of September 27 would see 240,000 striking workers on the avenues of New York. Frayne substantiated his optimism by reference to the special labor conference which had declared that "labor's protest will be overwhelming and decisive." On the appointed day, Wednesday, September 27, the Joint Labor Committee released figures to the press purporting to prove that 173,000 men and women had struck in sympathy with the transit workers.[46]

The sympathetic strike proved simultaneously to be the acme and the nadir of organized labor's pre-World War I organizing efforts in New York. While labor prepared to marshal its full power, management held fast, refusing to arbitrate even the facts in dispute as demanded by a citizen's committe which included George Creel, Amos Pinchot, Albert J. Nock, Rabbi Stephen S. Wise, Lincoln Steffens, and John Reed.[47] But before the walkout ended, the Amalgamated through its unrestrained use of threats succeeded in alienating all important sectors of the metropolitan community.

The general strike threat and the trolley workers' breach of contract brought a sharp and bitter response form the city's press. Newspapers devoted columns of type to informing the public of "alien labor agitators" from Cleveland, Detroit, Chicago, and Washington, D.C., who were subverting satisfied employees. Journalists and editorial writers suddenly uncovered varieties of insidious intrigue behind every development in the labor dispute.

The clamor against the sympathetic strike constantly rose. The *American* urged its working-class subscribers to forego "doing unionism more harm at a single blow than all its open foes could do." "A sympathetic strike," contended the *World,* "would be an abuse of liberty which could not fail to invite at the hands of society at large some regrettable reprisals." The *Tribune* labeled labor's threatened action the "most vicious, and indefensible exhibition of arbitrary, antisocial uses of power," and "its effects would damage labor and labor unionism to an incalculable degree." The *Herald* also spared no words, characterizing labor leaders as just "as dangerous to society as any preacher of redhanded anarchy; [to mention the sympathetic strike] is to suggest social revolution." The *Times* concluded that labor's proposed plans were the height of folly and wickedness as well as a crime and conspiracy against the "public peace and welfare."[48]

Mayor Mitchel's correspondence revealed a similar aversion among the community's leading citizens to the Amalgamated's tactics. Letter after letter demonstrated fear of social revolution. Correspondents urged the Mayor to clear out agitators, suppress the rioters, employ the National Guard, and treat the conflict as a civil war. Even E. H. Outerbridge, one of the Mayor's conciliators in the 1915–1916 garment trades dispute, advised Mitchel that Amalgamated organizers were fighting for "the right to insist that the only organizing shall be done by themselves and under their domination whether the men desire that or not." After the Mayor vigorously condemned working-class violence, criticized severely the strike leaders, and promised to protect private property, incoming correspondence generally applauded his toughness.[49] Newspaper editorials and letters to the Mayor hinted the fate of the transit workers.

As the community united against organized labor's threats, labor itself had second thoughts about the advisability of a general strike. On Thursday, September 28, the Building Trades Council of Greater New York, comprising some 150,000 men, decided to defer participation in the sympathy walkout. Their decision to postpone action reinforced the apprehension of other union locals troubled by their earlier decision to strike. The Building Trades' example proved contagious. Leaders of the labor movement—AFL Vice-President, Martin Lawlor, Ernest Bohm, William Fitzgerald, and Hugh Frayne, among others—one week later, on October 2, presided over the general strike's corpse. Citing the action of the building trades unions, they openly acknowledged the death of their grand strategy. As the Capmakers' journal commented pungently: "It takes more than vulgar bluff to subdue the thugs of corporate capital."[50] Organized labor in New York, with AFL approval, had approached the brink of radicalism and revolution. It then executed an abrupt about-face. "Brinkmanship" had failed.

Concentrated capital and united management again proved too adept, astute, and masterful in its strategy for disunited, uncertain, and poorly led labor. In the end, pay increases triumphed over working-class solidarity; "loyal" employees triumphed over "alien," outside influences; freedom of choice triumphed over the union shop; and the company union triumphed over the independent trade-union. The traction magnates gained every issue they contested. In late October, Governor Whitman, denying relief to petitioning transit workers, closed the last avenue of aid.[51]

Union officials instead of utilizing public sympathy to drive the companies to arbitration ultimately chose recklessly to coerce management through intimidation of the entire community by a city-wide strike. Amalgamated officials ignored, unwisely perhaps, the advice of the *New Republic*: "Labor must educate and inform the public, not defy and coerce it."[52]

But the *New Republic* together with hardheaded labor leaders did not perceive the impotence of municipal intervention in a dispute between unequally matched parties. In the first stages of the strike, labor leaders relied upon the intercession of Mitchel and Straus to gain their objectives. Only when the Mayor and the Commissioner proved powerless in their dealings with Shonts did organized labor actually consider the general strike a real possibility.

Statute law in Progressive America favored corporate management; capable company executives took full advantage. Shonts and Hedley might promise to respect their employees' right to organize freely but no written law thwarted their decision to violate their solemn word. Labor might protest management's establishment of company unions and its intimidation of independent union members, but no statute infringed management's freedom to deal arbitrarily with its labor force and its own property.[53]

Furthermore, municipal mediation as undertaken by Mitchel and Straus conceded management's right to organize employees into company unions. In competition between the independent union and the company union the companies possessed every advantage. Management, not union officials, controlled employment; it, not the union, could promise immediate wage increases and promotions; and the company, not the union, had unlimited resources. Thus when the strike ended, Shonts complimented his loyal employees, welcomed thousands of new men to the company's family, gained the endorsement of the company unions, and promised future wage increases.[54]

V

Where the garment workers had benefited from a fortuitous conjunction of circumstances, transit workers, express drivers, sanitation men, and hotel workers were less fortunate. They also demanded the right to organize and to bargain collectively. Their defeats, however, illustrated the shortcomings of middle-class reformers in dealing with industrial conflict. And in these instances internal union organization, community participation, and economic structure shaped the course of conflict to the disadvantage of the working class.

The defeated strikers were favored neither with resolute nor capable leaders. They produced no Rose Schneiderman, Abraham Rosenberg, Benjamin Schlesinger, or Joseph Schlossberg from their ranks; they lacked an Abraham Cahan, Morris Hillquit, or Meyer London to guide them; they had no kehillah to mediate in their behalf. They, their leaders, and their organizers could not count upon assistance from influential citizens. Nearly all their union officials and strike leaders came to New York as strangers to the community. Thus employers cast innumerable aspersions upon "alien" agitators seeking to disrupt satisfied and loyal employees.

Unlike the Jewish and Italian immigrant workers in the needle trades who were often effectively barred from prestigious occupations and who sought status through trade-union roles, transit and express workers represented older, more Americanized groups. Irish-Americans and German-Americans had wider latitude in which to develop their talents. The more capable among them forsook labor for the political arena and the business world.

The defeated strikers, moreover, lacked a philosophy which could suffuse initial failures with hope and transform a despairing present into the promise of a brave new world. Where the needle trade workers dwelled in a world of figurative class war and social revolution but acted temperately in practice, teamsters, waiters, and carmen shared few if any revolutionary sentiments but did upon occasion act destructively. And middle-class Progressive reformers refused, regardless of circumstance, to sanction violence.

The strikers among the teamsters, garbagemen, waiters, and transit workers could never win the community sympathy showered so profusely upon the garment workers. No exploited, overworked women and girls set middle-class hearts to crying. No stoop shouldered, tired looking Jewish immigrants (so romanticized by New York's settlement workers) won the admiration of nonworking-class reformers. During the defeated strikes the community saw, rightly or wrongly, only wide shouldered, brawny, healthy men who could wage their own battles which they sometimes did with fists and bricks. What the reformers saw during the unsuccessful strikes they did not always admire and often abjured.

Strike leaders, under intense pressure and unable to gain effective re-

form or community backing, necessarily replaced moderation with coercion. When the nonworking-class community failed to aid protesting
workers to gain better conditions, union strike power seemed the only
other alternative. But coercive action such as general strike threats only
served further to alienate reformers, community leaders, and municipal
officials.

The press reflected the strikers' failure to make sympathetic contact
with the community. Editorial opinion conditioned the public to expect
the worst from the men on strike. Few strikers were spared the wounds
inflicted by critical editorials. If the unions obtained any newspaper
support, for example in the *World* and the *American,* they quickly rebuffed their would-be journalistic friends.

Unlike the garment workers who literally had organized themselves,
providing from within their own ranks organizers and union leaders,
the teamsters, transit workers, and other defeated strikers relied heavily
on aid from old-line AFL unions. But the skilled-craft structure of the established AFL unions made it difficult for union organizers to attract
the devotion of largely unskilled workers who needed labor unity more
than working-class exclusiveness.

Above all, the strikers contended with resourceful adversaries. Powerful, oligarchic private enterprises and monopolistic public and semipublic concerns proved unshakeable in their opposition to unions. Protracted strikes by themselves did not weaken or defeat multimillion
dollar corporations. Neither new competitors nor financial ruin threatened management. Businessmen did not need organized labor to stabilize
shaky enterprises. Instead of offering their employees industrial democracy based upon law and order in industry, corporate management
proffered welfare capitalism founded upon employer autocracy. Industrial efficiency was to come through astute management. Eventually,
workers forced to their knees by economic pressure, or wooed by company
unions and welfare programs, or deserted by their quondam leaders,
conceded defeat and either returned to work without a union or suffered
unemployment and the blacklist. Where capital was already soundly
organized, labor organization was unwanted and unneeded.

Municipal intervention by Mayors Gaynor and Mitchel was of no
avail. Though both Gaynor and Mitchel publicly endorsed the workingman's right to organize independent unions, their intercession in the
express and traction strikes failed abjectly. Both Mayors, attempting to
be entirely impartial, granted management and labor equal organizing

rights; the independent union to compete with the company union. Events proved this competition unfair. Progressive reformers and municipal officials had yet to learn that third-party intervention did not work where the disputants were of unequal strength.

Even had New York's reform mayors been more aware of the realities of economic power, they would not have done better by the sanitation men, transit workers, and teamsters. Although only the garbagemen worked directly for the city, the services performed by teamsters and transitmen impinged upon what can be called the "public" sector of the economy, raising numerous political difficulties for Mayors Gaynor and Mitchel. Industrial conflict in the garment industry, which had little impact upon those not immediately involved, could not be compared to strikes in the "public" sector, which inconvenienced large portions of the community. More important, the conventional wisdom, then as now, deemed civil service employment a public trust and a strike by civil service workers a breach of faith as well as a defiance of legally-constituted authority, not a struggle for higher wages, improved conditions, or a better life.

Political reality was best demonstrated by Gaynor's rude crushing of the sanitation workers' strike and their union. Mayor Mitchel, more sympathetic to independent unionism than Gaynor, also felt compelled by public pressure and political expediency to limit the right of trade-unions to tie up metropolitan mass transportation. But transit workers who labored for private capitalists retained more freedom of action than sanitation men who worked for the city. Mitchel conceded that private employers might mistreat their workers, causing them to organize unions and to strike; Gaynor, however, refused to admit that municipal employees might have legitimate grievances. Private employment, then as now, imposed mutual obligations upon employers and employees whereas public employment seemed to place all the obligations upon the workers. Consequently, today just as was the case with New York's garbagemen in 1911, civil service workers have been denied the right to strike (today many states have criminal penalties against civil service strikers) and sometimes even the right to organize unions.

No simple solutions seem likely to ameliorate the predicament of public employees. Strikes probably never will be tolerated in the public sector although when civil service unions feel sufficiently powerful they may and often do risk public condemnation to impose their demands upon a defenseless public administration and a helpless community.

And in those cases where public employees, rightly or wrongly, legally or illegally, strike, despite mediation, conciliation, or arbitration, power as always will be the final arbiter.

In the last analysis, the reform impulse prevalent during the Progressive years generated organizational strikes but did not guarantee success for the principles of trade-unionism and industrial justice. In the years since, which have seen a New Deal, a Fair Deal, a New Frontier, and a Great Society, many more workers have fought for and gained just those principles but millions more find themselves still denied the right to organize and to strike.

Epilogue

THE GENERAL STRIKE FIASCO in the autumn of 1916 ended for a time the surge toward union organization by New York City's working-class masses. Within less than a year the nation was at war and the international crusade to save and spread democracy had become more important than either domestic reform or labor's organizing campaigns. Already by April, 1917, New York's immigrant clothing workers had created apparently stable and large trade-unions. With American belligerency, AFL affiliates, owing to their avid endorsements of Wilsonian diplomacy, came under benevolent federal guardianship. The AFL craft unions in New York and elsewhere surrendered the right to strike in return for federal sponsorship of unions and collective bargaining. Many employers, desperately short of labor and facing a national government which sanctioned independent trade-unionism, conceded union recognition, at least for the emergency. Those workers not fortunate enough to belong to trade-unions also benefited from war-induced labor scarcity, as employers offered higher wages, improved working conditions, and showed greater concern for their precious laborers. By the war's end labor in New York and in the nation had reached new heights.[1]

Ironically, however, the very forces which benefited organized labor in wartime America served in the following decade to weaken working-class organizations and to turn union brother against brother. American participation in international conflict brought in its wake the Hobbesian

Leviathan. Federal officials, local politicians, and private citizens joined hands to erase dissent and diversity. Criminal syndicalism laws, sedition acts, and other repressive measures were added to the statute books. Xenophobia and superpatriotism became the "American Way." And in all this the AFL cooperated gladly, bending every effort to win the war and to achieve social respectability.[2] The war was won. For organized labor, however, victory did not bring security and status.

The xenophobia of 1917–1919, which ostracized Wobblies and pacifists while intimidating German-Americans, turned upon organized labor in the early 1920's. A series of postwar strikes, beginning in 1919, engendered by runaway inflation ushered in the "Red Scare" and swayed the American community against organized labor. The propaganda and public relations techniques developed and perfected during the war to rewrite history and intensify hatred of Imperial Germany were utilized in peacetime America by employers to discredit striking workers and to link organized labor with treason and Bolshevism.

Throughout the 1920's, as desperately as the AFL tried to be "American," it never succeeded. Overtures to and a working alliance with the American Legion, virulent opposition to Soviet Russia and Bolshevism, the wooing of employers to join with labor in establishing a corporate society, all failed to win converts and respect for the AFL. Almost overnight, the Federation's war-induced, hothouse growth in membership vanished. By the decade's end, organized labor had fewer members than in 1919. With Republican political supremacy, the federal government and its courts added to labor's woes. The AFL, constantly on the defensive against management, government, and popular suspicions, could do little to extend organization into the unorganized sectors of New York's or the nation's economy.[3]

The Bolshevik Revolution, on the other hand, undermined the stability and strength of the needle trades' unions. Communist triumph in Russia divided the garment workers among themselves. Whereas prior to Lenin's rise to power a majority of Socialist workers in the garment industry dominated a smaller business unionist minority, after Soviet success the Socialists split into quarrelsome and self-destructive factions. Communists challenged democratic Socialists for trade-union supremacy. Dual unions flourished. Old friends became bitter ideological enemies. A new Communist elite and an old-guard Socialist leadership competed for the loyalty of the rank and file. And employers utilized working-class dissension to their own advantage, playing one trade-union faction against the other. With organized labor on the defensive everywhere during the "New Era," the needle trades' unions, divided internally, followed other labor organizations into decline and desuetude.[4]

The bright promise of a new and better world for the working class to be won through organized labor's initiative, a promise which had beckoned during the Progressive and war years, dimmed during the 1920's. By contrast with that waning light, the luster of "enlightened" capitalism grew even stronger. In the prosperity decade Americans came to a temporary accord with the industrial order; workers, won by relatively high wages, steady employment, and welfare capitalism, conceded to management primary control of industrial decisions. The war between industrial efficiency and industrial justice abated; the organizational impulse died; the 1920's were the age of Frederick Winslow Taylor, Theodore Shonts, and Frank Hedley rather than Julius Cohen. Only the collapse of prosperity and the failure of business to insure security renewed the open war between labor and capital.

Collective bargaining patterns developed before the First World War in the garment trades, however, persisted into the 1920's and 1930's, though greatly altered. Industrial stability remained the essential aim of labor-management negotiations. Worker organization and employer cooperation in an atomized, cutthroat, inherently unstable trade still held the key to both industrial efficiency and industrial justice. With the trade-unionists divided among themselves in the 1920's industrial stability even with full employer cooperation, which was not forthcoming, was unlikely. But employers and employees continued to recognize the vital interest and role of the community in labor disputes. In 1924 Governor Al Smith appointed a state committee to investigate the needle trades with a view to eliminating the severe competition which debased business and job security, wages, and working conditions. Arbitrators and mediators continued their efforts to preserve industrial peace and the community's well-being, while serving the seemingly exclusive goals of industrial efficiency and industrial justice. Later, in the depressed thirties, employers and unions again joined forces under Federal aegis to combat the spreading sweatshops. When New Deal labor legislation sanctioned collective bargaining which restricted competition, the organizational impulse again struck the garment industry and trade-unions grew and prospered. Labor organizations allied with larger employers to weed nonunion shops and workers out of the garment trades in order to realize Julius Henry Cohen's utopia of "law and order in industry."[5]

The same Federal labor legislation and New Deal attitudes which made possible revived union growth and collective bargaining in the needle trades presented employees of New York's large-scale, substantially capitalized enterprises with the opportunity to organize independent trade-unions. The New Deal brought statute law into accord with socio-economic reality, as public officials perceived that weak trade-unions could not compete equally with concentrated capital for the loyalty of the individual worker.

The very men and women who were introduced to social reform and the labor movement during the industrial conflicts which shook New York City during the Progressive years rose to positions of power within the nation, state, and city during the era of Franklin Roosevelt. New Deal United States Senator Robert F. Wagner, Sr., who in the early 1900's served as state senator from Manhattan's Yorkville district, co-directed the State Factory Investigating Commission (1911–1915), and sponsored most of the outstanding welfare and labor legislation in the state senate, in 1935 brought to fruition, through passage of the Wagner Act, Julius Henry Cohen's dream of "law and order in industry." Government, by adopting Wagner's legislative proposals, recognized that workers not only had the right to organize independent trade-unions without interference by management, but that management must also recognize such unions and bargain with them in good faith. Frances Perkins, ally of the striking immigrant garment workers of 1910–1916 and staff member of the State Factory Investigating Commission, as Roosevelt's Secretary of Labor utilized her New York experiences in pressing for the creation of an effective, public-spirited national labor movement. Harry Hopkins, veteran of lower east side social settlements and garment workers' labor wars, became a molder of national welfare policies and legislation. As Governor of New York State, Herbert Lehman brought to the Executive Mansion many graduates of the New York City school of reform to shape a progressive state labor policy. And Fiorello H. La Guardia, hero of the Italian immigrant working class and friend of the Jewish garment workers for aiding both ethnic groups in their struggle against the conservative officials of the UGWA (1913–1914), dominated the metropolitan scene after his election as Mayor in 1933. Moreover, labor leaders, who were just young men on the rise in the Progressive era, became dominant local and national figures during the New Deal. David

Dubinsky, elected to the ILGWU presidency in 1932, helped complete the process whereby Jewish Socialist garment workers became New Deal Democrats. And Sidney Hillman, who deserted Chicago for New York's lusher pastures in 1914, collaborated with Dubinsky and other local Jewish labor leaders in creating the American Labor Party as a halfway house between the Socialist Party and the regular Democratic organization. Hillman also achieved prominence as an adviser to Franklin Roosevelt and as the legendary "clear it with Sidney" behind-the-scenes manipulator at the 1944 Democratic national convention.

Thus, during the 1930's when transit workers, teamsters, and hotel and restaurant workers sought labor organization through the mass strike, they were more fortunate. This time with the backing of municipal, state, and federal officials the organizational impulse succeeded. During the depression decade, teamsters, waiters, cooks, and carmen achieved the lasting labor organization which had eluded them in the prosperous prewar years.[6]

History played its customary tricks upon the workers of New York City and the nation. The issues, tactics, and ideologies developed and utilized by labor to achieve betterment in prosperous, Progressive America fell into relative disuse in the even more prosperous twenties, only to come to life with new vigor in the troubled thirties. The organizational impulse, rather than dying during the prosperity decade, simply lay dormant until conditions changed to favor it. When depression and impending catastrophe undermined American faith in a business civilization, public attitudes, political leaders, and legislative enactments provided the working class with the benevolent environment in which to seek and to win industrial justice.

**Notes
Bibliography
Index**

Notes

Chapter 1

1. Samuel Gompers, *Seventy Years of Life and Labor* (New York, 1925), I, 61–62.

2. Robert Ernst, *Immigrant Life in New York City, 1825–1863* (New York, 1949), 112. Moses Rischin, *The Promised City: New York's Jews, 1870–1914* (Cambridge, Massachusetts, 1962), 171–194; Selig Perlman, "Jewish Unionism and American Labor," *Publications of the American Jewish Historical Society,* XLI (September 1951–June 1952), 297–337; Will Herberg, "The Jewish Labor Movement in the United States," *American Jewish Year Book,* LXXX (1952), 3–74.

3. Jacob Loft, *The Printing Trades* (New York, 1944), 286; Max Hall, ed., *Made in New York: Case Studies in Metropolitan Manufacturing* (Cambridge, Massachusetts, 1959), 209; Robert E. L. Knight, *Industrial Relations in the San Francisco Bay Area, 1900–1918* (Berkeley, California, 1960), 1, 375–377; Barbara W. Newell, *Chicago and the Labor Movement: Metropolitan Unionism in the 1930's* (Urbana, 1961), passim.

4. Chapters 6 and 7 describe labor's repeated threats during teamster and transit workers' strikes to employ sympathetic strikes and the general strike but its refusal to practice what it threatened.

5. See Chapter 7.

6. Philip S. Foner, *History of the Labor Movement in the United States,* Volume III: "The Policies and Practices of the American Federation of Labor, 1900–1909" (New York, 1964), Ch. 6, especially 150–153; Joseph Rayback, *A History of American Labor* (New York, 1959), 221–222; Thomas R. Brooks, *Toil and Trouble: A History of American Labor* (New York, 1964), 111.

7. Letters: Samuel Prince to Samuel Gompers, August 27, 1908, Files of the Office of the President, American Federation of Labor Papers, Wisconsin State Historical Society, (Madison, Wisconsin); D. J. Conroy to Gompers, October 24, 1908, ibid.; Elias Kaufman to Gompers, December 3, 1909, ibid.; Joseph Dehan to Gompers, December 30, 1912, ibid.; Martin Glynn to Gompers, November 12, 1912, ibid.; Bernard Sheintag to Gompers, October 8, 1917, ibid. Throughout the Progressive period Herman Robinson, AFL organizer for the New York City region and a City Commissioner of Licenses, reported regularly to Gompers on political affairs in the metropolis, ibid.

8. New York State Department of Labor, *Special Bulletin Number 66,* 1, 10; see Chapters 3–7.

9. In 1910 alone the increase in union membership totaled almost 100,000, and in 1913 it exceeded 100,000. In these two years the percentage increase in trade-union membership state-wide was 29.3 percent and 26.3 percent respectively. New York State Department of Labor, *Special Bulletin Number 46,* 27, and *Special Bulletin Number 60,* 1–2, 4–6; Leo Wolman, *The Growth of American Trade Unions, 1880–1923* (New York, 1924), 34–35, 50–52, 85–86, 106–108.

10. New York State Department of Labor, *Special Bulletin Number 60,* 4–6, 15; see also the Convention Proceedings and Reports of the International Ladies' Garment Workers' Union, the United Garment Workers of America, and the United Cloth Hat and Cap Makers' Union for the years 1909–1916.

11. In the first nine years of the Women's Trade Union League's existence the number of women in recognized trade-unions increased from 8,000 to 51,000. Between 1911 and 1913 membership in women's trade-unions in New York City doubled. New York Women's Trade Union League, *Annual Report, 1912–1913* (New York, 1913), 12; Mary Van Kleeck, *Women in the Bookbinding Trade* (New York, 1913), 175.

12. Quoted in Robert W. Iversen, "Morris Hillquit: American Social

Democrat" (Unpublished Doctoral Dissertation, State University of Iowa, 1951), 91.

13. United States Bureau of the Census, *Abstract of the Census with Supplement for New York for 1910* (Washington, 1913), 569–571; idem, *Report on Manufactures for 1919* (Washington, 1923), 22–223; Benjamin M. Selekman, "The Clothing and Textile Industries in New York and its Environs," *Regional Plan of New York and its Environs, Economic Series* [Monographs 7–9] (New York, 1925), 17.

14. United States Bureau of the Census, *Thirteenth Census of the United States Taken in the Year, 1910* [Abstract of the Census] (Washington, 1913), 448–449; idem, *Abstract for New York, 1910*, 702–703; idem, *Abstract of the Fourteenth Census* (Washington, 1923), 921; idem; *Report on Manufactures, 1919*, 22–223. See the series of monographs in *Regional Plan of New York and its Environs*, especially, A. F. Hinrichs, "The Printing Industry in New York and its Environs" (New York, 1924), 13–15; Vincent W. Lanfear, "The Metal Industry in New York and its Environs" (New York, 1924), 16–17; and Robert M. Haig and Roswell C. McCrea, "Major Economic Factors in Metropolitan Growth and Arrangement: A Study of Trends in the Economic Activities within the Region of New York and its Environs" (New York, 1928), passim.

15. Martin Segal, *Wages in the Metropolis: Their Influence on the Location of Industries in the Region* (Cambridge, Massachusetts, 1960), 14–16.

16. See the eight monographs in the series, *Regional Plan of New York*, especially Haig and McCrea, "Major Economic Factors"; Edgar M. Hoover and Raymond Vernon, *Anatomy of a Metropolis: The Changing Distribution of Jobs and People within the New York Metropolitan Region* (Cambridge, Massachusetts, 1959), 62–63, 65–67.

17. United States Immigration Commission, *Report on Immigrants in Manufacturing and Mining* (Washington, 1911), 384; see also the following monographs in the *Regional Plan Series*, A. F. Hinrichs, "Printing," 47; V. W. Lanfear, "Metals," 16–17; Mark C. Mills, "The Wood Industries in New York and Its Environs" (1924) 21; B. Selekman, "Clothing and Textiles," 34, 54, 81; Faith M. Williams, "The Food Manufacturing Industries in New York and Its Environs" (1924) 27.

18. United States Bureau of the Census, *Abstract for New York, 1910*, 702–703; idem, *Thirteenth Abstract*, 448–449; idem; *Fourteenth Abstract*, 921; Leo Wolman, "Labor in New York," in Alexander C.

Flick, ed., *History of the State of New York* (New York, 1937), X, 68.

19. United States Immigration Commission, *Report on Immigrants in Manufacturing,* 371, 375; Lucy W. Kellough, "The Tobacco Products Industry in New York and its Environs," *Regional Plan* (1924), 26–27; Charles B. Barnes, *The Longshoremen* (New York, 1915), 5–12; R. Ernst, *Immigrant Life,* 37–47, 122–161.

20. Robert F. Foerster, *The Italian Emigration of Our Times* (Cambridge, Massachusetts, 1919), 343, 356–357; United States Immigration Commission, *Immigrants in Manufacturing,* 371–375; Rudolph J. Vecoli, "*Contadini* in Chicago: A Critique of *The Uprooted,*" *Journal of American History,* LI (December, 1964), 404–417.

21. Liebmann Hersch, "International Migration of Jews," in Imre Ferencezi and Walter F. Willcox, eds., *International Migrations* (New York, 1931), II, 487–494, 503; I. M. Rubinow, "Economic Condition of the Jews in Russia," United States Bureau of Labor, *Bulletin Whole Number* 72 (September, 1907), 504–506, 522, 525; M. Rischin, *Promised City,* Ch. 4.

22. Harry A. Millis and Royal E. Montgomery, *Labor's Progress and Some Basic Labor Problems* (New York, 1938), 239.

23. Hyman Berman, "Era of the Protocol: A Chapter in the History of the ILGWU, 1910–1916" (Unpublished Doctoral Dissertation, Columbia University, 1955), 68–69; Samuel Waitzman, "The New York City Transit Strike of 1916" (Unpublished Master's Thesis, Columbia University, 1952), 29–30; Jesse E. Pope, "The Clothing Industry in New York," *University of Missouri Series in the Social Sciences,* I (Columbia, Missouri, 1905), 142.

24. Mary Van Kleeck, "Working Hours of Women in Factories," *Charities and the Commons,* XVII (October 6, 1906), 13–16. She discovered girls at work in the binding industry who labored 13 hours a day, 78 hours a week, and were discharged if they refused overtime.

25. New York State Factory Investigating Commission, *Preliminary Report* (Albany, 1912), I, 223; idem, *Third Report* (Albany, 1914), 86–88, 128–129; Louise C. Odencrantz, *Italian Women in Industry: A Study of Conditions in New York City* (New York, 1919), 90–92.

26. New York State Factory Investigating Commission, *Preliminary Report,* I, 72, 131–132, 314; II, 25.

27. Ibid., II, 33, 623; New York *Call,* March 25, 1911, 1; Ray Stannard Baker, "The Rise of the Tailors," *McClure's Magazine,* XXIV (December, 1904), 128.

28. State Licenses were easily obtainable and because the state lacked a sufficient force of inspectors, even the licensed houses went largely unsupervised. New York State Factory Investigating Commission, *Preliminary Report*, I, 86, 576; *Second Report*, II, 693; Elizabeth C. Watson, "Home Work in the Tenements," *The Survey*, XXV (February 4, 1911), 772; Mary Van Kleeck, *Artificial Flower Makers* (New York, 1913), 90, 136. Homeworkers in the flower industry outnumbered factory hands and by competing for work kept wage scales at a low level.

29. New York State Factory Investigating Commission, *Preliminary Report*, I, 91, 577–578, 582; *Second Report*, II, 698–699; IV, 1553, 1606–1608.

30. Ibid., II, 70; IV, 1555, 1609–1610; E. C. Watson, "Home Work," 778.

31. New York State Factory Investigating Commission, *Preliminary Report*, I, 91; *Second Report*, I, 98–99; IV, 1512.

32. Paul H. Douglas, *Real Wages in the United States, 1890–1926* (Boston, 1930), 41, 57–58, 582; Clarence D. Long, *Wages and Earnings in the United States, 1860–1890* (Princeton, 1961), 109–110; Albert Rees, *Real Wages in Manufacturing, 1890–1914* (Princeton, 1961), 4–5, 126.

33. New York State Factory Investigating Commission, *Fourth Report* (Albany, 1915), I, 1608–1609, 1619–1621; IV, 1668–1671; Robert C. Chapin, *The Standard of Living among Workingmen's Families in New York City* (New York, 1909), 234.

34. United States Immigration Commission, *Report on Immigrants in Manufacturing*, 376–382; idem, *Report on Immigrants in the Cities* (Washington, 1911), 44–46; United States Senate, 61st Congress: Second Session, *Senate Document Number 338*, "Reports of the Immigration Commission: Immigrants in the Cities" (Washington, 1911), 227–228, 233.

35. New York State Factory Investigating Commission, *Third Report*, 40–41; *Fourth Report*, I, 34–38; II, 193, 404; III, 1049, 1073, 1081; New York State Department of Labor, *Special Bulletin Number 92*, 6; C. B. Barnes, *Longshoremen*, 92; H. Berman, "Era of the Protocol," 68–69; M. E. Ravage, *An American in the Making: The Life Story of an Immigrant* (New York, 1917), 91–92; Mary Van Kleeck, *A Seasonal Industry: A Study of the Millinery Trade in New York City* (New York, 1917), 171; idem, *Women in Bookbinding* (New York, 1913), 85–86.

36. New York State Factory Investigating Commission, *Fourth Report*, V, 2810; L. Odencrantz, *Italian Women*, 151–152; M. Van Kleeck, *Artificial Flower Makers*, 60–62.

37. Percentage of Idleness in Representative Unions—New York City:

Year	End of June	End of December
1904	16.9	17.8
1905	11.1	6.7
1906	6.8	12.8
1907	10.0	34.2
1908	33.3	27.7
1909	19.0	18.0
1910	19.4	29.6
1911	25.2	36.7
1912	27.3	35.7
1913	26.5	46.4

The above Table is based upon figures in New York State Department of Labor, *Special Bulletin Number 58*, 5, 11, 20–21, and *Special Bulletin Number 85*, 50. Also see "Arbitration Proceedings: The Cloak and Suit Makers' Unions of New York and the Cloak, Suit and Skirt Manufacturers' Protective Association" [August 3–6, 1913] (Stenographic Copy, Tamiment Institute Library, New York), I, 117–118; L. Odencrantz, *Italian Women*, 116. Some of the high unemployment figures reported above resulted from large scale strikes but the figures do indicate unusual conditions of job insecurity.

38. Louis M. Rabinowitz, "Reminiscences," Number 248, 11, (Oral History Project, Columbia University); J. Loft, *Printing Trades*, 289; Roy Lubove, *The Progressives and the Slums* (Pittsburgh, 1962), passim.

39. Bayrd Still, *Mirror for Gotham: New York as Seen by Contemporaries from Dutch Days to the Present* (New York, 1956), 214; R. Ernst, *Immigrant Life*, 46–47; Oscar Handlin, *The Newcomers: Negroes and Puerto Ricans in a Changing Metropolis* (Cambridge, Massachusetts, 1959), Ch. 1; Niles Carpenter, "Immigrants and their Children," in United States Bureau of the Census, *Census Monograph VII* (Washington, 1927), 29; M. E. Ravage, *American in the Making*, 50. Ravage recalls how he viewed New York City from his Rumanian birthplace. "Everyone who went there became a millionaire overnight, and a doctor or a teacher into the bargain. There, in America, was my future."

40. United States Bureau of the Census, *Thirteenth Abstract and Supplement for New York,* 635–640; idem, *Fourteenth Abstract and Supplement for New York,* 710–715; *Report of the Enumeration of the Inhabitants of the State of New York, June 1, 1905* (Albany, 1906), 215–406, 472–629, 659–661; *Report of the Enumeration of Inhabitants of the State of New York, January 17, 1916* (Albany, 1916), 329–1114.

41. N. Carpenter, "Immigrants and Children," 137, 385; Walter Laidlaw, *The Population of New York City* (New York, 1932), 245; New York *Times,* July 6, 1962, 27.

42. Rose Cohen, *Out of the Shadow* (New York, 1918), 240–241.

43. Ibid.; M. Rischin, *Promised City,* Chs. 4–6; R. F. Foerster, *Italian Emigration,* 90–96; Works Progress Administration, Federal Writers' Project, *The Italians of New York* (New York, 1938), passim.

44. Robert E. Park and Herbert A. Miller, *Old World Traits Transplanted* (New York, 1921), 38–39, 234–236; O. Handlin, *Newcomers,* 39–40; R. Ernst, *Immigrant Life,* 37–47, 122–161, passim; M. Rischin, *Promised City,* 115–194.

45. N. Carpenter, "Immigrants and Children," 271.

46. L. Hirsch, "Jewish Migration," 474, 478, 519; Henry Chalmers, "The Number of Jews in New York City," *Publications of the American Statistical Association,* XIV (1914–1915), 68–75; M. Rischin, *Promised City,* 20, 33.

47. I. M. Rubinow, "Economic Condition of the Jews," 494–497; L. Hirsch, "Jewish Migration," 500–501, 505; N. Carpenter, *Immigrants and Children,* 287; J. C. Rich, "60 Years of the *Forward,*" *The New Leader* [Special Supplement] (June 3, 1957), 7, 31; *Documentary History of the ACWA, 1914–1916,* vi; Ray Stannard Baker, "Rise of the Tailors," 128; Sylvia Kopold and Ben Selekman, "The Epic of the Needle Trades," *The Menorah Journal,* XV (October, 1928), 293; M. Rischin, *Promised City,* 51–71.

48. I. M. Rubinow, "Economic Condition of the Jews," 548–551; Koppel Pinson, "Arkady Kremer, Vladimir Menen, and the Ideology of the Jewish 'Bund,'" *Jewish Social Studies,* VII (July, 1945), 236–237.

49. Harry S. Linfield, *The Communal Organization of the Jews in the United States, 1927* (New York, 1930), 129; Abraham Menes, "The East Side: Matrix of the Jewish Labor Movement," in Theodore Friedman and Robert Gordis, eds., *Jewish Life in America* (New York, 1955), 131–154; M. Rischin, *Promised City,* 171–194.

50. A. M. Ratti, "Italian Migration," 446–448; R. F. Foerster, *Italian*

Emigration, 94–96; John H. Mariano, *The Italian Contribution to American Democracy* (Boston, 1921), 65.

51. R. Vecoli, *"Contadini,"* 404–417.

52. Quoted in Park and Miller, *Old World Traits,* 238–239.

53. R. F. Foerster, *Italian Emigration,* 402–404, 422–426; United States Immigration Commission, *Abstract: Report on Immigrants in Manufacturing and Mining,* 143; Edwin Fenton, "Italian Immigrants in the Stoneworkers' Union," *Labor History,* III (Spring, 1962), 188–207.

54. "Arbitration Proceedings, The Cloak and Skirt Makers' Unions of New York; The Cloak and Skirt Makers' Protective Association," [August 3–6, 1913], I, 513–514; M. Rischin, *Promised City,* 91, 95–111.

55. Quoted in Bruno Lasker, Reminiscences No. 232, (Oral History Project, Columbia University), I, 173; Charles H. Towne, *This New York of Mine* (New York, 1931), II.

56. William Mailly, "The New York Rent Strike," *The Independent,* LXIV (January 16, 1908), 149; Robert L. Duffus, *Lillian Wald,* (New York, 1938), 27; E. E. Pratt, *Industrial Causes of Congestion of Population in New York City* (New York, 1911), 31–32, 35.

57. R. Lubove, *Progressives and Slums,* 1–48, 81–184, passim; M. Rischin, *Promised City,* 76–86; cf. James Ford, *Slums and Housing* (Cambridge, Massachusetts, 1946); Edith E. Wood, *The Housing of the Unskilled Wage Earner* (New York, 1919).

58. Charles E. Russell, *Bare Hands and Stone Walls* (New York, 1933), 80–81.

59. E. E. Pratt, *Industrial Causes,* 15, 28, 31–32; W. Laidlaw, *Population of New York,* 243; United States Immigration Commission, *Abstract: Report on Immigrants in the Cities,* 8–11.

60. M. E. Ravage, *American in the Making,* 66–67.

61. E. Hasanovitz, *One of Them* (Boston, 1918), 310; M. E. Ravage, *American in the Making,* 50, 66–67; L. Rabinowitz, Reminiscences No. 243.

62. John Collier and Edward M. Barrows, *The City Where Crime Is Play* (New York, 1914), 2–3; Richard J. Butler and Joseph Driscoll, *Dock Walloper: The Story of "Big Dick" Butler* (New York, 1933), 31; Elena Nichols, "The Effects of Italian Immigration on New York City," (Unpublished Master's Thesis, Columbia University, 1929), 2; O. Handlin, *Newcomers,* 38–39.

63. *University Settlement Studies,* II (July, 1906), 36–37; Frederick Shaw, *The History of the New York City Legislature* (New York, 1954), 101.

64. Gustavus Myers, *The History of Tammany Hall* (New York, 1917), 128–129; M. R. Werner, *Tammany Hall* (New York, 1928), 62–64; cf. Lee Benson, *The Concept of Jacksonian Democracy: New York as a Test Case* (Princeton, 1961), 165–207, for the origins of the Irish-Tammany alliance.

65. Collier and Barrows, *City Where Crime Is Play*, 2–3; Amos Pinchot, *A Letter to the County Chairmen and Other Chairmen* (New York, n.d.), 15.

66. *University Settlement Studies*, II, 36–37; Personal interviews with Rose Schneiderman (November 24, 1958), Pauline Newman, (December 10, 1958), Joseph Schlossberg, (November 20, 1958), and Louis Waldman (November 25, 1958) confirmed the J. B. Reynolds observations and conclusions.

67. Henry Bruere, Reminiscences No. 7, (Oral History Project, Columbia University), I, 14; Louis H. Pink, Reminiscences, ibid., I, 10; M. Rischin, *Promised City*, 205–208.

68. New York *Times*, February 11, 1900, 4; January 11, 1908, 8; March 30, 1908, 2; *University Settlement Studies*, II, 38; *The Survey*, XXVI (February 17, 1912), 1754; XXVII (April 8, 1913), 95; New York City Consumers' League to Women's Committee of the Socialist Party, November 9, 1912, Letter Books, Socialist Party: Local New York, (Tamiment Institute Library, New York); J. William Gillette, "Welfare State Trail Blazer: New York State Factory Investigating Commission, 1911–1915," (Unpublished Master's Thesis, Columbia University, 1956); Elizabeth F. Baker, *Protective Labor Legislation with Special Reference to Women in the State of New York* (New York, 1925), 170; R. L. Duffus, *Wald*, 76, 107; Fred R. Fairchild, *The Factory Legislation of the State of New York* (New York, 1906), 30–31, 85–88; Josephine Goldmark, *Impatient Crusader: Florence Kelley's Life Story* (Urbana, 1953), 81; Maud Nathan, *The Story of an Epoch-Making Movement* (New York, 1926), 78; Charles Stelzle, *A Son of the Bowery* (New York, 1926), 117; Louis Waldman, *Labor Lawyer* (New York, 1944), 34.

69. Letter, Mrs. Edith B. Barnum to the author, February 11, 1961; New York City Women's Trade Union League Papers, New York State Department of Labor Library, New York; Gladys Boone, *The Women's Trade Union Leagues in Great Britain and the United States of America* (New York, 1942).

70. Mary K. Simkhovitch, *Neighborhood: My Story of Greenwich*

House (New York, 1938), 161–162; Irwin H. Yellowitz, "Labor and the Progressive Movement in New York State, 1897–1916" (Unpublished Doctoral Dissertation, Brown University, June, 1961), 144–163.

71. See Chapters 3–7. Revealing memos by Robert Bruere, adviser to Mayor John Purroy Mitchel, can be found in the Mitchel Papers, Municipal Archives, New York City.

72. William R. Stewart, *The Philanthropic Work of Josephine Shaw Lowell* (New York, 1911), 371, 376; J. Riis, *How the Other Half Lives* (New York, 1900), 273; *The Survey*, XXII (April 10, 1909), 82.

73. *University Settlement Studies*, I (July, 1905), 68, 70, 73; C. B. Barnes, *Longshoremen*, 12; Charles S. Bernheimer, *The Russian Jew in the United States* (Philadelphia, 1905), 112; W. R. Stewart, *J. S. Lowell*, 412–413.

74. J. B. Reynolds' observations in *University Settlement Studies*, I (July, 1905), 60; Burton J. Hendrick, "Twilight of Tammany," 483; M. Rischin, *Promised City*, 189–201.

75. Quoted in Louis H. Pink, *Gaynor* (New York, 1931), 251; Julia S. Brown, "Factors Affecting Union Strength: A Case Study of the International Ladies' Garment Workers' Union, 1900–1940" (Unpublished Doctoral Dissertation, Yale University, 1942), 125–126; personal interviews with Rose Schneiderman, Pauline Newman, and Joseph Schlossberg.

Chapter 2

1. Ray Stannard Baker, "Parker and Theodore Roosevelt on Labor," *McClure's Magazine*, XXIV (November, 1904), 41; Richard Hofstadter, *The Age of Reform* (New York, 1955), 239–242.

2. See Chapters 4–7.

3. George K. Turner, "What Organized Labor Wants," *McClure's Magazine*, XXXII (November, 1908), 31; *Final Report and Testimony Submitted to Congress by the Commission on Industrial Relations* (Washington, 1916), II, 1526–1529, for the interchange on labor philosophy between Samuel Gompers and Morris Hillquit; cf. George W. Brooks, et al., *Interpreting the Labor Movement* (Champaign, 1952), passim; Marc Karson, *American Labor Unions and Politics, 1900–1918* (Carbondale, 1959), Ch. 1; H. Millis and R. Montgomery, *Labor's*

Progress and Some Problems (New York, 1938), passim; Selig Perlman, *A Theory of the Labor Movement* (New York, 1949), passim; Frank Tannenbaum, *A Philosophy of Labor* (New York, 1951), passim.

4. Quoted in Karson, *American Labor Unions,* 118–119; cf. Perlman, *Labor Theory,* passim.

5. Most of the material in this chapter is drawn from the publications and convention proceedings of the needle trades unions.

6. For Dyche's philosophy and essentially conservative approach see, *Final Report and Testimony, Commission on Industrial Relations,* X, 1038–1047, and John A. Dyche, *Bolshevism in American Labor Unions* (New York, 1926); Short biographical sketches of Thomas Rickert, William D. Mahon, James M. Lynch, Timothy Healy, and Ernest Bohm, conservative, American-born trade-unionists are contained in Solon De Leon, ed., *The American Labor Who's Who* (New York, 1925), 22, 101, 142, 144, 196.

7. *The Weekly Bulletin of the Garment Trades,* II (April 1, 1903), 4; (July 15, 1903), 4.

8. Ibid., III (January 13, 1904), 4.

9. *The Ladies' Garment Worker,* II (March 1, 1911), 4.

10. Ibid., (May 1, 1911), 5; III (October, 1911), 13; V (January, 1914), 11; (June, 1914), 9.

11. ILGWU, *Report and Proceedings of the 12th Convention* (June 1–13, 1914), 65, 79; *Weekly Bulletin,* II (October 7, 1903), 4.

12. New York *Call,* May 30, 1908, 4; ILGWU, *Proceedings, 12th Convention,* 65.

13. Short biographical sketches of Abraham Baroff, August and Frank Bellanca, Luigi Antonini, Pauline Newman, Benjamin Schlesinger, Joseph Schlossberg, Rose Schneiderman, and Morris Sigman, Jewish and Italian immigrant needle trades union leaders and Socialists, can be found in De Leon, *Labor Who's Who,* 7, 11, 14, 172, 205–207, 213.

14. See M. Dubofsky's forthcoming article "Success and Failure of Socialism in New York City, 1900–1918: A Case Study," to appear in *Labor History.*

15. Daniel Bell, "Marxian Socialism in the United States," in Donald D. Egbert and Stow Persons, eds., *Socialism and American Life* (Princeton, 1952), I, 217.

16. ILGWU, *Proceedings, 13th Convention* (Oct., 1916), 112–113.

17. M. Hillquit, "Socialism Up-to-Date," *Metropolitan Magazine,* XXXVI (Sept., 1912), 13–59.

18. Annie Skolnick to Socialist Party Central Committee, September 5, 1911, Socialist Party Papers (Tamiment Institute Library).

19. *Weekly Bulletin,* VII (June 12, 1908), 4.

20. Ibid. (March 6, 1908), 4; ILGWU, *Proceedings, 12th Convention,* 136; United Cloth Hat and Cap Makers' Union, *Proceedings, 9th Convention,* (May 1–9, 1913), 12; Interview with J. Schlossberg, November 20, 1958.

21. "Proceedings, 3rd Convention, (May 13–18, 1918)," in *Documentary History of the Amalgamated Clothing Workers of America, 1916–1918,* 16; ILGWU, *Proceedings, 14th Convention* (May 20–June 1, 1918), 290; *The Cap Makers' Journal,* III (June, 1905), 30.

22. *Advance,* I (August 31, 1917 , 4; *Ladies' Garment Worker,* VI (May, 1915), 7; Joseph Schlossberg to Algernon Lee, November 10, 1917, Algernon Lee Papers (Tamiment Institute Library).

23. *Ladies' Garment Worker,* VII (June, 1916) 2–3; for a concise account of the appeal of militant trade-unionism and socialism to the Jewish immigrant laborer see, Moses Rischin, *The Promised City: New York's Jews, 1870–1914* (Cambridge, Mass., 1962), 148–168, 193–194.

24. These topics are treated more thoroughly in Melvyn Dubofsky, "Organized Labor and the Immigrant in New York City, 1900–1918," *Labor History,* II (Spring, 1961), 182–201; "Organized Labor in New York City and the First World War, 1914–1918," *New York History,* XLII (October, 1961), 380–400.

25. John Frey, "Reminiscences No. 225" (Oral History Project, Columbia University); J. C. Rich, "60 Years of the *Jewish Daily Forward,"* 29; *The Weekly Bulletin,* VII (March 13, 1908), 4; XI (January 5, 1912), 4; United Cloth Hat and Cap Makers' Union, *Proceedings, 11th Convention* (May 1, 1917), 5; ILGWU, *Proceedings, 14th Convention,* 140.

26. J. Schlossberg to A. Lee, November 10, 1917, Lee Papers; *Ladies' Garment Worker,* IV (April, 1913), 3; New York *Call,* September 6, 1910, 1; United Cloth Hat and Cap Makers' Union, *Proceedings, 11th Convention,* 59.

27. *Weekly Bulletin,* XI (January 19, 1912), 4; Alice Henry, "The Way Out," *Life and Labor,* II (April, 1912), 121; Florence Peterson, "Causes of Industrial Unrest," *Annals of the American Academy of Political and Social Science,* CCLXXIV (March, 1951), 29; F. Tannenbaum, *Philosophy of Labor,* 66–67.

28. Sonya Levien, "The Little Prophet," *Metropolitan Magazine,*

XXXVII (March, 1913), 45; *Weekly Bulletin,* III (May 20, 1904), 4.

29. I (November 21, 1916), 1.

30. R. Cohen, *Out of the Shadow,* 74; anon., *Life and Labor,* II (April, 1912), 99.

31. *Ladies' Garment Worker,* V (December, 1914), 3; *Weekly Bulletin,* I (July 23, 1902), 2.

32. New York *Times,* April 3, 1911, 3.

Chapter 3

1. Julius Henry Cohen, "The Revised Protocol in the Dress and Waist Industry," *Annals of the American Academy of Political and Social Science,* LXIX (January, 1917), 183–196; idem., *A League to Enforce Industrial Peace* (New York, 1916), 35–36; idem., *They Builded Better Than They Knew* (New York, 1946), passim.; see article "Julius Henry Cohen" in *Who Was Who in America* (Chicago, 1960), 170.

2. Charles S. Bernheimer, *The Russian Jew in the United States* (Phila., 1905), Ch. 1; Isaac A, Hourwich, *Immigration and Labor* (New York, 1912), passim; Lewis B. Lorwin, *The Women's Garment Workers: A History of the International Ladies' Garment Workers Union* (New York, 1924), Chs. 1–4; James O'Neal, *A History of the Amalgamated Ladies' Garment Cutters' Union, Local 10* (New York, 1927), Ch. 1; Benjamin Stolberg, *Tailor's Progress* (New York, 1944), Ch. 1; Jesse Pope, "The Clothing Industry in New York," Ch. 1; Lazare Teper, *The Women's Garment Industry* (New York, 1937), passim. One estimate made in 1912 calculated that approximately 85 percent of the employees in the garment trades were Jewish, and most of the remaining 15 percent were Italian. Memo in the Paul Abelson Papers (Ithaca, New York State School of Industrial and Labor Relations Library).

3. H. Berman, "Era of the Protocol: A Chapter in the History of the ILGWU, 1910–1916" (Unpublished Doctoral Dissertation, Columbia University, 1955), Ch. 1; Moses Rischin, *The Promised City: New York's Jews, 1870–1914* (Cambridge, Mass., 1962), 64–65.

4. L. Teper, *Women's Garment Industry,* Ch. 1; M. Rischin, *Promised City,* 61–68; J. Seidman, *The Needle Trades* (New York, 1942), Ch. 1.

5. See Julius Henry Cohen's writings dealing with the problem: "The Revised Protocol"; *League to Enforce Industrial Peace;* and *Law and*

Order in Industry (New York, 1916). I am also indebted to Professor Jesse T. Carpenter, New York State School of Industrial and Labor Relations, for the insights I gleaned from his unpublished manuscript, "Competition and Collective Bargaining in the Needle Trades."

6. See pp. 59–60, 74–75, and 95–96.

7. Jacog Riis, *How the Other Half Lives* (New York, 1900), 124; Interview with J. Schlossberg, November 20, 1958; *Documentary History of the ACWA, 1914–1916,* vi; Ray S. Baker, "Rise of the Tailors," 128; S. Kopold and B. Selekman, "Epic of the Needle Trades," *The Memorial Journal,* XV (Oct., 1928), 299; E. Hasanovitz, *One of Them* (Boston, 1918), 172–173; J. C. Rich, "Sixty Years of the *Forward,*" 7.

8. Interviews with P. Newman, December 10, 1958, R. Schneiderman, November 24, 1958, and J. Schlossberg, November 20, 1958; ILGWU, *Proceedings, First–Tenth Conventions* (1900–1912); "Membership Reports," *12th Convention* (June 1–13, 1914), 137; *14th Convention* (May 20–June 1, 1918), 214.

9. For an interesting analysis of the temperament and aspirations of the Jewish immigrant see, Abraham Cahan, *The Rise of David Levinsky* (New York, 1917).

10. On internal dissension, see ILGWU, *Proceedings, 4th Convention* (June 1–4, 1903), 13; *Documentary History of the ACWA, 1914–1916,* viii; L. Lorwin, *Women's Garment Workers,* 120–126; Harry Lang, *"62": Biography of a Union* (New York, 1940), 54; for other problems see, New York *Times,* July 23, 1901, 3; July 21, 1902, 12; M. Rischin, *Promised City,* 175–183.

11. Undated manuscript concerning Morris Hillquit and Jewish labor in America in the Algernon Lee Papers; cf., Morris Hillquit, *Loose Leaves from a Busy Life* (New York, 1934), 29.

12. Lucy Robins Lang, *Tomorrow is Beautiful* (New York, 1938), 37; M. Rischin, *Promised City,* 190–194.

13. L. Lorwin, *Women's Garment Workers,* 99–143.

14. Interviews with P. Newman, R. Schneiderman, and J. Schlossberg; cf., L. Lorwin, *Women's Garment Workers,* 429–436; Joel Seidman, *The Needle Trades* (New York, 1942), Ch. 12.

15. Woods Hutchinson, "The Hygienic Aspects of the Shirtwaist Strike," *The Survey,* XXIII (January 22, 1910), 541–550; Marian F. Scott, "The Spirit of the Girl Strikers," *The Outlook,* XCIV (February 19, 1910), 394–395; Constance D. Leupp, "The Shirtwaist Makers'

Strike," *The Survey*, XXIII (December 18, 1909), 383–386; Melech Epstein, *Jewish Labor in U.S.A.* (New York, 1950), I, 338.

16. Gladys Boone, *The Women's Trade Union League* (New York, 1942), Chs. 2–3.

17. New York WTUL, *Annual Report, 1909–1910*, 11–12; G. Boone, *Women's Trade Union League*, 77–80.

18. New York *Call*, October 22, 1909, 1–2; L. Lorwin, *Women's Garment Workers*, 149–152.

19. W. Hutchinson, "Hygienic Aspects," 545–546.

20. New York *Call*, November 24, 1909, 1–2; C. Leupp, "Shirtwaist Strike," 383–386; Mary B. Sumner, "The Spirit of the Strikers," *The Survey*, XXIII (January 22, 1910), 551–555.

21. L. Lorwin, *Women's Garment Workers*, 154–155; New York *Call*, November 26, 1909, 1–2; November 27, 1909, 1.

22. For the founding and the dominant attitudes of the Manufacturers' Association, see H. Berman, "Era of the Protocol," 83–84.

23. New York *Call*, November 25, 1909, 1; November 26, 1909, 1–2; November 27, 1909, 1.

24. This was a paraphrase of the famous response of male strikers: "I'd rather starve walking than working." C. Leupp, "Shirtwaist Strike," 383; Interview with P. Newman.

25. McAlister Coleman, "All of Which I Saw," *The Progressive*, XIV (May, 1950), 24–25; New York *Call*, December 4, 1909, 1; December 8, 1909, 3; December 23, 1909, 1; W. Hutchinson, "Hygienic Aspects," 548.

26. New York *Times*, December 21, 1909, 1; December 24, 1909, 3; December 30, 1909, 3; January 4, 1910, 20; January 11, 1910, 5; New York *Call*, January 7, 1910, 1–2; C. Leupp, "Shirtwaist Strike," 385; M. Coleman, "All of Which I Saw," 25.

27. The Picket Corps involved more than forty members who served for seven months. New York WTUL, *Annual Report, 1909–1910*, 11–12.

28. New York *Times*, December 6, 1909, 1–2; December 14, 1909, 1; December 17, 1909, 6; New York *Call*, December 6, 1909, 1; December 14, 1909, 2; New York WTUL, *Annual Report, 1909–1910*, 12–14; W. Hutchinson, "Hygienic Aspects," 548.

29. New York *Times*, December 14, 1909, 1; December 17, 1909, 6; New York *Call*, December 14, 1909, 2.

30. New York *Times*, December 20, 1909, 1–2; December 21, 1909, 1; December 22, 1909, 8; December 24, 1909, 3; December 19, 1909, 2;

January 3, 1910, 1–2; New York *Call,* December 29, 1909, 2; January 3, 1910, 1–2; M. Rischin, *Promised City,* 148–149.

31. New York *American,* December 3, 1909, 18; January 14, 1909, 18; January 15, 1910, 16; New York *Post,* December 6, 1909, 8; December 16, 1909, 8; December 20, 1909, 6; December 21, 1909, 8; December 28, 1909, 8; New York *World,* December 15, 1909, 10; January 21, 1910, 8; January 31, 1910, 10.

32. Among the demands listed by Mrs. Weyl were: (1) recognition of the union; (2) abolition of inside contracting; (3) a 52-hour week, including a shorter day Saturday, and five paid holidays annually; (4) girls not to be kept in shops during dull seasons without work; and (5) equalization of wages for similar lines of work; New York *Times,* December 4, 1909, 20; for the insistence upon union recognition and union security, see also W. Hutchinson, "Hygienic Aspects," 550; M. F. Scott, "Spirit of the Strikers," 394; Ida Tarbell, "The Shirtwaist Strikers," *American Federationist,* XVII (March, 1910), 209.

33. The full case for both contending parties was presented in *The American Hebrew,* LXXXCI (December 17, 1909), 179–181; New York *Call,* December 6, 1909, 2; December 7, 1909, 1; December 8, 1909, 1; December 11, 1909, 1; December 14, 1909, 1–2.

34. New York State Department of Labor, *Bulletin No. 43* (March, 1910), 35; L. Lorwin, *Women's Garment Workers,* 162–163.

35. Lorwin, 164; New York *Call,* December 27, 1909, 1–2; December 28, 1909, 1–4; December 31, 1909, 1.

36. New York State Department of Labor, *Bulletin No. 43,* 35–43; New York *Times,* January 4, 1910, 20; New York *Call,* January 4, 1910, 1; January 6, 1910, 1; January 11, 1910, 1; January 12, 1910, 1.

37. New York *Call,* January 24, 1910, 1; February 2, 1910, 1; February 15, 1910, 1–2; L. Lorwin, *Women's Garment Workers,* 165.

38. I. Tarbell, "Shirtwaist Strikers," 209; Samuel Gompers, "The Struggle in the Garment Trades," *American Federationist,* XX (March, 1913), 190; Mary Sumner, "Strikers' Spirit," 555; New York *Call,* February 15, 1910, 2.

39. Union sources and metropolitan newspapers generally estimated the number of strikers at from 45,000 to 60,000. In August at the height of the strike, after some settlements had already been consummated, police estimated the number of strikers at 40,000; Police Reports in the Papers of Mayor William F. Gaynor, August 11, 1910, Municipal Archives, New York City (hereafter M/A); L. Lorwin, *Women's Garment*

Workers, 176–177; Morris Hillquit, *Not Guilty* (New York, 1915), 4–7; New York *Times,* July 8, 1910, 10; New York *Call,* July 8, 1910, 1; July 9, 1910, 1.

40. *The Ladies' Garment Worker,* I (April 1, 1910), 5. Among the headline speakers at the January mass meetings was Big Bill Haywood of the IWW; New York *Call,* February 1, 1910, 1.

41. ILGWU, *Proceedings, 10th Convention* (June 6–11, 1910), 47–48, 71–72; New York *Call,* June 30, 1910, 1–2; July 8, 1910, 1; July 9, 1910, 1; New York *Times,* July 8, 1910, 10; L. Lorwin, *Women's Garment Workers,* 189–182.

42. New York *Times,* July 12, 1910, 5; July 13, 1910, 3; New York *Call,* July 12, 1910, 1; July 13, 1910, 2; July 15, 1910, 1; July 16, 1910, 1–2; July 19, 1910, 1; July 21, 1910, 1–2; July 22, 1910, 1.

43. New York *Call,* July 28, 1910, 1; M. Rischin, *Promised City,* 250–251; Alpheus T. Mason, *Brandeis: A Free Man's Life* (New York, 1946), 300–302; Brandeis' conception of labor relations while advanced and liberal for 1910 was not as clearly conceived or as well developed as J. H. Cohen's. But Brandeis' eminent public reputation made his immediate, if not long, influence greater than Cohen's.

44. New York *Call,* August 1, 1910, 1–2; L. Lorwin, *Women's Garment Workers,* 189.

45. Ronald Sanders, "Abraham Cahan and the Jewish Labor Movement in New York, 1882–1914" (Master's Thesis, Columbia University, 1957); M. Rischin, *Promised City,* 124–127.

46. New York *Call,* July 30, 1910, 1–2; August 4, 1910, 1; H. Berman, "Era of the Protocol," 130–133.

47. Louis Waldman, *Labor Lawyer* (New York, 1944), 29.

48. M. Epstein, *Jewish Labor,* II, 24–26, 366–372; J. Seidman, *Needle Trades,* 98–105; David J. Saposs, "Benjamin Schlesinger," *Dictionary of American Biography,* VIII (1935), 436–437.

49. M. Hillquit, *Loose Leaves;* Harry Rogoff, *An East Side Epic: The Life and Work of Meyer London* (New York, 1930); Max and Edna A. Lerner, "Morris Hillquit," *Dictionary of American Biography,* XI (Supplement One, 1944), 402–405; Algernon Lee, "Meyer London," ibid., VI (1933), 372–374; see M. Rischin, *Promised City,* 241–248, for the relation of the strikers to the Jewish community.

50. Acting Mayor John Mitchel to Police Commissioner William F. Baker, August 12, 1910, Gaynor Papers, M/A; New York *Times,* July 10, 1910, 2; August 12, 1910, 14; August 13, 1910, 2; New York *Call,*

July 12, 1910, 1; August 4, 1910, 3; August 16, 1910, 1; August 24, 1910, 1; August 25, 1910, 1–2; *The Survey*, XXIV (August 13, 1910), 702.

51. New York *Times*, July 16, 1910, 6; July 25, 1910, 6; August 2, 1910, 6; August 5, 1910, 8; August 11, 1910, 6; August 27, 1910, 6; New York *Post*, July 29, 1910, 6; August 5, 1910, 6; August 29, 1910, 6; New York *Herald*, July 8, 1910, 8; New York *American*, August 2, 1910, 16.

52. *The Weekly Bulletin*, IX (August 26, 1910), 4; New York *Call*, August 27, 1910, 1; Elizabeth Wyatt, "The New York Cloakmakers' Strike," *McClure's Magazine*, XXXVI (April, 1911), 712.

53. New York *Times*, August 28, 1910, 1, 3; August 31, 1910, 5; September 2, 1910, 5; New York *Call*, September 2, 1910, 1–2; *The Weekly Bulletin*, IX (September 2, 1910), 4.

54. Letters, Louis Marshall to Meyer London, September 1, 1910, and Marshall to Gertrude Barnum, November 29, 1912, in Charles Reznikoff, ed., *Louis Marshall: Champion of Liberty* (Philadelphia, 1957), II, 1127–1129; New York *Call*, September 3, 1910, 1; A. Mason, *Brandeis*, 301; L. Lorwin, *Women's Garment Workers*, 194.

55. Letter, Louis Brandeis to Lawrence Abbot as quoted in A. Mason, *Brandeis*, 301; New York *Call*, September 3, 1910, 1; New York *Post*, September 3, 1910, 4; New York *Tribune*, September 4, 1910, 6.

56. H. Berman, "Era of the Protocol," contains the fullest discussion and history of the original Protocol.

57. *The Ladies' Garment Worker*, I (November 1, 1910), 2.

58. John B. Lennon, "Practical Trade Union of Cloakmakers," *American Federationist*, XVII (October, 1910), 891; Julius Henry Cohen, *Law and Order*, 22; idem.; *They Builded Better*, 195–196; H. Lang and Morris C. Feinstone, *Gewerkshaften: United Hebrew Trades* (New York, 1938), 59; Max Danish, *The World of David Dubinsky* (New York, 1957), 29.

Chapter 4

1. Philip S. Foner, *The Fur and Leather Workers' Union* (Newark, 1950), 41–44.

2. New York *Call*, June 15, 1912, 1; Foner, *Fur ... Workers*, 41–44.

3. The union's demands included union recognition, the closed shop, the 54-hour week, paid holidays, abolition of homework and of subcontracting, and sanitary conditions. Foner, *Fur . . . Workers,* 41–44; New York *Call,* June 20, 1912, 1; June 21, 1912, 1–2; June 22, 1912, 1–2.

4. New York *Call,* June 22, 1912, 1–2; Foner, *Fur . . . Workers,* 42, 49.

5. Rose Blank, "Strike of the Furriers," *Life and Labor,* II (December, 1912), 360–361; New York *Call,* July 17, 1912, 1; July 24, 1912, 3; August 5, 1912, 1; August 23, 1912, 1; the August 24 issue was a special strike edition, the entire proceeds of which went to the furriers. Among the contributors to the furriers' fund were the *Jewish Daily Forward,* $35,000; the United Hebrew Trades, $10,000; the Cap Makers' Union, $1500; and English-speaking unions of the AFL, $3000.

6. As quoted in M. Rischin, *The Promised City: New York's Jews, 1870–1914* (Cambridge, Mass., 1962), 242–243; article, "Judah L. Magnes," *Who Was Who in America* (Chicago, 1950), II, 340–341.

7. Letter, Charles S. Porter to Dr. Judah L. Magnes, August 14, 1912, Abelson Papers.

8. New York *Call,* August 22, 1912, 1; also see various notes and comments in Abelson Papers referring to the kehillah's role in the dispute; M. Rischin, *Promised City,* 254.

9. New York *Call,* August 23, 1912, 1–2; August 24, 1912, 1–2; August 25, 1912, 4; September 9, 1912, 1–2. The Furriers, in an agreement similar to the 1910 Protocol, achieved a permanent Board of Arbitration and a Joint Board of Sanitary Control. Strikes and lockouts were forbidden for the agreement's two years.

10. Letters, M. Sussman to Dr. J. L. Magnes, October 16, 1912; S. N. Samuels to Magnes, November 27, 1912; Copy of notice issued by M. Schoenholtz, President, Mutual Protective Fur Manufacturers' Association, November 26, 1912, Abelson Papers.

11. Unissued open letter from Dr. J. L. Magnes to the public, August[?], 1914, ibid.

12. Letters, Paul Abelson to Dr. J. L. Magnes, July 15, 1914; J. L. Magnes to P. Abelson, July 17, 1914; J. L. Magnes to Max Cohen, August 7, 1914; Adolph L. Engel to J. L. Magnes, August 17, 1914; A. W. Miller to J. L. Magnes, August 18, 1914, ibid.

13. New York *Call,* January 6, 1913, 2.

14. Harry Best, *The Men's Garment Industry of New York and the Strike of 1913* (New York, n.d.), 14–15; *The Weekly Bulletin*, XI (May 31, 1912), 4; (June 7, 1912), 4; XII (October 25, 1912), 1; *The Garment Worker*, XII (November 15, 1912), 1; (December 6, 1912), 1; (December 13, 1912), 1; (December 20, 1912), 1; (January 13, 1913), 1–2; New York *Call*, June 6, 1912, 2; December 24, 1912, 1; December 30, 1912, 1–2; New York *Times*, December 30, 1912, 1; December 31, 1912, 1–2.

15. H. Lang, *"62": Biography of a Union* (New York, 1942), 52, 55, 91; Harry Haskell, *A Leader in the Garment Workers: The Biography of Isadore Nagler* (New York, 1950), 28–29; L. Lorwin, *Women's Garment Workers* (New York, 1924), 220–221; Rose Schneiderman, "The League Goes into Action," *25th Anniversary: New York Women's Trade Union League* (New York, 1943), 7.

16. *The Ladies' Garment Worker*, II (October, 1911), 17–19; (November, 1911), 1–3; (December, 1911), 15; III (January, 1912), 12; (March, 1912), 6–7, 10–11; (May, 1912), 7–8; (November, 1912), 12, 17, 19; IV (January, 1913), 1; New York *Times*, January 7, 1913, 1; January 9, 1913, 5; January 10, 1913, 22; January 16, 1913, 3; New York *Call*, January 9, 1913, 1; L. Lorwin, *Women's Garment Workers*, 221–222, 225–226.

17. *Women's Wear Daily*, January 6, 1913, 1.

18. ILGWU, *Proceedings, 12th Convention* (June 1–13, 1914), 4; New York *Times*, January 16, 1913, 3; January 17, 1913, 10; New York *Call*, January 9, 1913, 1–2; January 10, 1913, 1; January 16, 1913, 1; January 17, 1913, 1.

19. *Documentary History of the A.C.W.A., 1914–1916*, xii, xvi–xviii; UGWA, *Proceedings, 16th Annual Convention* (August, 1910), 136–137; Personal Interview with Joseph Schlossberg, November 20, 1958.

20. *The Garment Worker*, XII (January 10, 1913), 1; New York *Times*, December 31, 1912, 1; January 5, 1913, 3; New York *Call*, December 31, 1912, 1; January 5, 1913, 1–2.

21. New York *Call*, 1; H. Best, *Men's Strike of 1913*, 16–17.

22. *The Garment Worker*, XII (January 17, 1913), 1; New York *Times*, January 6, 1913, 1–2; January 8, 1913, 6; New York *Call*, January 7, 1913, 2; January 12, 1913, 2; January 14, 1913, 2; H. Best, *Men's Strike of 1913*, 17–19.

23. Best, 18; M. Rischin, *Promised City*, 255.

24. H. Best, *Men's Strike of 1913*, 21.

25. *The Garment Worker,* XII (January 17, 1913), 1; (January 24, 1913), 1; New York *Times,* January 21, 1913, 24; New York *Call,* January 8, 1913, 1–2; January 14, 1913, 1–2; January 17, 1913, 1; January 23, 1913, 1; interview with J. Schlossberg.

26. Copy of letter, Mayor William F. Gaynor to Reverend John Howard Melish, January 8, 1913, Gaynor Papers, M/A; New York *Times,* January 15, 1913, 5; New York *Call,* January 27, 1913, 1; January 29, 1913, 1; *The Garment Worker,* XII (January 31, 1913), 2.

27. Ibid., 1–2; New York *Times,* January 27, 1913, 26.

28. New York *Times,* December 31, 1912, 6; January 2, 1913, 10; January 18, 1913, 12; January 19, 1913, 16; March 2, 1913, II, 6; January 4, 1913, 8.

29. New York *World,* January 5, 1913, 2; January 13, 1913, 10.

30. New York *Tribune,* January 15, 1913, 8; January 25, 1913, 8.

31. *The Garment Worker,* XII (January 24, 1913), 2; New York *Call,* January 23, 1913, 1; January 25, 1913, 2.

32. United Garment Workers' Conference, *Report for Conferees by Julius Henry Cohen* (January 27, 1913); *The Garment Worker,* XII (January 31, 1913), 1; H. Best, *Men's Strike of 1913,* 23; New York *Call,* January 27, 1913, 1.

33. *The Garment Worker,* XII (January 31, 1913), 4; (February 7, 1913), 4; (February 14, 1913), 1; New York *Call,* January 27, 1913, 1; January 28, 1913, 1–2; February 3, 1913, 1.

34. New York *Call,* February 10, 1913, 1; Socialist Party, Local New York, Letter Books, February 13, 1913 (Tamiment Institute); J. B. S. Hardman, *The Amalgamated: Today and Tomorrow* (New York, 1940), 18.

35. New York *Times,* February 20, 1913, 10; *The Garment Worker,* XII (February 21, 1913), 1.

36. Letter, Julius H. Cohen to Dr. J. L. Magnes, March 1, 1913, Abelson Papers; *The Garment Worker,* XII (February 14, 1913), 1; (February 21, 1913), 1; (February 28, 1913), 1; New York *Call,* February 14, 1913, 1; February 15, 1913, 1; February 25, 1913, 1–2; March 1, 1913, 1–2; New York *Times,* March 1, 1913, 1; H. Best, *Men's 1913 Strike,* 23.

37. "We throw down this treacherous settlement . . . because such a settlement is a shame and an insult to the whole organized labor movement of America." New York *Call,* March 2, 1913, 1–2; New York *Times,* March 2, 1913, 3; H. Best, *Men's 1913 Strike,* 21.

38. Interview with J. Schlossberg; New York *Call,* March 3, 1913, 1; J. B. S. Hardman, *The Amalgamated,* 18.

39. Copy of letter, Mayor William F. Gaynor to Police Commissioner Rhinelander Waldo, March 7, 1913, Gaynor Papers, M/A; *The Garment Worker,* XII (March 7, 1913), 1; *Documentary History of the ACWA, 1914–1916,* xviii–xix; Interview with J. Schlossberg.

40. *The Garment Worker,* XII (March 14, 1913), 1; New York *Times,* March 13, 1913, 22; New York *Call,* March 12, 1913, 1–2; J. B. S. Hardman, *The Amalgamated,* 18.

41. Letter, S. Meyerson to Dr. J. L. Magnes, February 16, 1914; copy of letter, Chairman, Clothing Trade Commission to J. H. Lavner, May 13, 1914; Letter, A. Miller to J. L. Magnes, May 23, 1914; copy of letter, Chief Representative, Clothing Trade Commission to Philip Cohen, July 23, 1914, Abelson Papers. Other general correspondence in the Abelson Papers sheds additional light on similar developments in the clothing trades.

42. Mary B. Bruere, "The White Goods Strikers," *Life and Labor,* III (March, 1913), 73–75; H. Berman, "Era of the Protocol," 179–180.

43. New York Women's Trade Union League, *Annual Report, 1912–1913,* 8; New York *Times,* January 18, 1913, 7; January 28, 1913, 22; February 8, 1913, 6. The city's leading clergymen, including Reverends John Haynes Holmes and Charles H. Parkhurst, established a public strike fund for the benefit of the girls. New York *Times,* February 17, 1913, 5, 12; New York *Post,* January 24, 1913, 8; February 8, 1913, 6; New York *World,* March 2, 1913, II, 2; Gertrude Barnum, "The Children's Crusade," *The Ladies' Garment Worker,* IV (February, 1913), 3; Rose Schneiderman, "The White Goods Workers," *Life and Labor,* III (May, 1913), 136; H. Berman, "Era of the Protocol," 181–183; H. Lang, "62," 110–111; Elting Morison, ed., *The Letters of Theodore Roosevelt* (Cambridge, Mass., 1954), VII, 696–701.

44. The employers' attorney, J. H. Cohen, was quoted to the effect that: "I could not . . . advise the Association to make an agreement with the union to increase wages and shorten hours unless the union could sufficiently control the workers to make the agreement general in the trade. I could not ask my association to cut its own throat. Competition in the industry is too strong. It is now up to the unions to demonstrate their strength." New York *Call,* January 17, 1913, 1; New York *Times,* January 17, 1913, 10; ILGWU, *Proceedings, 12th Convention* (June 1–13, 1914), 4; L. Lorwin, *Women's Garment Workers,* 223–225.

45. New York *Times,* January 19, 1913, 3; New York *Call,* January 18, 1913, 1; January 19, 1913, 1–2; United States Bureau of Labor Statistics, *Bulletin No. 146,* 16–17, 63–66.

46. *The Ladies' Garment Worker,* IV (March, 1913), 7–9; New York *Call,* February 12, 1913, 1; New York *Times,* February 12, 1913, 8.

47. Ibid.; New York *Call,* February 12, 1913, 1–2; February 19, 1913, 1; *The Ladies' Garment Worker,* IV (March, 1913), 5; H. Lang, "62," 131, 147–148.

48. For a full and detailed history of the Protocols see H. Berman, "Era of the Protocol"; on the schism in the UGWA, see M. Dubofsky, "Labor and the Immigrant in New York City," *Labor History,* II (Spring, 1961), 191–197.

Chapter 5

1. Copy of letter from Abraham Rosenberg and John Dyche to M. Silberman, August 24, 1912; copy of letter, General Manager, Cloak and Skirt Makers' Protective Association to the Joint Board of the Cloak and Skirt Makers' Union, January 12, 1912; unsigned memorandum, 1912–1913[?]; translation of article from the *New Post,* October 19, 1912, all in the Abelson Papers; *Ladies' Garment Worker,* III (February, 1912), 11, (October, 1912), 11–12; ILGWU, *Proceedings, 12th Convention* (June 1–13, 1914), 18.

2. H. Berman, "Era of the Protocol: A Chapter in the History of the ILGWU, 1910–1916" (Unpublished Doctoral Dissertation, Columbia University, 1955), contains the most complete and authoritative treatment of the Hourwich affair.

3. Cloak and Suit Industry, Board of Arbitration Minutes, October 12–13, 1913, 354–355, and Minutes, August 3–6, 1913, I, 21, 30, II, 130 (stenographic copy, New York State School of Industrial and Labor Relations Library); ILGWU, *Proceedings, 12th Convention,* (June 1–13, 1914), 19, 24–28, 32, 205; *Ladies' Garment Worker,* IV (June, 1913), 11, V (January, 1914), 12.

4. Arbitration Proceedings Between the Dress and Waist Manufacturers Association and Local 25, Waist and Dress Makers Union, Local 10, Cutters Union, and the International Ladies' Garment Workers Union (New York), November 6–7, 1914, 69–70, 126–127, 135–136, 177,

181 (stenographic copy, New York State School of Industrial and Labor Relations Library).

5. Clipping from *Women's Wear Daily,* January 8, 1915, in the Abelson Papers.

6. *Ladies' Garment Worker,* VI (March, 1915), 1; (June, 1915), 2, 12–15.

7. New York *Sun,* July 17, 1915, 6; New York *Times,* May 23, 1915, II, 2; July 8, 1915, 12; New York *Tribune,* July 3, 1915, 6; New York *World,* May 23, 1915, II, 2; June 14, 1915, 8; June 16, 1915, 8; July 5, 1915, 10; July 7, 1915, 8; July 14, 1915, 6; *The New Republic,* III (May 29, 1915), 84–85.

8. *Ladies' Garment Worker,* VI (July, 1915), 19–20. The union proposed that the dispute be submitted to a group of unbiased persons for adjudication. The offer was promptly seized by Mayor John Purroy Mitchel, who donated his services to bring the disputing parties together for peace conferences.

9. Copy of letters, Charles Heineman to Benjamin Schlesinger and Elmer Rosenberg, July 2, 1915; Benjamin Schlesinger and Elmer Rosenberg to Charles Heineman, July 2, 1915; Mayor John P. Mitchel to Felix Adler and to Louis Brandeis, July 9, 1915. The five conciliators were Felix Adler, Louis Brandeis, Henry Bruere, Charles L. Bernheimer, and Judge Walter C. Noyes; Mitchel Papers, M/A.

10. Richard B. Morris, "John Purroy Mitchel," *Dictionary of American Biography,* VII (1934), 37–38.

11. Letters, Charles Heineman to Mayor J. P. Mitchel, July 28, 1915; Benjamin Schlesinger to J. P. Mitchel, July 29, 1915, ibid.; *Ladies' Garment Worker,* VI (August, 1915), 3, 27–30.

12. Letter, Joseph S. Marcus to Mayor J. P. Mitchel, July 30, 1915, Mitchel Papers, M/A; New York *Post,* July 26, 1915, 6; New York *Times,* July 25, 1915, 14; New York *Tribune,* July 27, 1915, 6.

13. *Findings and Recommendations of the Council of Conciliation Appointed by Hon. John Purroy Mitchel* (handed down July 23, 1915, and accepted by the Union and the Association, August 4, 1915) (New York, 1915), 2, 8.

14. *Ladies' Garment Worker,* VI (August, 1915), 5; ILGWU, *Proceedings, 13th Convention* (October 16–28, 1916), 133.

15. *Ladies' Garment Cutter,* IV (February 12, 1916), 1; New York *Call,* February 8, 1916, 1; February 9, 1916, 1; February 12, 1916, 1.

16. Copy of letters, Mayor J. P. Mitchel to I. Ginsberg, to Benjamin

Schlesinger, to Felix Adler, to Henry Bruere, to Charles Bernheimer, February 8, 1916; Benjamin Schlesinger to J. P. Mitchel, Charles L. Bernheimer to J. P. Mitchel, Walter C. Noyes to J. P. Mitchel, February 9, 1916, Mitchel Papers, M/A.

17. *Ladies' Garment Worker,* VII (March, 1916), 20; (April, 1916), 1–3; *Ladies' Garment Cutter,* IV (March 11, 1916), 2–3; (March 25, 1916), 3; *Women's Wear Daily,* April 18, 1916, 1.

18. Copy of letters, Mayor J. P. Mitchel to Benjamin Schlesinger, to I. Gonnickman, and to E. J. Wile, April 24, 1916; Theodore Rousseau, Secretary to the Mayor, to Louis Brandeis, April 25, 1916; E. J. Wile to J. P. Mitchel, April 25, 1916; Theodore Rousseau to E. J. Wile, April 27, 1916; unsigned memoranda dated April 25 and April 26, 1916, Mitchel Papers, M/A.

19. The non-Protective Association manufacturers attempted to pressure the Mayor into exerting his influence in order to urge the union's leadership to relent in their general strike action. E. Lowenstein and Company to Mayor J. P. Mitchel, April 29, 1916, ibid.; *Ladies' Garment Worker,* VII (May, 1916), 20; (June, 1916), 12–13; *Ladies' Garment Cutter,* IV (April 29, 1916), 1; New York *Times,* May 3, 1916, 7; May 4, 1916, 1.

20. The strikers described their own plight as follows: "Our bosses send their children into the country; we send ours to the dispensary." *The Survey,* XXXVI (June 24, 1916), 321; *Ladies' Garment Cutter,* IV (July 15, 1916), 1.

21. *Ladies' Garment Worker,* VII (June, 1916), 1–2.

22. Among the signers of the Columbia letter were E. R. A. Seligman, John Dewey, Charles A. Beard, Carlton J. H. Hayes, Wesley F. Mitchell, Parker T. Moon, Franklin H. Giddings, James H. Robinson, Herbert L. Osgood, Robert L. Schuyler, and James T. Shotwell; New York *Times,* May 29, 1916, 5; May 26, 1916, 6; June 15, 1916, 22; the United Hebrew Trades, the ACWA, the Workmen's Circle, the Furriers' Union, and the Cloth Hat and Cap Makers' Union, all radical, immigrant-dominated groups, were raising funds for the strikers. The CFU and the Executive Council of the AFL also decided to begin fund raising campaigns. *Ladies' Garment Worker,* VII (June, 1916), 1–2, 22; (July, 1916), 11. A committee composed of prominent clergymen called upon the community to support materially the thousands of suffering strikers; New York *Times,* June 11, 1916, 11.

23. New York *Times* June 23, 1916, 22; July 1, 1916, 7; July 19, 1916, 6.

24. New York Women's Trade Union League, *Annual Report, 1915–1917*, 20; *Ladies' Garment Worker,* VII (July, 1916), 14; (August, 1916), 18; (September, 1916) 18–21. The unheard of, for that time, sum of $627,245.92 was expended by the ILGWU for the maintenance of the strikers.

25. New York *Times,* April 30, 1916, 18; New York *Tribune,* May 8, 1916, 10; New York *World,* May 27, 1916, 8; May 29, 1916, 8. All the editorials agreed that the union desired peace and the manufacturers initiated conflict.

26. New York *American,* June 24, 1916, 16; New York *Tribune,* June 15, 1916, 10; June 29, 1916, 10; July 21, 1916, 8; New York *World,* June 29, 1916, 10; July 7, 1916, 8; *The New Republic,* IV (June 24, 1916), 189.

27. The New York *Sun* feared that workers' demands would drive the garment industry from the city and said that actually, the workers "were a comfortably clad, well-fed looking lot of men and women;" June 20, 1916, 6; July 10, 1916, 14; cf. New York *Post,* June 15, 1916, 8; New York *Times,* May 27, 1916, 10; May 29, 1916, 10; June 3, 1916, 12; New York *Tribune,* May 30, 1916, 8; June 2, 1916, 10; New York *World,* July 11, 1916, 8.

28. *Ladies' Garment Worker,* VII (August, 1916), 17.

29. Letters, Lucien Breckenridge to Mayor J. P. Mitchel, June 12, 1916, June 15, 1916, and June 27, 1916; Benjamin Schlesinger and Morris Hillquit to Paul C. Wilson, June 30, 1916; copy of letter, J. P. Mitchel to Lazarus Joseph, June 12, 1916, Mitchel Papers, M/A.

30. Two memoranda of June 21, 1916 from Paul C. Wilson to Mayor J. P. Mitchel; there was considerable correspondence on this issue between the Mayor, the union, and the independent manufacturers. See especially, letters, Lazarus Joseph to J. P. Mitchel, June 14, 1916 and June 26, 1916, ibid.

31. Copy of letter, Mayor J. P. Mitchel to ILGWU, July 7, 1916; unsigned memorandum, July 10, 1916; memorandum, Paul C. Wilson to J. P. Mitchel, July 10, 1916; letter, Marcus M. Marks to J. P. Mitchel, July 11, 1916, ibid.; *Ladies' Garment Worker,* VII (August, 1916), 15.

32. Letter, Charles L. Bernheimer to Mayor J. P. Mitchel, July 13, 1916; Paul C. Wilson, memorandum of a telephone conversation with Robert Bruere, July 20, 1916, Mitchel Papers, M/A; *Ladies' Garment Worker,* VII (August, 1916), 15.

33. Memorandum of a telephone conversation between Paul C. Wilson and Robert Bruere, July 20, 1916, Mitchel Papers, M/A; *Ladies' Garment Worker,* VII (August, 1916), 16–18; *Ladies' Garment Cutter,* IV (July 29, 1916), 1–2, (August 5, 1916), 1–2; New York *Times,* July 23, 1916, 10; August 4, 1916, 2.

34. Copy of letter, Paul C. Wilson to David S. Ginsburg, July 27, 1916; Paul C. Wilson to A. Fensterstock, July 28, 1916; and the entire file of correspondence on this issue in the Mitchel Papers, M/A.

35. ILGWU, *Proceedings, 13th Convention* (October 16–28, 1916), 12; *Ladies' Garment Worker,* VII (September, 1916), 3, 10.

36. Selig Perlman and Philip Taft, *History of Labor in the United States 1896–1932* (New York, 1935), 289.

37. *Ladies' Garment Worker,* VI (June, 1915), 3.

38. H. Berman, "Era of the Protocol," 104, 419–420.

39. Julius Henry Cohen, *Law and Order in Industry* 22, and passim; idem. "Protocols in the Cloak, Suit, and Skirt Industry" [n.p.]; idem., *A League to Enforce the Industrial Peace* (New York, 1916), 35–36; idem. "The Revised Protocol," 4–5; Some authorities (see Berman, "Era of the Protocol," passim) maintain that labor organizations prospered in the garment trades because many of the manufacturers had risen from the ranks of labor and shared the religion and social problems of their fellow immigrant employees in an alien society. This may have been true to some extent, but more important were the manfacturers' basic lack of economic security and their very limited capital reserves.

Chapter 6

1. Louis Pink, *Gaynor* (New York, 1931); Richard B. Morris, "William F. Gaynor," *Dictionary of American Biography,* IV (1931–1932), 200–201.

2. Copy of letters, Mayor William F. Gaynor to William Gannell Brown, Esq. November 3, 1910; and Gaynor to Mortimer Heilbruner, March 30, 1911, Gaynor Papers, M/A.

3. New York *Call,* October 28, 1910, 1–2.

4. Ibid.; New York State Department of Labor, *Bulletin No. 46* (March, 1911), 32.

5. Interstate Commerce Commission, *First Annual Report of the Statistics of Express Companies in the United States for the Year Ending*

June 30, 1909 (Washington, 1909), 39–46; for the assets and the various holdings and profits of the express companies during the strike years, 1910–1911, see, idem., *Third Annual Report on the Statistics of Express Companies in the United States for the Year Ending June 30, 1911,* (Washington, 1911), 28–29.

6. Quoted in J. Rayback, *A History of American Labor* (New York, 1959), 211; For the prevailing labor relations philosophy of American businessmen in the late nineteenth century see Donald L. McMurry, *The Great Burlington Strike of 1888* (Cambridge, Mass., 1956), 273–275 and passim; and Edward C. Kirkland, *Industry Comes of Age: Business, Labor, and Public Policy, 1860–1897* (New York, 1961), 353–355.

7. These early conferences and negotiations were arranged through the efforts of the New York State Bureau of Mediation and Arbitration. The State Bureau advised the strikers not to negotiate on an individual basis though it suggested an *ad hoc* committee of drivers rather than an official trade-union delegation; New York State Department of Labor, *Bulletin No. 46,* 32.

8. Copy of letters, Mayor William F. Gaynor to Police Commissioner James C. Cropsey, November 1, 1910; Commissioner Cropsey to Mayor Gaynor, November 1, 1910; W. F. Gaynor to H. S. Julian, November 1, 1910, Gaynor Papers, M/A; New York State Department of Labor, *Bulletin No. 46,* 32; New York *Call,* October 31, 1910, 1; November 1, 1910, 1–2.

9. New York *Call,* November 1, 1910, 1.

10. New York State Department of Labor, *Bulletin No. 46,* 34–35.

11. Ibid., 35; New York *Call,* November 2, 1910, 1–2.

12. New York *Call,* November 3, 1910, 1–2, November 5, 1910, 1–2.

13. Copies of letters, Mayor William F. Gaynor to Frank H. Platt, both dated November 5, 1910, Gaynor Papers, M/A; New York State Department of Labor, *Bulletin No. 46,* 36.

14. New York *Call,* November 7, 1910, 1; November 8, 1910, 2.

15. Ibid., 1–2. In fact taxi drivers had joined the express company strikers.

16. Gaynor warned Wells-Fargo about the use of new drivers not licensed as required by law. He said that under these conditions the city could not continue to provide police protection for unlicensed drivers without just criticism. "Are you not able to see how demoralizing it would be to exempt you from the rule that applies by law to all without

discrimination?" Copy of letter, Gaynor to Wells-Fargo and Company, November 9, 1910, Gaynor Papers, M/A.

17. New York *World,* November 14, 1910, 10; New York *Times,* October 31, 1910, 8; New York *Post,* November 1, 1910, 8.

18. New York *Call,* November 9, 1910, 2; New York State Department of Labor, *Bulletin No. 46,* 40; Copy of letter, Mayor William F. Gaynor to Mayor H. O. Wittpen (Jersey City), November 9, 1910, Gaynor Papers, M/A.

19. Copy of letter, Mayor William F. Gaynor to Frank H. Hobbs, November 10, 1910, Gaynor Papers, M/A.

20. Letter, William Barrett, H. S. Julien, J. N. Smith, Frank H. Platt, and W. W. Stedman to Henry R. Towne, President, New York Merchants' Association, November 10, 1910, ibid.

21. New York State Department of Labor, *Bulletin No. 46,* 40–44; New York *Call,* November 11, 1910, 1–2; November 12, 1910, 1; November 13, 1910, 1–2.

22. Copy of letters, Mayor William F. Gaynor to William H. Ashton, November 14, 1910; John H. Hylan to W. F. Gaynor, November 14, 1910, Gaynor Papers, M/A.

23. Copy of letters, Mayor William F. Gaynor to Marcus M. Marks, November 18, 1910; Gaynor to H. S. Julien and William M. Barrett, November 17, 1910; Gaynor to William M. Barrett, November 18, 1910, ibid.

24. New York *Call,* November 15, 1910, 8; December 2, 1910, 1. Eventually the drivers gained a wage increase of from five to eight percent and an eleven-hour day. Adams Express Company employees received fewer concessions.

25. Copy of letter, Mayor William F. Gaynor to Police Commissioner James C. Cropsey, December 7, 1910, Gaynor Papers, M/A.

26. New York *Call,* March 11, 1911, 1; March 12, 1911, 1–2.

27. Copy of letter, Mayor William F. Gaynor to William H. Ashton, March 15, 1911, Gaynor Papers, M/A; New York *Call,* March 15, 1911, 2; March 16, 1911, 1.

28. New York *Call,* March 13, 1911, 1–2; March 16, 1911, 1.

29. Ibid., March 17, 1911, 1; March 18, 1911, 1; March 19, 1911, 1.

30. Even Dan Tobin, President of the International Brotherhood of Teamsters, ordered that no sympathetic strike take place in favor of the Adams Company employees and that all local contracts with employers be respected; ibid., March 18, 1911, 1–2.

31. Copy of letter, Mayor William F. Gaynor to William H. Ashton, March 20, 1911, Gaynor Papers, M/A.

32. New York *Call,* March 22, 1911, 1; March 23, 1911, 1; March 24, 1911, 1.

33. Letter, Department of Sanitation Commissioner William Edwards to Mayor William F. Gaynor, January 21, 1910, Gaynor Papers, M/A.

34. Commissioner William Edwards to Mayor William F. Gaynor (two letters), July 6, 1911; Mayor Gaynor to Commissioner Edwards, July 6, 1911, ibid.

35. Gaynor proclaimed: "The City is not in the position of a private employer and cannot make any terms with its employees it sees fit." *The Survey,* XXVII (November 25, 1911), 1244–1245.

36. Ibid., 1243; *American Federationist,* XIX (February, 1912), 16–17.

37. *The Survey,* XXVII (November 25, 1911), 1245–1246; New York *Call,* November 9, 1911, 1; November 11, 1911, 1–2; November 21, 1911, 1.

38. New York *World,* November 25, 1911, 10; November 11, 1911, 8; New York *Tribune,* November 12, 1911, 8. "Organized strikes among men of the city departments . . . cannot be condoned whatever their grievances may be;" New York *Herald,* November 10, 1911, 10. The *Herald* added: "A little specific clubbing by the police has worked wonders. . . . If a club is not effective, there is the riot gun." November 14, 1911, 10. "The right to strike of public employees is more than doubtful." New York *Times,* November 12, 1911, 14; November 13, 1911, 8. "In no labor dispute in recent memory has there been shown greater impudence, nor callous indifference to the rights of the public or slighter justification than in the strike of the Street Cleaning Department's drivers." New York *Sun,* November 15, 1911, 8; New York *Post,* November 11, 1911, 8; November 14, 1911, 6. The strikers "should be put down with a strong hand, and rioters and murderers punished with the full penalties of the law." New York *World,* November 12, 1911, II, 1.

39. Copy of letter, Mayor William F. Gaynor to Commissioner William Edwards, November 8, 1911; Commissioner Edwards to Mayor Gaynor, November 9, 1911, Gaynor Papers, M/A; New York *Call,* November 10, 1911, 1–2, November 11, 1911, 1–2.

40. Copy of letters, Mayor William F. Gaynor to W. F. Clark, November 13, 1911; Gaynor to Reverend Howard Melish, November 13, 1911; and Gaynor to Marcus M. Marks, November 13, 1911, Gaynor Papers,

M/A; New York *Call,* November 12, 1911, 1–2; November 14, 1911, 1–2.

41. New York *Call,* November 15, 1911, 1–2.

42. Ibid., November 14, 1911, 1; November 15, 1911, 1.

43. Both on November 15 and November 16 the strikers voted overwhelmingly to continue their walkout until night work was abolished; ibid., November 16, 1911, 2.

44. Letters, James Creelman, President, Municipal Civil Service Commission, to Mayor William F. Gaynor, November 14, 1911; Commissioner William Edwards to Mayor Gaynor, November 14, 1911; copy of letter, Mayor Gaynor to Commissioner Edwards, November 16, 1911; Commissioner Edwards to Mayor Gaynor, November 27, 1911, Gaynor Papers, M/A.

45. For a report on the removals of strikers from the civil service lists, see James Creelman to Mayor William F. Gaynor, May 16, 1912, ibid.; New York *Call,* November 19, 1911, 2; November 23, 1911, 3.

46. The Civil Service Reform Commission commended Gaynor for his handling of the strike. Elliot H. Goodman to Mayor William F. Gaynor, December 8, 1911, Gaynor Papers, M/A.

47. New York *Call,* May 30, 1912, 1; May 31, 1912, 1–2.

48. Quoted in Matthew Josephson, *Union House; Union Bar: The History of the Hotel and Restaurant Employees and Bartenders' International Union, A.F.L.-C.I.O.* (New York, 1956), 83, 85.

49. Exploitation of waiters was no myth. At the Hotel Belmont, they received $25 monthly plus meals and tips, were fined 25¢ for dropping a piece of silver, or being late, or talking too much to customers, or for numerous other minor infractions. One waiter was fined $2 for drinking leftover coffee, and two others were fined $1 each for observing but failing to report the incident; ibid., 83–86.

50. Ibid., 96.

51. The history of the IWW is covered in the author's forthcoming book on that organization to be published by Quadrangle Books in the fall of 1969.

52. M. Josephson, *Union House,* 97; New York *Call,* May 30, 1912, 1; May 31, 1912, 1–2; June 1, 1912, 1–2.

53. New York *Call,* June 2, 1912, 1–2; M. Josephson, *Union House,* 97–98.

54. New York *Herald,* June 4, 1912, 10; New York *Times,* June 1, 1912, 10; June 4, 1912, 10.

55. On Wednesday, June 5 the Socialist Party held a mass meeting at Carnegie Hall to bolster the morale of a sagging cause; New York *Call,* June 6, 1912; on the following Wednesday, the *Call* issued a special strike edition, the proceeds of which went to the strikers. See also ibid., June 10, 1912, 1–2; June 12, 1912, 2; June 13, 1912, 2.

56. Ibid., June 15, 1912, 2; June 18, 1912, 1; June 19, 1912, 2; June 26, 1912, 3; M. Josephson, *Union House,* 98.

57. New York *Call,* January 1, 1913, 1; January 2, 1913, 1; January 8, 1913, 1; January 11, 1913, 1.

58. Ibid., January 12, 1913, 4.

59. Ibid., January 15, 1913, 3; January 14, 1913, 2; January 16, 1913, 1; January 24, 1913, 1; January 25, 1913, 1; February 1, 1913, 1.

Chapter 7

1. *The Independent,* XXXCII (September 25, 1916), 460; *Rules and Regulations for the Government of the Operating Officers and Employees of the Interborough Rapid Transit Company Subway Division to Take Effect January 1, 1916* (New York, n.d.); Samuel Waitzman, "New York City Transit Strike of 1916" (Unpublished Master's Thesis, Columbia University, 1952), 29–30.

2. *The New Republic,* VIII (August 12, 1916), 28–29.

3. *Conferences Between the Management, the Board of Directors of New York Railways Company and Representatives of its Employees* [Proceedings, August 17–September 6, 1916], (New York, 1916), ix; *Annual Report of the Interborough Rapid Transit Company for the Year Ended June 30, 1917* (New York, 1917); New York Railways Company, *Annual Report, 1913–1918* (New York, 1918), 5, 22–23.

4. William B. Shaw, "Theodore P. Shonts," *Dictionary of American Biography,* IX (1935–1936), 123–124; "Frank Hedley," *Who Was Who In America* (Chicago, 1960), 386.

5. New York Railways Company, *Annual Report, 1913–1914* (New York, 1914), 26–27.

6. The development of management's welfare approach can be followed best in *New York Railway Employees Magazine,* I (April, 1914), 2–3; (October, 1914), 12; (November, 1914), 2; (February, 1915), 5; II (August, 1915), 3; (January, 1916), 3.

7. Ibid., I (April, 1914), 3; *Interborough Bulletin,* IV (April, 1914),

6; V (August, 1915), 6; VI (February, 1916), 2; (March, 1916), 2–3.

8. Copy of letter, Committee of Trainmen to Thomson Investigating Commission, June 21, 1916, Mitchel Papers, M/A.

9. S. DeLeon, *American Labor Who's Who* (New York, 1925), 144; "William D. Mahon," *Who Was Who in America* (Chicago, 1943–50), 341.

10. New York *Call*, July 24, 1916, 1; July 27, 1916, 1; July 28, 1916, 1; July 30, 1916, 1–2; August 1, 1916, 1.

11. Copy of notice from Frank Hedley to all Employees, July 30, 1916, Mitchel Papers, M/A; New York Railways Company, *Annual Report, 1916–1917* (New York, 1917), 16; *New York Railway Employees' Magazine*, III (August, 1916), 4; *Interborough Bulletin*, VI (August, 1916), 21.

12. Letter, W. D. Mahon to Mayor John P. Mitchel, August 2, 1916, Mitchel Papers, M/A; New York *Call*, August 2, 1916, 1; *The New Republic*, VIII (August 12, 1916), 29.

13. Letters, W. D. Mahon to Mayor John P. Mitchel, August 2, 1916; Mahon to Mitchel, August 3, 1916, Mitchel Papers, M/A.

14. Letters, Theodore P. Shonts to Mayor John P. Mitchel, August 3, 1916; Shonts to Mitchel, August 4, 1916; William O. Wood to J. P. Mitchel, August 4, 1916, ibid.; *Settlement of the August 4th Strike on the New York Railways Company* (New York, 1916), 1–3.

15. New York *Call*, August 4, 1916, 1; Public Service Commission, First District, New York State, *Report on the Street Railway Strike of 1916* (New York, 1916), 4; letter, William Fellowes Morgan, President, Merchants' Association, to Mayor John P. Mitchel, August 4, 1916, Mitchel Papers, M/A; S. Waitzman, "Transit Strike of 1916," 22; *The New Republic*, VIII (October 7, 1916), 235; New York *American*, August 7, 1916, 14; New York *Herald*, July 31, 1916, 10; August 3, 1916, 8; August 4, 1916, 8; August 5, 1916, 8; New York *Post*, August 1, 1916, 8; August 3, 1916, 8; New York *Times*, August 1, 1916, 8; August 4, 1916, 8; August 6, 1916, II, 2; New York *Tribune*, August 1, 1916, 10; August 6, 1916, 2; New York *World*, August 3, 1916, 10.

16. Memorandum by Mayor Mitchel, Mitchel Papers, M/A.

17. Abram I. Elkus, "Oscar Straus," *Dictionary of American Biography*, IX (1935–1936), 130–132.

18. Two memoranda of August 6, 1916 in Mitchel Papers, M/A; Public Service Commission, *1916 Transit Strike*, 12; *Settlement of August 4 Strike*, 4–7.

19. Copy of letters, W. D. Mahon, William B. Fitzgerald, Hugh

Frayne, and Louis Fridiger to Mayor John P. Mitchel and Oscar S. Straus, August 6, 1916; Theodore P. Shonts to J. P. Mitchel and Oscar S. Straus, August 6, 1916; Mitchel Papers, M/A.

20. *Settlement of August 4 Strike,* 4–11; Public Service Commission, *Transit Strike of 1916,* 12–16; New York, *Call,* August 8, 1916, 1.

21. Letters, Charles E. Chapin to Mayor J. P. Mitchell, August 8, 1916; Louis Wiley to Mitchel, August 8, 1916; William G. Willcox to Mitchel, August 8, 1916; Samuel Levy to Mitchel, August 8, 1916; C. W. Lincoln to Mitchel, August 8, 1916; Seth Low to Mitchel, August 9, 1916; Thomas W. Whittle to Mitchel, August 9, 1916; these are just a sample of the favorable correspondence the Mayor received from influential New Yorkers. Mitchel Papers, M/A; *The New Republic,* VIII (August 12, 1916), 29; New York *Times,* August 8, 1916, 8.

22. Copy of letter, Representative Employees of the New York Railways Company to Theodore P. Shonts, August 5, 1916; T. P. Shonts to Mayor John P. Mitchel, August 16, 1916, Mitchel Papers, M/A; *Settlement of August 4 Strike,* 11–18, 21–35, 38–39; New York Railways Company, *Annual Report, 1916–1917,* 15; New York *Call,* August 15, 1916, 1–2; August 10, 1916, 1.

23. New York *Call,* August 16, 1916, 1; August 19, 1916, 1–2; *The New Republic,* VIII (August 19, 1916), 52; *Conferences Between the Management, the Board of Directors of New York Railways Company, and Representatives of the Employees* (New York, 1916), 32–33. Organizer Fitzgerald insisted that "it was our thought of trying to work out together for the men who were desirous of doing business in a collective way, a mutual understanding in the proper way."

24. Transcript of the August 21 Conference with Mayor Mitchel, Mitchel Papers, M/A; *Settlement of August 4 Strike* [n.p.]; New York *Call,* August 22, 1916, 1–2.

25. Copy of letter, Committee of Trainmen to Public Service Commission, August 4, 1916, Mitchel Papers, M/A; *Interborough Bulletin,* VI (August 16, 1916), 2; IRT, *Annual Report, 1916–1917,* 25–26.

26. *The Effort to Tie-Up the Street Railroad System of New York* (New York, 1916), 5–9, 13–17; *Conferences Between the Management,* 168, 340–341; New York *Call,* August 25, 1916, 1; September 2, 1916, 1–2.

27. *Effort to Tie-Up,* 13–17; New York *Call,* September 6, 1916, 1–2.

28. Letter, Theodore P. Shonts to Mayor John P. Mitchell, September

4, 1916; Printed copies of Brooklyn *Eagle* editorials [n.d.], Mitchel Papers, M/A; *Effort to Tie-Up*, 5, 21–27, 32–36.

29. Copy of letter, Frederick Whitridge to W. B. Fitzgerald and P. J. O'Brien, September 6, 1916; Frederick W. Whitridge to Mayor John P. Mitchel, September 9, 1916, Mitchel Papers, M/A; *Conferences Between the Management*, 365–370.

30. New York *Call*, September 6, 1916, 1–2; September 7, 1916, 1–2; September 8, 1916, 1–2; September 9, 1916, 1.

31. New York *Herald*, September 13, 1916, 8; September 14, 1916, 8; New York *Post*, September 6, 1916, 8; September 7, 1916, 8; September 8, 1916, 8; September 11, 1916, 8; September 13, 1916, 8; New York *Times*, September 7, 1916, 8; September 8, 1916, 6; September 11, 1916, 8; September 13, 1916, 8; New York *Tribune*, September 7, 1916, 8; New York *World*, September 6, 1916, 6; September 7, 1916, 10.

32. Letter, Frank Morrison to Samuel Gompers, September 10, 1916, AFL Papers (Madison); New York *Call*, September 10, 1916, 1; September 11, 1916, 1–2.

33. Letters, Frederick W. Whitridge to Mayor John P. Mitchel, September 10, 1916; D. C. Imboden to Mitchel, September 6, 1916; Dr. M. E. Walton to Mitchel, September 7, 1916; D. Louis Moore to Mitchel, September 14, 1916; H. A. Boude to Mitchel, September 13, 1916; Milton S. Gordon to Mitchel, September 13, 1916; James McLoughlin to Mitchel, September 14, 1916, Mitchel Papers, M/A.

34. Railway Employees of All Companies to Mayor John P. Mitchel, September 11, 1916, ibid.

35. New York *Call*, September 13, 1916, 1; S. Waitzman, "1916 Transit Strike," 59–63.

36. Letter, Railroad Employees of Greater New York to Mayor John P. Mitchel, September 15, 1916; transcript of Conference between Mayor J. P. Mitchel and Representatives of the Interborough Rapid Transit Employees, September 15, 1916, Mitchell Papers, M/A.

37. New York *Call*, September 16, 1916, 1–2; *Ladies' Garment Cutter*, IV (September 16, 1916), 2.

38. Transcript of Conference between Mayor John P. Mitchel, Police Commissioner Arthur Woods, Timothy Healey, Hugh Frayne, T. V. O'Connor, Ernest Bohm, William B. Fitzgerald, and James P. Holland, September 18, 1916, Mitchel Papers, M/A; New York *Call*, September 18, 1916, 1–2, September 19, 1916, 1–2.

39. New York *Call*, September 9, 1916, 2.

40. Transcript of Conference between Mayor John P. Mitchel, Public Service Chairman Oscar Straus, and Theodore P. Shonts, September 20, 1916, Mitchel Papers, M/A.

41. Transcript of Conference between Mayor John P. Mitchel, Chairman Oscar Straus, and the Citizen's Committee on the Traction Strike, September 21, 1916, ibid.

42. Transcript of Conference between Mayor John P. Mitchel, Chairman Oscar Straus, the Citizen's Committee on the Traction Strike, Samuel Gompers, Hugh Frayne, William V. Fitzgerald, Louis Fridiger, T. V. O'Connor, James P. Holland, and others, September 21, 1916, 11–53, ibid.

43. Ibid., 14.

44. Labor Officials reasoned, or rather rationalized, that a general suspension of work would not entail any breach of existing labor contracts as would a general strike.

45. New York *Call,* September 22, 1916, 1–2; September 23, 1916, 1–2; *Ladies' Garment Cutter,* IV (September 30, 1916), 2.

46. *Ladies' Garment Cutter,* IV (September 23, 1916), 1; (September 30, 1916), 1; New York *Call,* September 26, 1916, 1–2; September 28, 1916, 1–2.

47. Copy of Open Letter, Citizen's Committee on the Traction Strike to Theodore P. Shonts, September 25, 1916, Mitchel Papers, M/A.

48. New York *American,* September 26, 1916, 18; October 3, 1916, 18; New York *World,* September 21, 1916, 8; September 22, 1916, 6; September 23, 1916, 6; September 24, 1916, II, 2; New York *Tribune,* September 12, 1916, 8; September 22, 1916, 8; September 23, 1916, 8; September 25, 1916, 8; September 27, 1916, 10; New York *Herald,* September 21, 1916, 8; September 24, 1916, 16; September 25, 1916, 8; New York *Sun,* September 25, 1916, 12; New York *Times,* September 21, 1916, 10; September 25, 1916, 8.

49. Letter, E. H. Outerbridge to Mayor John P. Mitchel, September 23, 1916. The complete file of correspondence on the traction strike in the Mitchel Papers, M/A, is even more denunciatory of the strikers.

50. *The Headgear Worker,* I (October–November, 1916, 5; New York *Call,* September 29, 1916, 1; October 3, 1916, 2–3.

51. New York *Call,* October 10, 1916, 1; October 13, 1916, 1; October 25, 1916, 1; October 30, 1916, 1–2.

52. *The New Republic,* VIII (October 7, 1916), 235–237.

53. John P. Roche, "Entrepreneurial Liberty and the Fourteenth Amendment," *Labor History,* IV (Winter, 1963), 11–15, 22, 31.

54. *New York Railway Employees' Magazine,* III (September, 1916), 2; (October, 1916), 2; Petition from General Committee, Brotherhood of New York Railway Company Employees to Mayor John P. Mitchel, July 5, 1917, Mitchel Papers, M/A.

Epilogue

1. Joseph Rayback, *A History of American Labor* (New York, 1959), 273–279.

2. Ibid., 280–290; William Preston, Jr., *Aliens and Dissenters: Federal Suppression of Radicals, 1903–1933* (Cambridge, Mass., 1963), Chs. 4 and 8, and passim.

3. James Morris, *Conflict Within the AFL* (Ithaca, 1958), 55–85; Philip Taft, *The A.F. of L. from the Death of Gompers to the Merger* (New York, 1959), 1–2, 5–6, 8–12, 15–20, 21–25; Charles O. Gregory, *Labor and the Law* (New York, 1946), Chs. 7–8; Arthur M. Schlesinger, Jr., *The Crisis of the Old Order, 1919–1933* (Boston, Mass., 1957), 111–114.

4. L. Lorwin, *The Women's Garment Workers* (New York, 1924), 353–359; J. Seidman, *The Needle Trades* (New York, 1942), 153–184; B. Stolberg, *Tailor's Progress,* 108–155; P. Taft, *AFL from Death of Gompers,* 12.

5. J. Seidman, *Needle Trades,* 164–165, 186–208; B. Stolberg, *Tailor's Progress* (New York 1924), 136–137, 202–260.

6. P. Taft, *AFL from Death of Gompers,* Chs. 4–5, 10; J. Morris, *Conflict Within AFL,* Ch. 6; Arthur M. Schlesinger, Jr., *The Coming of the New Deal* (Boston, Mass., 1959), 397–406.

Bibliography

Note on Sources

THIS BIBLIOGRAPHICAL NOTE is intended to be a brief guide to the source materials essential to the writing of this book and also to distinguish this work from others of a similar nature. This book naturally benefited from the labors of other students of the New York labor movement, particularly Moses Rischin, Hyman Berman, and Irwin Yellowitz. It also built upon a solid foundation of literature dealing with the Jewish-American labor movement in the needle trades. But this study differs in important respects from earlier works.

Rischin in *The Promised City* is concerned primarily with the total Jewish community and treats the Jewish labor movement only incidentally. My emphasis, by contrast, is on the Jewish working class and its unions, and includes a detailed analysis of their efforts to organize the needle trades.

Berman's unpublished dissertation, "Era of the Protocol," is an excellent analysis of internal union development, but is limited to just one union, the ILGWU. I have been able to supplement his account with some important new sources of the ILGWU's struggles; these include the papers of Mayor John Purroy Mitchel and the labor arbitrator Paul Abelson. Moreover, unlike both Rischin and Berman, I analyze the organizational battles of the non-Jewish, nongarment workers in the city's labor force.

Yellowitz in his *Labor and the Progressive Movement* approaches the labor movement from a perspective entirely different from those of

Rischin and Berman. He concentrates upon the relationship between organized labor and middle- and upper-class social reformers as both groups lobbied to obtain labor legislation at the statewide level. But his study slights labor's efforts to organize trade-unions and neglects the Jewish socialist garment workers, perhaps the most forceful and creative element within the labor movement.

I found sources for the workers' side of the story limited. The New York City Central Federated Union left behind no records, the papers of several important leaders in the needle trades unions were destroyed or lost, and still others are unavailable, whatever the reason. The official publications of the building trades unions and other of the more conservative AFL unions consist mostly of job notices, wage rate schedules, and lists of unfair employers, and contain almost nothing on the philosophy or attitude of the organizations. However, the journals of the garment workers' unions and their convention proceedings, on which I relied greatly, offer what the craft unions' publications do not. There, philosophy, attitudes, strategy, and tactics can be clearly followed. The numerous popular magazines of the Progressive era also devoted considerable attention to industrial conflicts in New York, particularly those of the garment workers, and present case studies of the middle-class Progressive mentality. New York's daily newspapers do the same, and the excellent Socialist Party daily, *The Call,* contains detailed and unsurpassed reports, many quite objective, on the strikes and other events of importance in the history of New York labor.

Manuscript sources provide a mixed bag. The American Federation of Labor papers are disappointing; neither the Samuel Gompers Letterbooks in Washington, D.C. nor the AFL Official Correspondence in Madison, Wisconsin contain important materials concerning the strikes of 1909–1916. Equally disappointing for the same period were the papers of Joseph Barondess (New York Public Library), a former Jewish labor leader, and Morris Hillquit (Wisconsin State Historical Society), Socialist Party leader and attorney for most of the New York City needle trades' unions. On the other hand, the papers and records of the New York City Socialist Party (Tamiment Institute Library) provide revealing insights into the world of labor. Socialist records indicate that the party leadership, while mostly middle class (attorneys and dentists), depended on a Jewish working-class base, and that the garment workers' unions turned out the vote which Jewish precincts delivered. The outstanding manuscript sources were the Paul Abelson papers (in the personal possession

of Professor Jesse T. Carpenter of the New York State School of Industrial and Labor Relations) and the papers of New York Mayors William
F. Gaynor and John Purroy Mitchel (Municipal Archives). These papers,
utilized neither by Berman nor Yellowitz, detail the unexpected extent
of municipal intervention in major labor disputes and reveal better than
any other New York City sources the achievements and failures of urban
reformers in dealing with industrial conflicts. A complete list of the
sources used in this book follows.

Primary Sources

Manuscript Materials

PAUL ABELSON PAPERS. New York State School of Industrial and Labor
Relations, Ithaca, New York.
AMERICAN ASSOCIATION FOR LABOR LEGISLATION PAPERS. New York
State School of Industrial and Labor Relations, Ithaca, New York.
AMERICAN FEDERATION OF LABOR PAPERS. Wisconsin State Historical
Society, Madison.
JOSEPH BARONDESS PAPERS. Manuscript Division, New York Public
Library.
AUGUST CLAESSENS PAPERS. Tamiment Institute Library, New York.
MAYOR WILLIAM F. GAYNOR PAPERS. Municipal Archives, New York
City.
MORRIS HILLQUIT PAPERS. Wisconsin State Historical Society, Madison.
ALGERNON LEE PAPERS. Tamiment Institute Library, New York.
MEYER LONDON PAPERS. Taminent Institute Library, New York.
MAYOR JOHN PURROY MITCHEL PAPERS. Municipal Archives, New
York City.
SOCIALIST PARTY: LOCAL NEW YORK, PAPERS AND MINUTE BOOKS.
Tamiment Institute Library, New York.
WOMEN'S TRADE UNION LEAGUE OF NEW YORK, PAPERS. New York
State Department of Labor Library, New York.

Government Documents

CARPENTER, NILES. *Immigrants and their Children, 1920* (Bureau of
the Census. Census Monographs VII), Washington: Government
Printing Office, 1927.
EDWARDS, ALBA M. "Comparative Occupation Statistics for the United

States, 1870–1940," *Sixteenth Census of the United States,* Washington: Government Printing Office, 1943.

INTERSTATE COMMERCE COMMISSION. *First Annual Report on the Statistics of Express Companies in the United States as of June 30, 1909,* Washington: Government Printing Office, 1911.

———. *Third Annual Report on the Statistics of Express Companies in the United States as of June 30, 1911,* Washington: Government Printing Office, 1913.

RUBINOW, I. M. "Economic Conditions of the Jews in Russia," *Bulletin of the Bureau of Labor, No. 72* (September, 1907), 487–583, Washington; Government Printing Office, 1907.

UNITED STATES BUREAU OF THE CENSUS. *Thirteenth Census of the United States Taken in the Year 1910* (with Abstract of Census and Supplement for New York), Washington: Government Printing Office, 1913.

———. *Fourteenth Census of the United States Taken in the Year 1920* (with Abstract of Census and Supplement for New York), Washington: Government Printing Office, 1923.

UNITED STATES BUREAU OF LABOR STATISTICS. "Conciliation, Arbitration, and Sanitation in the Dress and Waist Industry of New York City," *Bulletin Whole Number 145* (April 10, 1914), Washington: Government Printing Office, 1914.

———. "Wages and Regularity of Employment in the Dress and Waist Industry: New York," *Bulletin Whole Number 146* (April 28, 1914), Washington: Government Printing Office, 1914.

———. "Collective Agreements in the Men's Clothing Industry," *Bulletin Whole Number 198* (September, 1916), Washington: Government Printing Office, 1916.

UNITED STATES SENATE: 61st Congress; 2nd Session, "Report on Conditions of Woman and Child Wage-Earners in the United States," *Senate Document No. 645,* Washington: Government Printing Office, 1910, 19 volumes.

———. 61st Congress; 2nd Session, "Reports of the Immigration Commission: Immigrants in the Cities," *Senate Document No. 338,* Washington: Government Printing Office, 1911.

———. 61st Congress; 2nd Session, "Reports of the Immigration Commission: Immigrants in Industry" (Parts 5, 6, and 7), *Senate Document No. 633,* Washington: Government Printing Office, 1911.

———. 61st Congress; 2nd Session, "Abstracts of Reports of the Immigration Commission on Immigrants in the United States," *Senate*

Document No. 747, Washington: Government Printing Office, 1911–1912, 15 volumes.

―――. 64th Congress; 1st Session, "Final Report and Testimony Submitted to Congress by the Commission on Industrial Relations Created by the Act of August 23, 1912," *Senate Document No. 415,* Washington: Government Printing Office, 1916, 20 volumes.

New York State Documents

NEW YORK STATE. *Report of the Enumeration of the Inhabitants of the State of New York, June 1, 1905,* Albany: Brandow Printing Company, 1906.

―――. *Report of the Enumeration of the Inhabitants in the State of New York, January 17, 1916,* Albany: J. B. Lyon Company, 1916, 2 volumes.

NEW YORK STATE DEPARTMENT OF LABOR. *Special Bulletins 43–85,* Albany: J. B. Lyon Company, 1910–1918.

NEW YORK STATE FACTORY INVESTIGATING COMMISSION. *Preliminary Report.* Albany: The Argus Company, 1912, 3 volumes.

―――. *Second Report,* Albany: J. B. Lyon Company, 1913, 4 volumes.

―――. *Third Report,* Albany: J. B. Lyon Company, 1914.

―――. *Fourth Report,* Albany: J. B. Lyon Company, 1915, 5 volumes.

NEW YORK STATE PUBLIC SERVICE COMMISSION, FIRST DISTRICT. *Report on the Surface Transit Strike in New York City,* New York, 1916.

Convention Proceedings

AMALGAMATED CLOTHING WORKERS OF AMERICA. *Official Convention Proceedings* in *Documentary History of the Amalgamated Clothing Workers of America, 1914–1919.*

AMERICAN FEDERATION OF LABOR. *Report of the Proceedings of the Annual Convention, 1900–1918.*

INTERNATIONAL LADIES' GARMENT WORKERS' UNION. *Report and Proceedings of Annual Conventions, 1903–1918.*

NEW YORK STATE FEDERATION OF LABOR. *Official Convention Proceedings, 1900–1918.*

SOCIALIST LABOR PARTY. *Proceedings of the 10th Annual Convention, 1900.* Typewritten Copy, Tamiment Institute Library, New York.

SOCIALIST PARTY OF AMERICA. *Proceedings of the Socialist Unity Convention, 1901.* Typewritten Copy, Tamiment Institute Library, New York.

UNITED CLOTH HAT AND CAP MAKERS OF NORTH AMERICA. *Official Convention Proceedings, 1902, 1911–1918.*
UNITED GARMENT WORKERS OF AMERICA. *Official Convention Proceedings, 1901, 1906–1914.*

Union and Trade Journals

The Advance
American Federationist
Cap-Makers' Journal
Daily Trade Record
The Fur Worker
The Headgear Worker
Interborough Bulletin
Labor Temple Bulletin
The Ladies' Garment Cutter
The Ladies' Garment Worker

Legislative Labor News and Labor Advocate
New York Railways Employees' Magazine
The Painter and Decorator
The Weekly Bulletin of the Clothing Trades (The Garment Worker)
Women's Trade Union League Bulletin
Women's Wear Daily

Newspapers

New York *American*
New York *Call*
New York *Herald*
New York *Evening Post*
New York *Sun*

New York *Evening Telegram*
New York *Times*
New York *Tribune*
New York *World*

Periodicals

The American Hebrew
Charities
Charities and the Commons
Forum
Independent
Life and Labor
McClure's Magazine

Metropolitan Magazine
The New Republic
Outlook
Review of Reviews
The Survey
University Settlement Studies
World's Work

Arbitration Proceedings

"Arbitration Proceedings, The Cloak and Skirt Makers' Unions of New York, the Cloak, Suit, and Skirt Manufacturers' Protective Association" (August 3–6, 1913). Stenographic Copy, Tamiment Institute Library, New York, 2 volumes.

"Board of Arbitration Meetings, Local 25, Dress and Waistmakers' Union, New York City and the Associated Dress and Waist Manufacturers' Association" (1913–1915). Stenographic Reports, New York State School of Industrial and Labor Relations, Ithaca, New York.

Conferences between the Management, the Board of Directors of New York Railways Company and Representatives of Its Employees (August 17–September 6, 1916), New York, 1916.

"Findings and Recommendations of the Council of Conciliation Appointed by Honorable John Purroy Mitchel, Handed Down July 23, 1915, and Accepted by the Union and the Association, August 4, 1915." Stenographic Copy in the Mitchel Papers, Municipal Archives, New York City.

"Meetings of the Board of Arbitrators with the Representatives of the Skirt and Cloak Makers' Unions of New York, the Cloak, Suit, and Skirt Manufacturers' Protective Association" (October 12–13, 1913). Stenographic Report, New York State School of Industrial and Labor Relations, Ithaca, New York.

"United Garment Workers' Conference, Report for Conferees by Julius Henry Cohen, January 27, 1913." Stenographic Copy, Tamiment Institute Library, New York.

Personal Interviews

PAULINE NEWMAN
December 10, 1958
JOSEPH SCHLOSSBERG
November 20, 1958

ROSE SCHNEIDERMAN
November 24, 1958
LOUIS WALDMAN
November 25, 1958

Reminiscences and Autobiographies

BERNHEIMER, CHARLES S. *Half a Century of Community Service,* New York: Association Press, 1948.

BUTLER, RICHARD J., and DRISCOLL, JOSEPH. *Dock Walloper: The Story of "Big Dick" Butler,* New York: G. P. Putnam's Sons, 1933.

CLAESSENS, AUGUST. *Didn't We Have Fun,* New York: The Rand School Press, 1953.

COHEN, JULIAN H. *They Builded Better Than They Knew,* New York: Julian Messner, Inc., 1946.

COHEN, ROSE. *Out of the Shadow,* New York: George H. Doran Company, 1918.

COLUMBIA UNIVERSITY. Oral History Project, Reminiscences:

HENRY BRUERE	LOUIS H. PINK
"Number 7," 2 volumes.	"Number 31," 2 volumes.
JOHN P. FREY	LOUIS M. RABINOWITZ
"Number 225," 4 volumes.	"Number 243."
BRUNO LASKER	LAWRENCE VEILLER
"Number 232," 3 volumes.	"Number 5," 2 volumes

CURRAN, HENRY H. *Pillar to Post,* New York: Charles Scribner's Sons, 1941.

FREEMAN, JOSEPH. *An American Testament,* New York: Farrar and Rinehart Inc., 1936.

GOMPERS, SAMUEL. *Seventy Years of Life and Labor.* New York: E. P. Dutton and Company, 1925, 2 volumes.

HASANOVITZ, ELIZABETH. *One of Them,* Boston: Houghton Mifflin Company, 1918.

HILLQUIT, MORRIS. *Loose Leaves from a Busy Life,* New York: The Macmillan Company, 1934.

KLEIN, HENRY H. *My Last Fifty Years,* New York: Isaac Goldman Company, 1935.

LA GUARDIA, FIORELLO H. *The Making of an Insurgent, 1882–1919,* Philadelphia: J. B. Lippincott Company, 1948.

LANG, LUCY ROBINS. *Tomorrow Is Beautiful,* New York: The Macmillan Company, 1948.

RAVAGE, M. E. *An American in the Making: The Life Story of an Immigrant,* New York: Harper and Brothers, 1917.

REZNIKOFF, CHARLES and NATHAN. *Early History of a Sewing-machine Operator,* New York: Charles Reznikoff, 1936.

RUSSELL, CHARLES E. *Bare Hands and Stone Walls,* New York: Charles Scribner's Sons, 1933.

SIMKHOVITCH, MARY K. *Neighborhood: My Story of Greenwich House,* New York: W. W. Norton and Company, Inc., 1938.

SMITH, ALFRED E. *Up to Now: An Autobiography,* New York: The Viking Press, 1929.

STELZLE, CHARLES. *A Son of the Bowery,* New York: George H. Doran Company, 1926.

STEWART, WILLIAM R. *The Philanthropic Work of Josephine Shaw Lowell,* New York: The Macmillan Company, 1911.

WALD, LILLIAN D. *The House on Henry Street,* New York: Henry Holt and Company, 1915.

WALDMAN, LOUIS. *Labor Lawyer,* New York: E. P. Dutton and Company, Inc., 1944.

ZAUSNER, PHILIP. *Unvarnished: The Autobiography of a Union Leader,* New York: Brotherhood Publishers, 1941.

Other

The American Labor Year Book (1916–1918). New York: The Rand School of Social Science, 1916–1918, 2 volumes.

Annual Report of the Interborough Rapid Transit Company for the Year Ended June 30, 1917. New York: John Ward and Son, 1917.

BAKER, RAY STANNARD. "The Rise of the Tailors," *McClure's Magazine,* XXIV (December, 1904), 126–139.

BARNES, CHARLES B. *The Longshoremen,* New York: The Russell Sage Foundation, 1915.

BERNHEIMER, CHARLES S. *The Russian Jew in the United States,* Philadelphia: The J. C. Winston Company, 1905.

———. *The Shirt Waist Strike,* New York: University Settlement, 1910.

BEST, HARRY. *The Men's Garment Industry of New York and the Strike of 1913,* New York: University Settlement Society, 1913[?].

BETTS, LILLIAN W. "Italian Peasants in a New-law Tenement," *Harper's Bazaar,* XXXVIII (August, 1904), 802–805.

BLANK, ROSE. "The Strike of the Furriers in New York," *Life and Labor,* II (December, 1912), 357–361.

BRUERE, MARTHA B. "The Triangle Fire," *Life and Labor,* I (May, 1911), 137–141.

———. "The White Goods Strikers," *Life and Labor,* III (March, 1913), 73–75.

BYRNES, CLARA. *Block Sketches of New York City,* New York: Radbridge Company, 1918.

CHAPIN, ROBERT C. *The Standard of Living Among Workingmen's Families in New York City,* New York: The Russell Sage Foundation, 1909.

CLAESSENS, AUGUST, and FEIGENBAUM, WILLIAM M. *The Socialists in the New York Assembly,* New York: The Rand School of Social Science, 1918.

CLARK, SUE A., and WYATT, EDITH. "The Shirtwaist-makers and Their Strike," *McClure's Magazine*, XXXVI (November, 1910), 70–86.
———. "Women Laundry Workers in New York," *McClure's Magazine*, XXXVI (February, 1911), 401–414.
COHEN, JULIUS HENRY. *A League to Enforce Industrial Peace*, New York: Academy of Political Science, 1916.
———. *Law and Order in Industry*, New York: The Macmillan Company, 1916.
———. "The Protocols in the Cloak, Suit, and Skirt Industry and in the Dress and Waist Industry." Reprinted from *Transactions of the Efficiency Society, Inc.*, January 28, 1913.
———. "The Revised Protocol in the Dress and Waist Industry." Reprinted from the *Annals of the American Academy of Political and Social Science* (January, 1917).
COLLIER, JOHN, and BARROWS, EDWARD M. *The City Where Crime Is Play*, New York: The People's Institute, 1914.
DE SCHWEINITZ, KARL. "Tammany by Default," *The Survey*, XXXIX (November 17, 1917), 162–164.
DEWHURST, MARY. "The Cloak Makers' Strike," *The Outlook*, CXIII (July 12, 1916), 606–609.
The Effort to Tie-up the Street Railroad System of New York City, New York: Interborough Rapid Transit Company, 1916.
FISHBERG, MAURICE. "The Russian Jew in America," *Review of Reviews*, XXVI (September, 1902), 315–318.
GOMPERS, SAMUEL. "The Struggle in the Garment Trades," *American Federationist*, XX (March, 1913), 185–202.
HARD, WILLIAM. "The New York Mayoralty Campaign," *The New Republic*, XII (October 6, 1917), 270–273.
HENDRICK, BURTON J. "The Twilight of Tammany," *World's Work*, XXVII (February, 1914), 432–440.
HENRY, ALICE. "The Way Out," *Life and Labor*, II (April, 1912), 120–121.
HERZFELD, ELSA G. *Family Monographs*, New York: The James Kempster Printing Company, 1905.
HILLQUIT, MORRIS. *Not Guilty*. New York: International Ladies' Garment Workers' Union, 1915.
———. "Socialism Up to Date," *Metropolitan Magazine*, XXXVI (September, 1912), 12–13, 59–60.
HUTCHINSON, WOODS. "The Hygienic Aspects of the Shirtwaist Strike," *The Survey*, XXIII (January 22, 1910), 541–550.

LAIDLAW, WALTER. "The Jews of New York," *American Hebrew,* LXX-VI (May 19, 1905), 785–792.

LENNON, JOHN B. "The Practical Trades Unionism of the Cloakmakers' Strike," *American Federationist,* XVII (October, 1910), 890–891.

LEUPP, CONSTANCE D. "The Shirtwaist Makers' Strike," *The Survey,* XXIII (December 18, 1909), 383–386.

LEVIEN, SONYA. "The Little Prophet of the Immigrants," *Metropolitan Magazine,* XXXVII (March, 1913), 45–46.

MAILLY, WILLIAM. "The New York Rent Strike," *The Independent,* LXIV (January 16, 1908), 148–152.

———. "The Triangle Trade Union Relief," *American Federationist,* XVIII (July, 1911), 544–547.

MALKIEL, THERESA S. *The Diary of a Shirtwaist Striker,* New York: The Co-operative Press, 1910.

MANGANO, ANTONIO. "Associated Life of Italians in New York City," *Charities,* XII (1904), 476–480.

MYERS, GUSTAVUS. "The Secrets of Tammany's Success," *Forum,* XXXI (June, 1901), 488–500.

NEW YORK RAILWAYS COMPANY. *Annual Reports, 1913–1918,* New York: John Ward and Son, 1913–1918.

ODENCRANTZ, LOUISE C. *Italian Women in Industry: A Study of Conditions in New York City,* New York: Russell Sage Foundation, 1919.

PINCHOT, AMOS. *A Letter to County Chairmen and Other Chairmen,* New York: [n.p.], 1913.

PRATT, EDWARD E. *Industrial Causes of Congestion of Population in New York City,* New York: Columbia University, 1911.

RIPLEY, WILLIAM Z. "Race Factors in Labor Unions," *Atlantic Monthly,* XCIII (March, 1904), 299–308.

Rules and Regulations for the Government Operating Officers and Employees of the Interborough Rapid Transit Company, Subway Division, to Take Effect, January 1, 1916, New York: IRT, 1915–1916.

SCHNEIDERMAN, ROSE. "The White Goods Workers of New York," *Life and Labor,* III (May, 1913), 132–136.

SCOTT, MIRIAM F. "The Spirit of the Girl Strikers," *The Outlook,* XCIV (February 19, 1910), 392–397.

———. "What the Women Strikers Won," *The Outlook,* XCV (July, 2, 1910), 480–481.

SERGEANT, ELIZABETH S. "Toilers of the Tenements," *McClure's Magazine,* XXXV (July, 1910), 231–248.

Settlement of the August 4th Strike on the New York Railway Company, New York: [n.p.], 1916.

STEINER, EDWARD A. "The Russian and Polish Jew in New York," *The Outlook,* LXXII (November 1, 1902), 528–539.

SUMNER, MARY B. "The Spirit of the Strikers," *The Survey,* XXIII (January 22, 1910), 550–555.

———. "A Strike for Clean Bread," *The Survey,* XXIV (June 18, 1910), 483–488.

TARBELL, IDA M. "The Shirt-waist Strikers," *American Federationist,* XVII (March, 1910), 209–210.

TRACHTENBERG, ALEXANDER. *The American Socialists and the War,* New York: The Rand School of Social Science, 1917.

TURNER, GEORGE KIBBE. "What Organized Labor Wants: An Interview with Samuel Gompers," *McClure's Magazine,* XXXII (November, 1908), 25–31.

VAN KLEECK, MARY. *Artificial Flower Makers,* New York: The Russell Sage Foundation, 1913.

———. *A Seasonal Industry: A Study of the Millinery Trade in New York City,* New York: The Russell Sage Foundation, 1917.

———. *Women in the Bookbinding Trade,* New York: The Russell Sage Foundation, 1913.

———. "Working Hours of Women in Factories," *Charities and the Commons,* XVII (October 6, 1906), 13–21.

WATSON, ELIZABETH C. "Home Work in the Tenements," *The Survey,* XXV (February 4, 1911), 772–782.

THE WOMEN'S TRADE UNION LEAGUE OF NEW YORK. *Annual Reports, 1906–1917,* New York: WTUL, 1907–1917.

WYATT, EDITH. "The New York Cloak-makers' Strike," *McClure's Magazine,* XXXVI (April, 1911), 708–714.

Secondary Sources

Books

ABBOTT, EDITH. *Women in Industry,* New York: D. Appleton and Company, 1910.

ADAMS, THOMAS S., and SUMNER, HELEN L. *Labor Problems,* New York: The Macmillan Company, 1908.

ALBION, ROBERT G. *The Rise of New York Port, 1815–1860,* New York: Charles Scribner's Sons, 1939.

BAKER, ELIZABETH F. *Protective Labor Legislation with Special Reference to Women in the State of New York,* New York: Columbia University Press, 1925.

BIMBA, ANTHONY. *The History of the American Working Class,* New York: International Publishers, 1927.

BOONE, GLADYS. *The Women's Trade Union Leagues in Great Britain and the United States of America,* New York: Columbia University Press, 1942.

BOWERS, DAVID F., ed. *Foreign Influences in American Life,* Princeton: Princeton University Press, 1944.

BRISSENDEN, PAUL F. *The I.W.W.: A Study of American Syndicalism,* New York: Russell and Russell, Inc. 1957.

BROOKS, GEORGE W. et. al., eds. *Interpreting the Labor Movement,* Champaign, Illinois: Industrial Relations Research Association, 1952.

BUDISH, J. M., and SOULE, GEORGE. *The New Unionism in the Clothing Industry,* New York: Harcourt, Brace, and Howe, 1920.

CAHAN, ABRAHAM. *The Rise of David Levinsky,* New York: Harper and Brothers, 1917.

CARROLL, MOLLIE R. *Labor and Politics,* Boston: Houghton Mifflin Company, 1923.

CARSEL, WILFRED. *A History of the Chicago Ladies' Garment Workers' Union,* Chicago: Normandie House, 1940.

CHINITZ, BENJAMIN. *Freight and the Metropolis: The Impact of America's Transport Revolutions on the New York Region,* Cambridge, Mass.: Harvard University Press, 1960.

CROCKETT, ALBERT S. *Peacocks on Parade,* New York: Sears Publishing Company, Inc., 1931.

DANISH, MAX D. *The World of David Dubinsky,* Cleveland: The World Publishing Company, 1957.

DAVIE, MAURICE R. *World Immigration,* New York: The Macmillan Company, 1936.

DOUGLAS, PAUL H. *Real Wages in the United States, 1890–1926,* Boston: Houghton Mifflin Company, 1930.

DREISER, THEODORE. *The Color of a Great City,* New York: Boni and Liverwright, 1923.

DUFFUS, ROBERT L. *Lillian Wald,* New York: The Macmillan Company, 1938.

DULLES, FOSTER RHEA. *Labor in America,* New York: Thomas Y. Crowell Company, 1949.

EGBERT, DONALD D., and PERSONS, STOW. *Socialism and American Life,* Princeton: Princeton University Press, 1952, 2 volumes.

EPSTEIN, MELECH. *Jewish Labor in U.S.A.,* New York: Trade Union Sponsoring Committee, 1950–1953, 2 volumes.

ERICKSON, CHARLOTTE. *American Industry and the European Immigrant,* Cambridge, Mass.: Harvard University Press, 1957.

ERNST, ROBERT. *Immigrant Life in New York City, 1825–1863,* New York: King's Crown Press, 1949.

FAIRCHILD, FRED R. *The Factory Legislation of the State of New York,* New York: American Economic Association, 1906.

FERENCZI, IMRE, and WILLCOX, WALTER F., eds. *International Migrations,* New York: National Bureau of Economic Research, 1931, 2 volumes.

FINE, NATHAN. *Labor and Farmer Parties in the United States, 1828–1928,* New York: The Rand School of Social Science, 1928.

FLICK, ALEXANDER C., ed. *History of the State of New York,* New York: Columbia University Press, 1937, 10 volumes.

FOERSTER, ROBERT F. *The Italian Emigration of Our Times,* Cambridge, Mass.: Harvard University Press, 1919.

FONER, PHILIP S. *The Fur and Leather Workers' Union,* Newark: Nordan Press, 1950.

FORD, JAMES. *Slums and Housing,* Cambridge, Mass.: Harvard University Press, 1946, 2 volumes.

FRANKLIN, ALLAN. *The Trail of the Tiger,* New York: [n.p.], 1928.

GOLDMAN, ERIC F. *Rendezvous with Destiny: A History of Modern American Reform,* New York: Alfred A. Knopf, 1953.

GOLDMARK, JOSEPHINE. *Impatient Crusader: Florence Kelley's Life Story,* Urbana: University of Illinois Press, 1953.

GREEN, CHARLES H. *The Headwear Workers: A Century of Trade Unionism,* New York: Marstin Press, 1944.

GREEN, MARGUERITE. *The National Civic Federation and the American Labor Movement, 1900–1925,* Washington, D.C.: Catholic University Press, 1956.

GREGORY, CHARLES O. *Labor and the Law,* New York: W. W. Norton and Company, 1946.

GROAT, GEORGE G. *Trade Unions and the Law in New York,* New York: Columbia University Press, 1905.

HAIG, ROBERT M., and MCCREA, ROSWELL C. *Regional Plan of New York and Its Environs,* New York: Committee on Regional Plan of New York and Its Environs, 1924–1928, 9 volumes.

HALL, MAX, ed. *Made in New York: Case Studies in Metropolitan Manufacturing,* Cambridge, Mass.: Harvard University Press, 1959.

HANDLIN, OSCAR. *Adventure in Freedom: Three Hundred Years of Jewish Life in America,* New York: McGraw-Hill Book Company, 1954.

———. *The Newcomers: Negroes and Puerto Ricans in a Changing Metropolis,* Cambridge, Mass.: Harvard University Press, 1959.

———. *The Uprooted,* Boston: Little, Brown and Company, 1951.

HAPGOOD, NORMAN, and MOSCOWITZ, HENRY. *Up from the City Streets: Alfred E. Smith,* New York: Harcourt, Brace and Company, 1927.

HARDMAN, J.B.S., ed. *The Amalgamated: Today and Tomorrow,* New York: The Amalgamated Clothing Workers of America, 1940.

———, ed. *The Book of the Amalgamated in New York, 1914–1940.* New York: The Amalgamated Clothing Workers of America, 1940

HARRIS, HERBERT. *American Labor,* New Haven: Yale University Press, 1939.

HART, SMITH. *The New Yorkers,* New York: Sheridan House, 1938.

HASKEL, HARRY. *A Leader of the Garment Workers: The Biography of Isadore Nagler,* New York: Amalgamated Ladies' Garment Cutters' Union, Local 10, 1950.

HAYNES, GEORGE E. *The Negro at Work in New York City,* New York: Columbia University Press, 1912.

HAYS, SAMUEL P. *The Response to Industrialism, 1885–1914,* Chicago: University of Chicago Press, 1957.

HENRY, ALICE. *The Trade Union Woman,* New York: D. Appleton and Company, 1915.

———. *Women and the Labor Movement,* New York: George H. Doran Company, 1923.

HIGHAM, JOHN. *Strangers in the Land: Patterns of American Nativism,* New Brunswick, New Jersey: Rutgers University Press, 1955.

HOFSTADER, RICHARD. *The Age of Reform: From Bryan to F.D.R.,* New York: Alfred A. Knopf, 1955.

HOOVER, EDGAR M., and VERNON, RAYMOND. *Anatomy of a Metropolis: The Changing Distribution of Jobs and People within the New York Metropolitan Region,* Cambridge, Mass.: Harvard University Press, 1959.

HOURWICH, ISAAC A. *Immigration and Labor,* New York: G. P. Putnam's Sons, 1912.

HOWE, WIRT. *New York at the Turn of the Century, 1899–1916,* Toronto: Privately Printed, 1946.

HURWITZ, HOWARD, L. *Theodore Roosevelt and Labor in New York State, 1880–1900,* New York: Columbia University Press, 1943.

HURWITZ, MAXIMILIAN. *The Workmen's Circle: Its History, Ideals, Organization and Institutions,* New York: The Workmen's Circle, 1936.

JONES, MALDWYN A. *American Immigration,* Chicago: University of Chicago Press, 1960.

JOSEPHSON, MATTHEW. *Sidney Hillman: Statesman of Labor,* New York: Doubleday and Company, Inc., 1952.

———. *Union House, Union Bar: The History of the Hotel and Restaurant Employees' and Bartenders' International Union, AFL-CIO,* New York: Random House; 1956.

KARSON, MARC. *American Labor Unions and Politics, 1900–1918,* Carbondale: Southern Illinois University Press, 1958.

KING, WILLFORD I. *The Wealth and Income of the People of the United States,* New York: The Macmillan Company, 1915.

KIPNIS, IRA. *The American Socialist Movement, 1897–1912,* New York: Columbia University Press, 1952.

KIRKLAND, EDWARD C. *Industry Comes of Age: Business, Labor, and Public Policy, 1860–1897,* New York: Holt, Rinehart, and Winston, 1961.

KNIGHT,ROBERT E. L. *Industrial Relations in the San Francisco Bay Area, 1900–1918,* Berkeley, California: University of California Press, 1960.

KUHN, HENRY, and JOHNSON, OLIVE M. *The Socialist Labor Party, 1890–1930,* New York: Labor News Company, 1931.

LAIDLAW, WALTER. *Statistical Sources for Demography of New York City,* New York: 1920 Census Committee, 1922.

LANG, HARRY. *"62": Biography of a Union,* New York: Undergarment and Negligee Workers' Union, Local 62, 1940.

———, and FEINSTONE, MORRIS. *Gewerkshaften: United Hebrew Trades,* New York: United Hebrew Trades, 1938.

LEARSI, RUFUS. *The Jews in America: A History,* Cleveland: The World Publishing Company, 1954.

"Let Us Review the Scene" with William M. Feigenbaum. New York: Social Democratic Federation, 1951.

LEUCHTENBERG, WILLIAM L. *The Perils of Prosperity, 1914–1932,* Chicago: University of Chicago Press, 1958.

LINFIELD, HARRY S. *The Communal Organization of the Jews in the United States,* New York: The American Jewish Committee, 1930.

LINK, ARTHUR S. *American Epoch,* New York: Alfred A. Knopf, 1955.

LOFT, JACOB. *The Printing Trades,* New York: Farrar and Rinehart, Inc., 1944.

LONG, CLARENCE D. *Wages and Earnings in the United States, 1850–1890,* Princeton: Princeton University Press, 1960.

LORWIN, LEWIS L. *The Women's Garment Workers: A History of the International Ladies' Garment Workers' Union,* New York: B. W. Huebsch, Inc., 1924.

LUBOVE, ROY. *The Progressives and the Slums,* Pittsburgh: University of Pittsburgh Press, 1962.

MCMURRY, DONALD L. *The Great Burlington Strike of 1888,* Cambridge, Mass.; Harvard University Press, 1956.

MARIANO, JOHN H. *The Italian Contribution to American Democracy,* Boston: The Christopher Publishing House, 1921.

MASON, ALPHEUS T. *Brandeis: A Free Man's Life,* New York: The Viking Press, 1946.

MILLIS, HARRY A., and MONTGOMERY, ROYAL E. *Labor's Progress and Some Basic Labor Problems,* New York: McGraw-Hill Book Company, 1938.

MORRIS, JAMES O. *Conflict within the AFL,* Ithaca: Cornell University Press, 1958.

MOWRY, GEORGE E. *The Era of Theodore Roosevelt, 1900–1912,* New York: Harper and Brothers, 1958.

MYERS, GUSTAVUS. *The History of Tammany Hall,* New York: Boni and Liverwright, 1917.

NATHAN, MAUD. *The Story of an Epoch-Making Movement,* New York: Doubleday, Page and Company, 1926.

NEVINS, ALLAN, and KROUT, JOHN A., eds. *The Greater City: New York, 1898–1948,* New York: Columbia University Press, 1948.

NEWELL, BARBARA W. *Chicago and the Labor Movement: Metropolitan Unionism in the 1930's,* Urbana: University of Illinois Press, 1961.

ONEAL, JAMES. *A History of the Amalgamated Ladies' Garment Cutters' Union, Local 10,* New York: Amalgamated Ladies' Garment Cutters' Union, Local 10, 1927.

PARK, ROBERT E., and MILLER, HERBERT A. *Old World Traits Transplanted,* New York: Harper and Brothers, 1921.

PELLING, HENRY. *American Labor,* Chicago: University of Chicago Press, 1960.

PERLMAN, SELIG. *A History of Trade Unionism in the United States,* New York: The Macmillan Company, 1923.

———. *A Theory of the Labor Movement,* New York: Augustus M. Kelley, 1949.

———, and TAFT, PHILIP. *History of Labor in the United States, 1896–1932,* New York: The Macmillan Company, 1935.

PETERSON, H. C., and FITE, GILBERT C. *Opponents of War, 1917–1918,* Madison: University of Wisconsin Press, 1957.

PINK, LOUIS H. *Gaynor,* New York: The International Press, 1931.

PISANI, LAWRENCE F. *The Italians in America,* New York: Exposition Press, 1957.

POPE, JESSE, E. "The Clothing Industry in New York," *University of Missouri Series in the Social Sciences, Volume I,* Columbia, Missouri: University of Missouri Press, 1905.

PORTER, KENNETH W. *John Jacob Astor: Business Man,* Cambridge, Mass.: Harvard University Press, 1931, 2 volumes.

PRESTON, WILLIAM JR. *Aliens and Dissenters: Federal Suppression of Radicals, 1903–1933,* Cambridge, Mass.: Harvard University Press, 1963.

RAYBACK, JOSEPH C. *A History of American Labor,* New York: The Macmillan Company, 1959.

REES, ALBERT. *Real Wages in Manufacturing, 1890–1914,* Princeton: Princeton University Press, 1961.

RIIS, JACOB A. *How the Other Half Lives,* New York: Charles Scribner's Sons, 1900.

RISCHIN, MOSES. *The Promised City: New York's Jews, 1870–1914,* Cambridge, Mass.: Harvard University Press, 1962.

ROBINSON, DONALD B. *Spotlight on a Union: The Story of the United Hatters, Cap and Millinery Workers' Union,* New York: The Dial Press, 1948.

ROBINSON, DWIGHT E. *Collective Bargaining and Market Control in the Coat and Suit Industry,* New York: Columbia University Press, 1949.

ROGOFF, ABRAHAM M. *Formative Years in the Jewish Labor Movement in the United States (1890–1900),* New York: [n.p.], 1945.

ROGOFF, HARRY. *An East Side Epic: The Life and Work of Meyer London,* New York: The Vanguard Press, 1930.

SAPOSS, DAVID J. *Left Wing Unionism,* New York: International Publishers, 1926.

SAYRE, WALLACE S., and KAUFMAN, HERBERT. *Governing New York City: Politics in the Metropolis,* New York: Russell Sage Foundation, 1960.

SCHLESINGER, ARTHUR M., JR. *The Crisis of the Old Order, 1919–1933,* Boston: Houghton Mifflin and Company, 1957.

———. *The Coming of the New Deal,* Boston: Houghton Mifflin and Company, 1959.

SCHLOSSBERG, JOSEPH. *The Rise of the Clothing Workers,* New York: Amalgamated Clothing Workers of America, 1921.

———. *The Workers and Their World,* New York: American Labor Party Committee, 1935.

SEGAL, MARTIN. *Wages in the Metropolis: Their Influence on the Location of Industries in the Region,* Cambridge, Mass.: Harvard University Press, 1960.

SEIDMAN, JOEL. *The Needle Trades,* New York: Farrar and Rinehart, Inc., 1942.

SEIDMAN, HAROLD. *Labor Czars,* New York: Liverwright Publishing Corporation, 1938.

SHANNON, DAVID A. *The Socialist Party of America,* New York: The Macmillan Company, 1955.

SHAW, FREDERICK. *The History of the New York City Legislature.* New York: Columbia University Press, 1954.

SIMKHOVITCH, MARY K. *The City Worker's World in America,* New York: The Macmillan Company, 1917.

SMITH, MORTIMER. *William Jay Gaynor: Mayor of New York,* Chicago: Henry Regnery Company, 1951.

STELLA, ANTONIO. *Some Aspects of Italian Immigration to the United States,* New York: G. P. Putnam's Sons, 1924.

STEVENS, GEORGE A. *New York Typographical Union No. 6,* Albany: J. B. Lyon Company, 1913.

STILL, BAYRD. *Mirror for Gotham: New York as Seen by Contemporaries from Dutch Days to the Present,* New York: New York University Press, 1956.

STOLBERG, BENJAMIN. *Tailor's Progress,* New York: Doubleday, Doran and Company, 1944.

STRONG, EARL D. *The Amalgamated Clothing Workers of America,* Grinnell, Iowa: Herald-Register Publishing Company, 1940.

SWANBERG, W. A. *Citizen Hearst: A Biography of William Randolph Hearst,* New York: Charles Scribner's Sons, 1961.

SYMES, LILLIAN, and CLEMENT, TRAVERS, *Rebel America: The Story of Social Revolt in the United States,* New York: Harper and Brothers, 1934.

TANNENBAUM, FRANK. *A Philosophy of Labor,* New York: Alfred A. Knopf, 1951.

TEBBEL, JOHN. *The Life and Good Times of William Randolph Hearst,* New York: E. P. Dutton and Company, 1952.

TEPER, LAZARE. *The Women's Garment Industry,* New York: ILGWU, 1937.

THOMAS, BRINLEY. *Migration and Economic Growth: A Study of Great Britain and the Atlantic Economy,* Cambridge: Cambridge University Press, 1954.

TOWNE, CHARLES H. *This New York of Mine,* New York: Cosmopolitan Book Corporation, 1931.

WARE, LOUISE. *Jacob A. Riis,* New York: D. Appleton-Century Company, 1938.

WARNE, FRANK J. *The Immigrant Invasion,* New York: Dodd, Mead and Company, 1913.

WERNER, M.R. *Tammany Hall,* New York: Doubleday, Doran and Company, 1928.

WIEBE, ROBERT E. *Businessmen and Reform,* Cambridge, Mass.: Harvard University Press, 1962.

WILLIAMS, PHYLLIS. *South Italian Folkways in Europe and America,* New Haven: Yale University Press, 1938.

WINKLER, JOHN K. *William Randoph Hearst: A New Appraisal,* New York: Hastings House, 1955.

WOLFSON, THERESA. *The Woman Worker and the Trade Unions,* New York: International Publishers, 1926.

WOLMAN, LEO. *The Clothing Workers of Chicago, 1910–1922,* Chicago: Amalgamated Clothing Workers of America, 1922.

———. *The Growth of American Trade Unions, 1880–1923,* New York: National Bureau of Economic Research, 1924.

WOOD, EDITH E. *The Housing of the Unskilled Wage Earner,* New York: The Macmillan Company, 1919.

WORKS PROGRESS ADMINISTRATION. *The Italians of New York,* New York: Random House, 1938.

ZARETZ, CHARLES E. *The Amalgamated Clothing Workers of America,* New York: Ancon Publishing Company, 1934.

Articles

BEST, HARRY. "Extent of Organization in the Women's Garment Making Industries of New York," *American Economic Review,* IX (December 1919), 776–792.

———. "The Melting Pot in the United States," *Social Forces,* XIV (May, 1936), 591–596.

BLUMENSON, S. L. "Revolt of the Reefer-makers," *Commentary,* VIII (July, 1949), 62–70.

CHALMERS, HENRY. "The Number of Jews in New York City," *Publications of the American Statistical Association,* XIV (1914–1915), 68–75.

COLEMAN, MCALISTER. "All of Which I Saw," *The Progressive,* XIV (May, 1950), 24–27.

COMMONS, JOHN R. "The New York Building Trades," *Quarterly Journal of Economics,* XVIII (May, 1904), 409–434.

ECKLER, A. ROSS, and ZLOTNICK, JACK. "Immigration and the Labor Force," *Annals of the American Academy of Political and Social Science,* CCLXII (March, 1949), 92–101.

DOUGLAS, PAUL H., and LAMBERSON, F. "The Movement of Real Wages, 1890–1918," *American Economic Review* (September, 1921), 409–426.

ERLICH, VICTOR. "Jewish Labor and the 'Daily Forward'," *Modern Review,* I (September, 1947), 533–542.

HANDLIN, OSCAR, and MARY, F. "Ethnic Factors in Social Mobility," *Explorations in Entrepreneurial History,* IX (October, 1956), 1–7.

HANSEN, ALVIN. "Factors Affecting Real Wages," *American Economic Review,* XV (March, 1925), 25–42, 294.

HARDMAN, J. B. S. "Jewish Workers in the American Labor Movement," *YIVO Annual of Jewish Social Science,* VII (1952), 229–254.

HERBERG, WILL. "The Jewish Labor Movement in the United States," *American Jewish Year Book,* LXXX (1952), 3–74.

HUTHMACHER, J. JOSEPH. "Urban Liberalism and the Age of Reform," *Mississippi Valley Historical Review,* XLIX (September, 1962), 231–241.

JONES, F. W. "Real Wages in Recent Years," *American Economic Review,* VII (June, 1917), 317–330.

KOPOLD, SYLVIA, and SELEKMAN, BEN. "The Epic of the Needle Trades," *The Menorah Journal,* XV (October, 1928), 293–307.

LOFT, JACOB. "Jewish Workers in the New York City Men's Clothing Industry," *Jewish Social Studies,* II (January, 1946), 62–63.

MANN, ARTHUR. "Gompers and the Irony of Racism," *Antioch Review,* XIII (Summer, 1953), 203–214.

MENES, ABRAHAM. "The East Side: Matrix of the Jewish Labor Movement," *Jewish Life in America* (Theodore Friedman and Robert Gordis eds.), 1955, 131–154.

PERLMAN, SELIG. "The Basic Philosophy of the American Labor Movement," *Annals of the American Academy of Political and Social Science,* CCLXXIV (March, 1951), 57–63.

———. "Jewish Unionism and American Labor," *Publications of the American Jewish Historical Society,* XLI (September, 1951–June, 1952), 297–337.

PETERSON, FLORENCE. "Causes of Industrial Unrest," *Annals of the American Academy of Political and Social Science,* CCLXXIV (March, 1951), 25–31.

PINSON, KOPPEL S. "Arkady Kremer, Vladimir Medem, and the Ideology of the Jewish 'Bund'," *Jewish Social Studies,* VII (July, 1945), 233–264.

RICH, JACOB C. "The Jewish Labor Movement in the United States," *The Jewish People: Past and Present,* II (1948), 399–430.

———. "60 Years of the Jewish Daily *Forward,*" *The New Leader* [Special Supplement] (June 3, 1957).

ROCHE, JOHN P. "Entrepreneurial Liberty and the Fourteenth Amendment," *Labor History,* IV (Winter, 1963), 1–31.

RUBINOW, I. M. "The Recent Trend of Real Wages," *American Economic Review,* IV (December, 1914), 793–817.

SMITH, JOHN S. "Organized Labor and Government in the Wilson Era; 1913–1921: Some Conclusions," *Labor History,* III (Fall, 1962), 265–286.

SOROKIN, PITIRIM A. "Leaders of Labor and Radical Movements," *American Journal of Sociology,* XXXIII (November, 1927), 382–411.

WEINRYB, BERNARD D. "The Adaptation of Jewish Labor Groups to American Life," *Jewish Social Studies,* VIII (October, 1946), 219–244.

WEINSTEIN, JAMES. "The Socialist Party: Its Roots and Strength, 1912–1919," *Studies on the Left,* I (Winter, 1960), 5–27.

Unpublished Materials

BERMAN, HYMAN. "Era of the Protocol: A Chapter in the History of the International Ladies' Garment Workers' Union, 1910–1916," Doctoral Dissertation, Columbia University, 1956.

BROWN, JULIA S. "Factors Affecting Union Strength: A Case Study of the International Ladies' Garment Workers' Union, 1900–1940," Doctoral Dissertation, Yale University, 1942.

GILLETTE, J. WILLIAM. "Welfare State Trail Blazer: New York State Factory Investigating Commission, 1911–1915," Master's Thesis, Columbia University, 1956.

HEER, JEAN M. "Industrial Home Work in New York City," Master's Thesis, Columbia University, 1925.

HOLBROOK, JOHN F. "The Clothing Industry and the Immigrant Jew in New York City," Master's Thesis, Columbia University, 1950.

JOHNSON, MICHAEL. "The Federal Judiciary and Radical Unionism: A Study of the U.S. *v.* W. D. Haywood, et al.," Master's Thesis, Northern Illinois University, 1963.

IVERSEN, ROBERT W. "Morris Hillquit: American Social Democrat," Doctoral Dissertation, State University of Iowa, 1951.

MINKOFF, S. N. "An Introduction to Socialist Opinion in the United States on the Question of War, 1913–1918," Tamiment Institute Library, 1935.

NICHOLS, ELENA. "The Effects of Italian Immigration on New York City," Master's Thesis, Columbia University, 1929.

RAPPAPORT, JOSEPH. "Jewish Immigrants and World War One: A Study of American Yiddish Press Reactions," Doctoral Dissertation, Columbia University, 1951.

SANDERS, RONALD. "Abraham Cahan and the Jewish Labor Movement in New York, 1882–1914," Master's Thesis, Columbia University, 1957.

WAITZMAN, SAMUEL. "The New York City Transit Strike of 1916," Master's Thesis, Columbia University, 1952.

YELLOWITZ, IRWIN. "Labor and the Progressive Movement in New York State, 1897–1916," Doctoral Dissertation, Brown University, 1961.

Index

Cahan, Abraham, 60–61, 148; and
cloakmakers' strike, 63; and social-
ism, 33; and trade-unions, 46
Call, New York, 78, 113, 123
Central Federated Union, 47, 54,
105, 132, 142, 144
Central Labor Union of Brooklyn,
144
Chamber of Commerce, New York,
41, 76, 80
child labor, 10
Child Labor Committee, New York,
24
cigar makers, 1
Citizens' Committee for Locked-Out
Cloak and Suit Makers, 94
Citzens' Committee on the Traction
Strike, 143
Civil Service Commission, 119
class conflict, 31, 35; *see also* strikes
and ideology
Cloak, Suit, and Skirt Manufacturers'
Protective Association; and 1910
cloakmakers' strike, 59–60, 64,
65; and 1916 cloakmakers' strike,
92–97; and Mayor's Council of
Conciliation, 90; and Protocolism,
65, 86, 88–89
cloakmakers; and general strike, 93,
144; and 1910 strike, 58–65, 174n.
and 1916 strike, 93–97
Cloakmakers' Joint Board, New
York, 62, 87
closed shop, 2, 38, 56–57, 60–61,
109, 133
Clothing Contractors Association, 79
clothing industry (men's and
women's), *see* needle trades
Cobb, Henry E., Dr., 78
Cohen, Isadore, 68
Cohen, Julius Henry, 41, 154, 155;
and 1910 cloakmakers' strike, 64–
65; and industrial relations, 40–
41, 44, 101, 175n.; and 1913
needle trades strikes, 75, 77, 79,
80–81, 180n.; and Protocolism,
87–88
Coleman, McAlister, 53
collective bargaining, 1, 2, 56, 59–60,
65, 70, 95–96, 106–107, 134, 154
"Columbus tailors," 42
Commercial Advertiser, New York,
61
Committee of Five, 81–82
Communists, 153
company unions, 114, 149; *see also*
IRT *and* Mitchel, John Purroy *and*
transit workers

Consumers' League, 24, 94
contractors (garment), 42–43, 44
contracts, labor, 2, 138–140, 142,
144, 194n.
corruption and unions, 3
craft unions, 1, 2–3, 29, 102, 149,
151
Creel, George, 145
Cutting, R. Fulton, 78, 81, 82

Debs, Eugene, 33
DeLeon, Daniel, 33, 47, 63
Democratic Party, *see* Tammany Hall
Dodge, Cleveland H., 78
Douglas, George W., Canon, 78
Douglas, Paul H., 11
Dreier, Margaret, 50,
Dreier, Mary, 50, 51
Dubinsky, David, 156
Dyche, John, 30, 31, 49; and ideo-
logy, 30, 32; and Protocolism, 86;
and 1913 tailors' strike, 82

Edwards, William, 116, 117, 118,
119–120
Elster, Joseph, 121
Emery, John J., 55
Ethical Culture Society, 41
Ettor, Joseph J., 122, 124
express companies, 104–115
express drivers, 104–105; *see also*
express companies *and* Ashton,
William *and* Gaynor, William F.

factory legislation, 8–9, 24
Feigenbaum, Benjamin, 63
Filene, A. Lincoln, 60
Fitzgerald, William V., 130, 131,
138, 139, 146, 192n.
Flynn, Elizabeth Gurley, 122, 124
Forward, 60–61, 62, 80, 81
Frayne, Hugh; and furriers' strike,
68; and general strike, 142, 144–
145, 146; and transit strike, 135
Fridiger, Louis, 135
Fur Manufacturers' Protective Asso-
ciation, 68, 70, 71, 72
Fur Worker, The, 38
furriers' strike, 68–71, 72, 177n.
Fusion, 89

garment trades; *see* needle trades
garment workers; and Communism,
153–154; and socialism, 47, 170n.;
and strikes, 58–65, 72–84, 93–97,
174n.; reasons for success, 98–101;
and unions, 4, 42–44, 47, 85; and
working conditions, 8, 45